Amirreza Tahamtan

Web Service Composition Based Interorganizational Workflows

Amirreza Tahamtan

Web Service Composition Based Interorganizational Workflows:

Modeling and Verification

With a Preface by Johann Eder

Südwestdeutscher Verlag für Hochschulschriften

Impressum/Imprint (nur für Deutschland/ only for Germany)
Bibliografische Information der Deutschen Nationalbibliothek: Die Deutsche Nationalbibliothek verzeichnet diese Publikation in der Deutschen Nationalbibliografie; detaillierte bibliografische Daten sind im Internet über http://dnb.d-nb.de abrufbar.
Alle in diesem Buch genannten Marken und Produktnamen unterliegen warenzeichen-, marken- oder patentrechtlichem Schutz bzw. sind Warenzeichen oder eingetragene Warenzeichen der jeweiligen Inhaber. Die Wiedergabe von Marken, Produktnamen, Gebrauchsnamen, Handelsnamen, Warenbezeichnungen u.s.w. in diesem Werk berechtigt auch ohne besondere Kennzeichnung nicht zu der Annahme, dass solche Namen im Sinne der Warenzeichen- und Markenschutzgesetzgebung als frei zu betrachten wären und daher von jedermann benutzt werden dürften.

Verlag: Südwestdeutscher Verlag für Hochschulschriften Aktiengesellschaft & Co. KG
Dudweiler Landstr. 99, 66123 Saarbrücken, Deutschland
Telefon +49 681 37 20 271-1, Telefax +49 681 37 20 271-0, Email: info@svh-verlag.de
Zugl.: Wien, Uni Wien, Diss., 2009

Herstellung in Deutschland:
Schaltungsdienst Lange o.H.G., Berlin
Books on Demand GmbH, Norderstedt
Reha GmbH, Saarbrücken
Amazon Distribution GmbH, Leipzig
ISBN: 978-3-8381-0670-0

Imprint (only for USA, GB)
Bibliographic information published by the Deutsche Nationalbibliothek: The Deutsche Nationalbibliothek lists this publication in the Deutsche Nationalbibliografie; detailed bibliographic data are available in the Internet at http://dnb.d-nb.de.
Any brand names and product names mentioned in this book are subject to trademark, brand or patent protection and are trademarks or registered trademarks of their respective holders. The use of brand names, product names, common names, trade names, product descriptions etc. even without a particular marking in this works is in no way to be construed to mean that such names may be regarded as unrestricted in respect of trademark and brand protection legislation and could thus be used by anyone.

Publisher:
Südwestdeutscher Verlag für Hochschulschriften Aktiengesellschaft & Co. KG
Dudweiler Landstr. 99, 66123 Saarbrücken, Germany
Phone +49 681 37 20 271-1, Fax +49 681 37 20 271-0, Email: info@svh-verlag.de

Copyright © 2009 by the author and Südwestdeutscher Verlag für Hochschulschriften Aktiengesellschaft & Co. KG and licensors
All rights reserved. Saarbrücken 2009

Printed in the U.S.A.
Printed in the U.K. by (see last page)
ISBN: 978-3-8381-0670-0

Acknowledgements

I am deeply grateful to my Ph.D. supervisor and teacher Prof. Johann Eder for his invaluable guidance, perfectionism and generosity. I have not only learned a lot about computer sciences but also a lot about good personality.

A special thank to Prof. Erich Schikuta for peer-reviewing of this book and for his support and friendliness.

I owe a special note of gratitude to my colleagues at the Dept. of Knowledge and Business Engineering of the University of Vienna for their support, feedback, answering my questions and proofreading.

I want to extend many thanks to the team of the European project WS-Diamond for their cooperation.

I would like to thank Dr. Marek Lehmann and Dr. Horst Pichler for their collaboration and cooperation.

Preface by Johann Eder

Process orientation has become one of the most important architectural concepts for the design and implementation of information systems. For intra-organizational business processes workflow systems have achieved a prominent position. They support process oriented enterprise administration as they provide the logistics infrastructure to coordinate and drive functional activities - performed by man or machine. Workflow systems allow for modelling of processes, they enact the execution of the individual activities in the modelled order, and they precisely document the execution of processes leading to great improvements in planning and controlling business processes.

A similar support for inter-organizational business processes is still subject of ongoing research efforts. Some difficult challenges are in the composition of inter-organizational business processes out of component processes of participating organizations. Web Services are helpful for easing the barrier of syntactic differences. However, the distributed coordination of inter-organizational workflows, which typically do not have and should not have a central coordination unit, the balance between openness for interoperability and the protection of trade secrets, and the questions of compatibility of business procedures for composing larger processes are great challenges for research and development. And this book contributes greatly to this endeavour in four research fields.

Workflow Views are introduced to provide abstractions of intra-organizational workflows with the aim of defining the dynamic interfaces and protocols needed for cooperation without exhibiting the internal details of the workflow. Views also have a long tradition in databases for lowering the degree con coupling between components.

Federated Choreographies are an innovative way of attacking three problems: First if choreographies for coordinating processes are only defined by protocols between two partners, the process orientation of the inter-organizational workflow gets lost. Here choreographies are modelled as processes. Second, for inter-organizational business processes, the involved parties are independent business entities - so there is no central coordinator and all modelling and enacting of processes has to take that into account and allow for a completely distributed approach. Third, the participating parties are not equally close to each other. This requires that the knowledge needed about other participants has to be variable. An approach, where there is only one global process and the individual internal processes would fall short.

Conformance deals with whether processes, in particular internal workflows and inter-organizational business processes, fit together. Conformance is a quite difficult formal issue. The survey shows different notions of conformance - in particular structural conformance - and explores their relationships and properties.

A particular notion of conformance is temporal conformance, i.e. to analyze whether the combination of the individual workflows does not violate temporal constraints and allows to meet the deadlines imposed on the global processes.

All these four aspects covered in this book contribute to a better understanding of the challenges for inter-organizational workflows and provide solutions which can be used for actually implementing systems.

Vienna, Klagenfurt, 2009-04-15
Johann Eder

Contents

1. Introduction   1

2. Workflow Technology   5
   - 2.1. Workflow Terminology 6
   - 2.2. Benefits of Workflows 8
   - 2.3. Types of Workflows 9
   - 2.4. Workflow Components 9
   - 2.5. Workflow Reference Model 10
   - 2.6. Workflow Control-Flow Structures 11
   - 2.7. Workflow Conformance Classes 14
   - 2.8. Workflow Interoperability 15

3. Workflow Modeling Languages   17
   - 3.1. Petri-Nets 17
     - 3.1.1. Behavioral Properties 20
   - 3.2. Workflow-Nets 21

4. Interorganizational Workflows   23
   - 4.1. Related Works 23

5. Workflow Views   35
   - 5.1. Related Works 37
   - 5.2. Correctness of Views 42
   - 5.3. Construction of Views 43
     - 5.3.1. Concatenation of Operators 51

6. Web Services and Web Service Standards   55
   - 6.1. Web Services 55
   - 6.2. SOAP 56
   - 6.3. WSDL 57
   - 6.4. UDDI 60
     - 6.4.1. UDDI Architecture 61
     - 6.4.2. Comparison of UDDI 62

6.5.	WS-BPEL		63
	6.5.1. Business Processes in WS-BPEL		65
		6.5.1.1. Partner Links	66
		6.5.1.2. Partners	66
		6.5.1.3. Variables	66
		6.5.1.4. Correlation and Correlation Sets	67
		6.5.1.5. Fault Handlers	67
		6.5.1.6. Compensation Handlers	68
		6.5.1.7. Event Handlers	69
		6.5.1.8. Activities	70

7. An Architecture for Interorganizational Workflows 75
7.1. Choreographies and Orchestrations 75
7.2. Federated Choreographies 85
    7.2.1. Advantages of the Federated Choreographies 91
    7.2.2. Metamodel of the Federated Choreographies 92
    7.2.3. Graph Representation of the Control Flow 96
    7.2.4. Mapping onto WF-nets 96

8. Conformance of the Federated Choreographies 99
8.1. Different Notions of Process Equivalence 99
    8.1.1. Bisimulation 99
    8.1.2. Trace Equivalence 110
    8.1.3. Testing Equivalence 110
    8.1.4. Failure Equivalence 112
    8.1.5. Observation Equivalence 113
    8.1.6. Weak Observation Equivalence 115
    8.1.7. Logical Equivalence 116
    8.1.8. Classification of the Equivalence Relationships 116
    8.1.9. Kennaway Equivalence 118
    8.1.10. Darondeau Equivalence 119
8.2. Structural Conformance of the Federated Choreographies 120
    8.2.1. Conformance Algorithm 123
8.3. Temporal Conformance 129
    8.3.1. Related Works 130
    8.3.2. Best Case, Worst Case Time Management of the Federated Choreographies 132
        8.3.2.1. Prerequisites 132
        8.3.2.2. The Proposed Approach 135
        8.3.2.3. Methods 138
        8.3.2.4. Temporal Conformance Checking Algorithm 141

		8.3.2.5.	Implementation and Proof of Concept 143

- 8.3.2.5. Implementation and Proof of Concept 143
- 8.3.2.6. Proof of Termination and Complexity Analysis 146
- 8.3.3. Interval-Based Calculations of Temporal Conformance 148
  - 8.3.3.1. Calculation of Timed Graphs and Temporal Conformance Checking 150
- 8.3.4. Calculation of Temporal Execution Plans of Views 151
  - 8.3.4.1. Calculation of Timed Graphs of Views 151
- 8.3.5. Probabilistic Time Management of the Federated Choreographies . . 153
  - 8.3.5.1. Probabilistic Model Description 158
  - 8.3.5.2. Histogram Operations 160
  - 8.3.5.3. Calculation of Probabilistic Timed Graphs 161
  - 8.3.5.4. The Proposed Approach 163
  - 8.3.5.5. Methods 163
  - 8.3.5.6. Temporal Conformance Checking Algorithm 166
  - 8.3.5.7. Proof of Termination and Complexity Analysis 172
  - 8.3.5.8. Run-time Applications 172
- 8.3.6. Temporal Aspects of BPEL Processes 173
- 8.4. Correctness of View-Based Interorganizational Workflows 174

9. A General Case of Interorganizational Workflows 179
- 9.1. A More General Architecture for Interorganizational Workflows 179
- 9.2. Conformance Issues 180
  - 9.2.1. Structural Conformance 181
  - 9.2.2. Temporal Conformance 181
    - 9.2.2.1. Best Case, Worst Case Calculations 181
    - 9.2.2.2. Probabilistic Calculations 184

10. Conclusions 187

A. Calculation of Timed Graphs 191

B. Calculation of The Probabilistic Values 199

Chapter 1

Introduction

Interorganizational workflows are workflows that facilitate the cooperation and provide a framework for collaboration among autonomous organizations. Partners of an interorganizational workflow belong to autonomous and organizationally independent and possibly geographically distant entities that cooperate with each other and work together in order to reach the overall defined goals. In contrast to workflows within single organizations, interorganizational workflows are more challenging because privacy and access permission to partners from outside of an organization play an essential role. On the one hand, organizations want to isolate their private workflow in order to protect their business know-how and business logic and on the other hand they have to expose some parts of their private workflow to external partners in order to enable interaction and communication. This book proposes the application of workflow views to achieve this goal. Workflow views are handy and powerful tools that define visible parts of a process for external partners which are needed for interaction whilst keep the internal business logic hidden from outside observers. This book proposes a method for correct construction of workflow views and interorganizational workflows. Application of workflow views give organizations the ability to balance the need for cooperation and protection of know-how.

Web services and web service technology are suitable means for many application domains such as business process management, business-to-business interactions, distributed computing, e-commerce and many more. Because of the useful characteristics of web services and web service related technologies such as modularity and loosely coupledness which enable cheaper to implement and maintain systems and the trend in academia and industry towards software oriented architecture and web services, it is assumed that partners of interorganizational workflows use web services and web services related technologies for both definition of communication protocol and implementation of private workflows.

A web service is a stand alone entity that is operational in isolation and as well can be a part of a bigger system. A web service interacts and cooperates with other web services within a system in order to reach the common goals of a business process. What makes web services specially advantageous and a useful technology is their capability of being composed into more complex orchestrated and choreographed systems in a modular and recursive fashion. In such a way available web services are building blocks of more complex systems for more sophisticated requirements. This capability eliminates the need for designing and implementing all systems from scratch. Instead such systems can be put together using available web services. It is obvious that web service composition reduces the cost of process design, implementation and maintenance in organizations. In a recursive fashion choreographies and orchestrations can again be exposed to and used by other more complex choreographies and orchestrations. Choreographies are in charge of describing the interaction among partners and orchestrations are internal and private processes owned by one partner which in addition to other tasks are in charge of realization of choreographies.

The central requirement for a functioning interorganizational workflow is an architectural model that meets the requirements of real life applications. Besides, It must be ensured that an Interorganizational workflow is consistent and conformant with respect to the local and global constraints, i.e. the correctness criteria must be verified. Execution of the model must not lead to any conflicts or errors.

This book introduces a nouvelle architecture for web service composition based interorganizational workflows, called *federated choreographies*, that provides a more realistic approach for requirements of real life scenarios and offers advantages for organizations and businesses. In addition, different techniques for checking the structural and temporal conformance of the model are proposed.

For structural conformance different notions of process equivalence are studied and an algorithm based on branching bisimulation for checking the structural conformance of the federated choreographies is proposed. By structural conformance it can be ensured that structures of processes that participate in an interorganizational workflow are conformant. In other words, it is checked if the structural requirements (e.g. execution order of activities) imposed by one process are not violated by other processes.

Temporal conformance guarantees the correct temporal execution of the flow. Temporal conformance of an interorganizational workflow must not only consider local constraints (e.g. assigned deadline) but also global constraints (e.g. restrictions imposed by workflows of other interacting partners). Temporal conformance checking helps process designers to detect possible temporal failures early enough such that corrective actions can be triggered in order to guarantee the correct temporal execution of the flow. In this approach, valid temporal execution plans for all involved activities are calculated. The calculated plans can be monitored at run time and possible deviations from the valid temporal intervals can be detected. This technique gives process designers and managers tools to predict the future behavior of a flow and possible upcoming temporal failures. Prediction of future upcoming failures is obviously a great advantage to avoid them which reduces the cost of process execution. If a temporal failure has not yet been occurred, counter-measures can be triggered early enough to prevent the error and in case of already occurrence of a temporal failure exception handling mechanisms must be triggered. In order to cater for different requirements and model the uncertainties incorporated with temporal conformance checking and temporal information, several approaches are proposed for modeling temporal information and checking the temporal conformance. Approaches based on fixed temporal values, interval based temporal values and a probabilistic approach for modeling the uncertainties coupled with activity durations and branching probabilities are presented for modeling and handling different requirements.

Both structural and temporal conformance checking are performed at design time and can be monitored at run time. By application of the proposed algorithms at design-time, possible structural and temporal errors can be detected and consequently corrected. Error detection at design-time reduce the cost of process because of two reasons: first, errors detected at run-time are usually more costly than those detected at design-time and cause less costs for process reengineering and second, triggering of exception handling mechanisms can be avoided which are, in turn, coupled with additional costs.

This book provides a summary on the state of the art of the most important standards of the web service technology such as SOAP, UDDI, WSDL and WS-BPEL. Because of the prominence of WS-BPEL in the industry as well as academia and its status as a de-facto standard, WS-BPEL is handled in more depth. WS-BPEL can be used for modeling choreographies and orchestrations as abstract and executable processes respectively. Business processes modeled by WS-BPEL can be temporally annotated in order to ensure the temporal conformance of interacting and cooperating processes in a web service composition scenario. The underlying techniques for checking the temporal conformance are handled in this book.

The main contributions of this work are:

- A nouvelle hierarchical architecture for web service composition based interorganizational workflows
- Techniques for a correct construction of workflow views
- A technique and algorithm for automated checking of the structural conformance of the model
- Different approaches for checking the temporal conformance of the model that cater for different sets of requirements
- A temporal conformance checking tool
- Introduction of underlying techniques for time management of business processes in WS-BPEL

This book is structured as follows:

Chapter 2: gives an overview on workflow and workflow-related technology and provides a motivation for application of workflow technology.

Chapter 3: presents the formal and mathematical foundations of workflow modeling languages that are used throughout this work: Petri-nets and workflow-nets.

Chapter 4: presents the concept of interorganizational workflows and summarizes and compares the related research works in this field.

Chapter 5: discusses why workflow views should be used in interorganizational workflows, provides a summary and comparison of related works and proposes techniques for a correct construction of views.

Chapter 6: motivates the use of web services and represent the state of the art of the underlying standards for web services and web service technology.

Chapter 7: discusses the available approaches for web services composition, clarifies the related concepts and presents a nouvelle, hierarchical architecture for web service composition based interorganizational workflows.

Chapter 8: provides a discussion for the conformance issues of the proposed architecture, introduces different notions of process equivalence, presents an algorithm for structural conformance checking and proposes several approaches for temporal conformance checking.

Chapter 9: provides a more general architecture for web service based interorganizational workflows and presents its conformance checking techniques.

The techniques and methods presented in this book are not only limited to the proposed architecture but they also can be applied on a broad range of scenarios involving web services, web service composition, intraorganizational and interorganizational workflows and business process management. Moreover, the proposed approach is platform and language independent and algorithms work in a distributed manner.

Chapter 2

Workflow Technology

The concept of workflow has been used in many contexts within and outside the field of computer science. It is an important and beneficial technology with a huge influence on organizational performance in many fields such as business process management (BPM), web service technology, office automation, distributed information systems and e-business applications. Many firms, vendors and institutions are involved with workflow and workflow-related technologies. The Workflow Management Coalition (WfMC) [15], founded in 1993, is a non-profit, international organization of workflow specialists that serve as the standardization body. According to the glossary of terminology [20] published by the workflow management coalition , a *workflow* [20] is :

"automation of a business process, in whole or part, during which documents, information or tasks are passed from one participant to another for actions according to a set of procedural rules".

A *business process* [20] is defined as:

"A set of one or more linked procedures or activities which collectively realize a business objective or policy goal, normally within the context of an organizational structure defining functional roles and relationships."

In other words, a workflow can be understood as an automation of a process that handles the created data, e.g. documents, in order to meet the defined business goals. The state of the data is changed after the data has been processed by different activities (steps of the workflow). Modern workflow systems are capable of modeling and execution of complex processes which can be modeled and verified by different calculi [61, 276, 279, 163] such as pi-calculus [226, 269] and event calculus [80, 81]. A *worfkflow management systems (WfMS)* [20] is defined by the workflow management coalition as:

"A system that defines, creates and manages the execution of workflows through the use of software, running on one or more workflow engines, which is able to interpret the process definition, interact with workflow participants and, where required, invoke the use of IT tools and applications".

A workflow management system is composed of software components and has administrative and supervisory functions. It is in charge of interpretation of process definition, creation, execution and management of process instances and interaction among participants and applications. A wokflow management system assigns activities (manual or automated) to participants (human or machines) for execution. It monitors the execution as well as satisfaction of constraints and is in charge of triggering alarms and exception handling mechanisms if a constraint is violated.

2.1. Workflow Terminology

A workflow is based on processes. According to workflow management coalition's terminology and glossary, A *process* [20] is defined as:

"The representation of a business process in a form which supports automated manipulation, such as modeling, or enactment by a workflow management system. The process definition consists of a network of activities and their relationships, criteria to indicate the start and termination of the process, and information about the individual activities, such as participants, associated IT applications and data, etc."

A process is composed of activities. An *activity* [20] is:

"A description of a piece of work that forms one logical step within a process. An activity may be a manual activity, which does not support computer automation, or a workflow (automated) activity. A workflow activity requires human and/or machine resources(s) to support process execution; where human resource is required an activity is allocated to a workflow participant."

An activity is either a *manual activity* [20], defined as:

"An activity within a business process which is not capable of automation and hence lies outside the scope of a workflow management system. Such activities may be included within a process definition, for example to support modeling of the process, but do not form part of a resulting workflow"

or an *automated activity* [20], defined as:

2.1. Workflow Terminology

"An activity which is capable of computer automation using a workflow management system to manage the activity during execution of the business process of which it forms a part"

After processes and activities have been defined, an *instance* [20] of them is created by the workflow management system :

"The representation of a single enactment of a process, or activity within a process, including its associated data. Each instance represents a separate thread of execution1 of the process or activity, which may be controlled independently and will have its own internal state and externally visible identity, which may be used as a handle, for example, to record or retrieve audit data relating to the individual enactment."

A process often calls another *sub-process* [20], which is:
"A process that is enacted or called from another (initiating) process (or sub process), and which forms part of the overall (initiating) process. Multiple levels of sub process may be supported"

Basically, A workflow management systems is designed for automation of tasks of its participants. A *workflow participant* [20] is:
"A resource which performs the work represented by a workflow activity instance. This work is normally manifested as one or more work items assigned to the workflow participant via the worklist"

A workflow participant may participate in a workflow by his *organizational role* [20]:
"A group of participants exhibiting a specific set of attributes, qualifications and/or skills"

Workflow participants are assigned *work items* [20]:

"The representation of the work to be processed (by a workflow participant) in the context of an activity within a process instance"

The assigned wok items to a workflow participant can be grouped into *worklists* [20]:

"A list of work items associated with a given workflow participant (or in some cases with a group of workflow participants who may share a common worklist). The worklist forms part of the interface between a workflow engine and the worklist handler"

And finally a *worklist handler* [20] is needed for the interaction:

"A software component that manages the interaction between the user (or group of users) and the worklist maintained by a workflow engine. It enables work items to be passed from the workflow management system to users and notifications of completion or other work status conditions to be passed between the user and the workflow management system"

2.2. Benefits of Workflows

Workflow technology provides many benefits to organizations as a consequence of process automation and process management capabilities. These include but not limited to:

Decreased error rate: **Automation of repetitive activities which are usually tiresome and error-prone for human participants leads to a decrease or even elimination of errors.**

Increased productivity: **Automation of routine tasks on the other hand results in an improved productivity in organizations because cases can be handled faster and with a greater efficiency.**

Faster handling of cases: **In addition to the fact that computer based systems are much more faster than humans in processing tasks, workflow management systems provides possibilities for parallel processing that again reduces the required time for handling cases.**

Less organizational overhead: **Application of workflow management systems in an organization reduces the organizational overhead and drops the organizational and managerial costs.**

Increased revenue: **Workflow management systems enable organizations to be available for customers 24 hours a day and 7 days a week. Inquiries such as purchase requests can be accepted and processed at any time which results in a higher revenue.**

Process analysis and process optimization: **Workflow management systems provide logging possibilities which assist process designers and process managers to analyze the process, identify the bottlenecks and consequently optimize the process.**

Shift of the organizational attention: **By automatization and optimization of processes, resources become free such that the organization can concentrate on issues like innovation, adjustment to future demands and emerging markets which ensure mid-term and long-term competitiveness.**

Better planning capabilities: **Workflow management systems provide decision support and better planing skills. As the knowledge where business is made and how processes are handled is available more easily.**

Process flexibility: Organizations are better equipped for modification and change of processes as a response to different market requirements.

2.3. Types of Workflows

Production Workflows: This type of workflows shows repetitive characteristics of tasks. Production workflows [175, 197, 139] are used for automation of repetitive tasks and minimization of human interventions in a business process with high quality and precision. Activities of a production workflow and their attributes are known a priori.

Administrative Workflows: In contrast to production workflows whose focus is on productivity, the focus of administrative workflows [173, 69, 24] is on flexibility. They are used for automatization of manual processes in administrative environments such as offices. Processes are often defined using forms.

Ad-Hoc Workflows: These workflows are very flexible workflows. The process definition of the ad-hoc workflows [147, 134, 63, 147] can be modified and changed frequently as a consequence of changes in the environment. In other types of workflow, normally there are a limited number of workflow definitions and many instances of each definition. In ad-hoc workflows as many workflow instances as workflow definitions may exist.

Collaborative Workflows: The focus of collaborative workflows [152, 167, 282, 225] is on communication and inter-group collaboration in order to achieve the goals of the group. Collaborative workflows support team work and are also called groupware.

2.4. Workflow Components

A workflow management systems is composed of several components. Some of the major components are *workflow engine* and *workflow enactment system*. A workflow engine is responsible for creation and cancelation of the process, scheduling of the activities and communication with external entities. It provides the run-time environment for a workflow instance. A workflow engine has a kind of application tool invocation capability and may be distributed over several machines and work in a non-centralized manner.

A workflow enactment service consists of one or more workflow engines and provides mainly the run-time environment for a process. It links the roles to the actual agents (human or machine). In other words, it defines which role a specific participant has in the process. Besides, it is responsible for interpretation and instantiation of the process and also controls the worklists of the participants. The control data of a workflow enactment service may be distributed over several workflow engines.

2.5. Workflow Reference Model

The workflow management coalition defines five interfaces for the interoperability between various workflow components at different levels. The workflow reference model and the relationship between its different interfaces is depicted in figure 2.1.

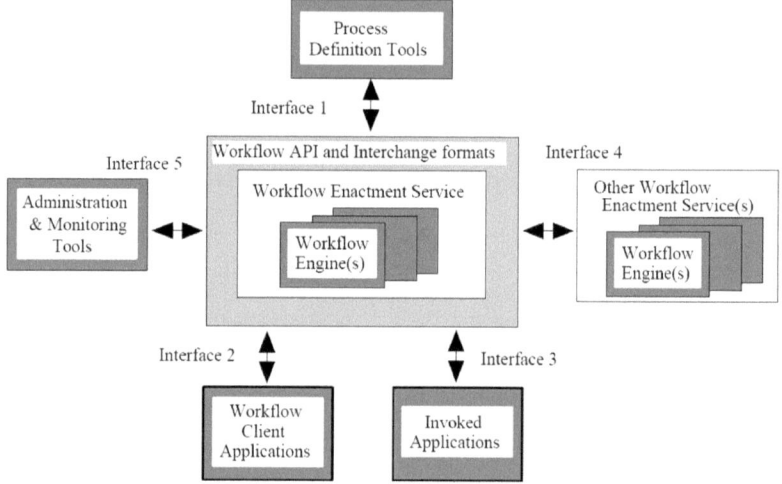

Figure 2.1.: The Workflow Reference Model (image from [15])

Interface 1: Process Definition: **This** interface separates the build-time environment from the run-time environment. The defined process in the build-time environment can be exported to the run-time environment and used as input. The build-time environment offers modeling tools for workflow processes.

Interface 2: Workflow Client Application: **This** interface specifies the communication protocol and controls and manages the interaction between an engine and client applications. There are multiple interaction mechanisms covering diversity of workflow implementations.

Interface 3: Invoked Application: **The** communication protocol between an engine and other (external) applications in the environment is defined through this interface. The environment includes local applications, the platform on which the engine resides as well as other accessible platforms.

Interface 4: Other Workflow Enactment Services: **Through** this interface the interaction protocol between a workflow engine and an external workflow engine is defined

2.6. Workflow Control-Flow Structures

and handled. The interaction between two workflow engines includes enactment and invocation of activities and sub-processes, status control of invoked activities and sub-processes, synchronization, coordination, process definition and transfer of required data. For this aim it is necessary to provide common interpretation and run-time support for transfer of required data.

Interface 5: Administration and Monitoring Tools: This interface handles the interaction between a workflow engine and administration and monitoring tools and enables a shared usage of administration and monitoring tools among several workflow engines. The administration and monitoring tools may be an independent entity or part of a workflow enactment service. Security and authorization issues also fall into the administration and monitoring tools responsibilities.

2.6. Workflow Control-Flow Structures

A major aspect for medeling a workflow process is its control flow. It must be clear in which order the activities are executed and when the thread of control is passed from one activity to another. The control flow structures are

Sequence
Some activities are executed in a chain under a single thread of execution, i.e. one after another. It is important to note that the successor activity can not start execution unless its predecessor has finished execution. See figure 2.2 for an example. The activity *Process request* can start execution as soon as its predecessor, activity *Receive request*, has finished execution.

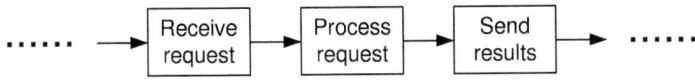

Figure 2.2.: Sequence

AND-split
AND-split is a structure in a workflow where one path (a thread of execution) splits into two or more paths. Each path, then, will be executed in parallel with the other paths of the AND-split structure. See figure 2.3 for an example of this structure. After the AND-split, two paths are executed simultaneously. The request is approved (activity *Approve request*) and then the contract is sent (activity *Send contract*). In parallel to this thread of execution, the purchase history of the buyer is updated (activity *Update history*).

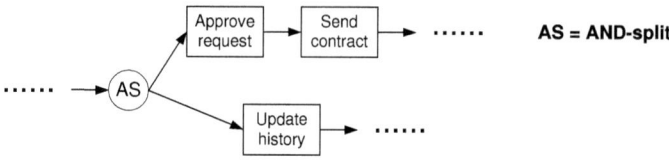

Figure 2.3.: AND-split

AND-join

In an AND-join multiple parallel paths merge again to one path. AND-join waits for all of its incoming paths to finish execution and then commits. In other words, the length of the path between an AND-split and AND-join is equal to the length of its longest path. Figure 2.4 demonstrates an example of an AND-join. Only after two paths have finished execution, i.e. the request has been approved, the contract sent and the purchase history of the buyer has been updated, the AND-join commits. The successor activity of the AND-join (activity *Plan production*) can start execution after the AND-join has committed.

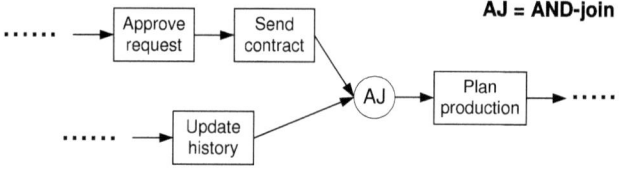

Figure 2.4.: AND-join

XOR-split

XOR-split offers some alternative paths for execution. Based on some conditions evaluated at run-time, a branch of the XOR-split is taken and executed. Figure 2.5 illustrates an example of the XOR-split. After the request has been received (activity *Receive request*), the request may be approved (activity *Approve request*) or rejected (activity *Reject request*). Approval or rejection of the request is based on some conditions that are not shown in this example.

2.6. Workflow Control-Flow Structures

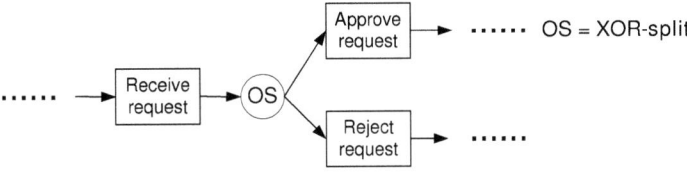

Figure 2.5.: XOR-split

XOR-join

XOR-join is the counterpart of a XOR-split. Similar to AND-join, in this structure paths of a XOR-split, representing alternative behavior of the flow, again merge into one path. Unlike AND-split, there is no need for synchronization. In other words, the duration of the structure between a XOR-split and a XOR-join equals the duration of the executed path. Obviously, this duration can not be known a priori at design-time because one can not know which path may be taken and executed at run-time. Figure 2.6 illustrates an application of XOR-join. After the request has been approved (activity *Approve request*) or has been rejected (activity *Reject request*), the result of the decision is sent to the buyer (activity *Send results*). The XOR-split waits only for one of its incoming paths to commit. It is clear that the request is either approved or rejected but not both.

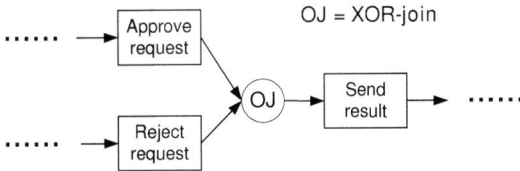

Figure 2.6.: XOR-join

LOOP

Sometimes it is needed to iterate an activity or a group of activities. In a workflow, similar to many programming languages, this iteration can be implemented by a loop. The defined activity or a group of activities are iterated as long as the exit condition from the loop is not yet satisfied. Figure 2.7 demonstrates such a scenario. In this scenario, a buyer looks for and finds a supplier for his required item (activity *Find supplier*), then the buyer sends a request for his item to the supplier (activity *Send request*) and then receives the results (approval or rejection) from the supplier (activity *Receive result*). The buyer iterates these three activities as long as he has received an approval for his request. As soon as a supplier approves the request the loop terminates and the order is placed at the supplier in the next step (activity *Place order*).

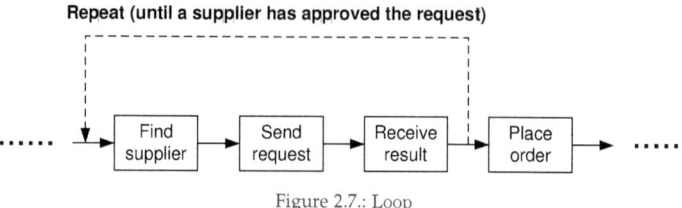

Figure 2.7.: Loop

2.7. Workflow Conformance Classes

The workflow management coalition in its published standards [21] identifies three conformance classes for structure of a workflow, which are:

Full-blocked: This conformance class requires that for each AND-split there is a counterpart AND-join and for each XOR-split there is a counterpart XOR-join. In other words, each outgoing path from a split-structure (AND-split, XOR-split) must eventually reach its counterpart join-structure (AND-join, XOR-join). Figure 2.8 depicts a portion of a full-blocked workflow description. As it can be seen there is a counterpart join-structure for each split-structure.

Loop-blocked: In the loop-blocked class, loops must be nested properly and the activities must form a directed acyclic graph (DAG). Arbitrary cycles are prohibited.

Non-blocked: This conformance class imposes no restriction on the structure of a workflow process. activities and transitions may form an arbitrary structure.

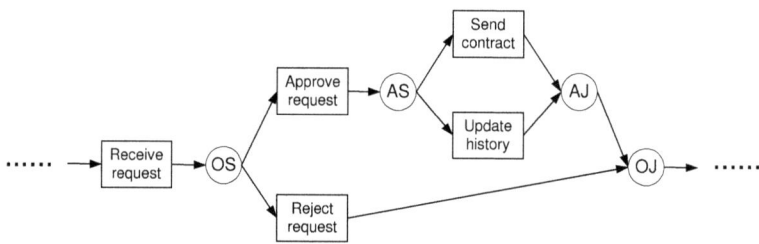

Figure 2.8.: A Full-blocked workflow

2.8. Workflow Interoperability

The interoperability of workflow systems is an important issues to be considered when two or more workflows cooperate and work together. Such a scenario may arise in different applications and domains for example a distributed implementation over several workflow systems or in interorganizational workflows where several autonomous workflow systems of different organizations cooperate and collaborate in order to reach the common goals of a business process. (See chapter 4 for interorganizational workflows).

The workflow management coalition's white paper on interoperability [19] identifies several levels of interoperability:

No interoperability: Two different workflow systems have no communication and interaction and are fully isolated from each other.

Coexistence: Only the run-time environment is shared by several workflow systems but there is no interaction between workflow systems. When for example a process is partially implemented by different workflow systems, each part with a different system, the underlying systems coexist with each other.

Unique gateways[1]: In this level of interoperability cooperating workflow systems route operations between engines and instances and furthermore translate and deliver workflow relevant and application data.

Common gateway API: This level assumes that the common subset of used gateways by workflow systems can be supported by a standard and gateways share a common application programming interface (API).

Limited common API subset: In this level the shared APIs allow direct interaction between workflow systems.

Complete workflow API: In this interoperability level all workflow systems share a single standard API, granting access to all of operations by any workflow system.

Shared definition formats: Different workflow systems use the same process definition format. When a process is defined on one workflow system, it can be reused by other systems as well.

Protocol compatibility: This level assumes standardized API client/server communication between workflow systems.

Common look and feel utilities: This level requires that the user interfaces of different workflow systems are the same or at least look and feel the same to the user.

---

[1] A gateway is a mechanism that allows specific workflow products to move work between each other[19]

Chapter 3

Workflow Modeling Languages

Workflow processes can be modeled by different languages and formalism. Each language and formalism has its own strengths and weaknesses. The characteristics of each formalism make it suitable for some application domains while maybe not enough expressive or too complex for other problems. The choice of the modeling language shall be done in the context of the modeling task.

Web Services Flow Language (WSFL) [176], Web Services for Business Process Design (XLANG) [255], Business Process Modeling Notation (BPMN) [23], Yet Another Workflow Language (YAWL) [260] and XML Process Definition Language (XPDL) [22] belong to these languages. In the following sections, two formalisms that are used in this work have been formalized. For a specification of other languages and formalisms please refer to the references.

3.1. Petri-Nets

Petri-nets [198, 26, 229, 218] and their subclasses such as workflow-nets (abbreviated WF-nets) [250, 100] and labeled Place/Transition nets (abbreviated Labeled P/T nets) [46] are a convenient modeling language for workflows and workflow based applications and are widely used and vastly studied in the literature. This is because petri-nets are a highly expressive language, both graphically and mathematically, with a well-defined structure and are supported by many tools and applications. These characteristics make petri-nets suitable for many application areas such as embedded systems [230], communication protocols [50], fault-tolerant and fault detection systems [280], manufacturing systems [267], software engineering [119, 277], multiprocessor systems [125], database systems [127, 199, 283], parallel computing [40, 73], discrete event systems [92, 128], dataflow systems [171, 248], logic-based systems [281, 251], compiler technology [186], information systems [240, 93, 137, 206, 236, 33], formal methods [150, 210], control, robotic and flexible manufacturing systems [68], decision support systems [258], artificial intelligence [216, 190], multi-agent systems [183, 85], knowledge representation [153], expert systems [178], neural networks [75], business process management [239, 91, 87], workflow management systems [237, 35, 179] and web service technology [254, 241, 253]. On the other hand, a major difficulty when applying petri-nets is its complexity which causes an overhead for modeling the problem at hand. It should be noted that however, petri-nets provide a strong and expressive formalism for different application domains, based on the context the problem may be solved and modeled more efficiently with less complex formalisms such as directed graphs.

Definition 3.1: **(Petri-net)**
A petri-net as defined in [198] is a 5-tuple $N = (P, T, F, W, M_0)$, where

- P is a finite set of places
- T is a finite set of transitions
- $F \subseteq (P \times T) \cup (T \times P)$ is a set of flow relations
- $W : F \to \mathbb{N}$ is a weight function
- $M_0 : P \to \mathbb{N}_0$ is the initial marking

where $\mathbb{N}$ is the set of natural numbers and $\mathbb{N}_0$ denotes $\mathbb{N} \cup \{0\}$

A petri-net is composed of two different kinds of nodes:

1. Places

2. Transitions

The set of places and transitions are non-empty and disjoint, i.e. $P \cap T = \emptyset \land P \cup T \neq \emptyset$. The flow relations are arcs that connect places with transitions or vice versa. A flow relation may have an assigned weight. A flow relation with the weight w is equal to the w parallel flow relations. The initial marking denotes the distribution of tokens over places. In other words, the initial marking assigns an integer $i \in \mathbb{N}_0$ to each place where i indicates the number of tokens in that place, i.e. a place can have zero, one or many tokens. Petri-nets that allow for weights $w > 1$ are called generalized petri-nets, whereas petri-nets that allow for only weights $w = 1$ are called ordinary petri-nets. It has been shown that generalized petri-nets are equivalent to ordinary petri-nets. However, generalized petri-nets provide more convenience at use [132, 162]. Graphically, places are depicted as circles, transitions as black boxes, flow relations as arcs and tokens as black dots. Note that the roles of places and transitions must be interpreted differently in different application domains and based on the application they may have different semantics. For example, in a petri-net model of a workflow application, transitions represent tasks and places the pre and post conditions of the tasks. However in another scenario the transitions may be the processing steps and places the required input and the produced output respectively. Figure 3.1 illustrates a very simple example of a petri-net.

3.1. Petri-Nets

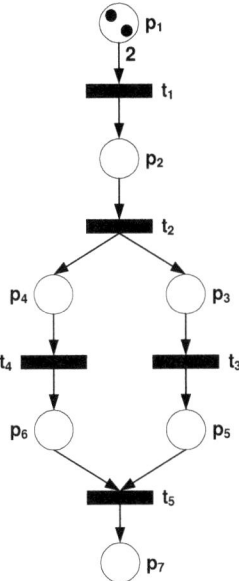

Figure 3.1.: An example of a petri-net

In a petri-net, a place with no incoming flow relation is called the source place (in Figure 3.1 place p_1) and the place with no outgoing flow relations is called the sink place (place p_7). Place p_1 is the input place of the transition t_1 and place p_2 is its output place. The flow relation from place p_1 to transition t_1 has the weight 2 and all other flow relations have the weight 1 and hence omitted in the figure 3.1 . The distribution of the tokens represents the marking. The marking of a petri-net can be shown by a column vector M where the number of tokens in the i-th place is assigned to the i-th row of the vector. The initial marking is typically presented by M_0.

The dynamic behavior of petri-nets can be described by its state change. A state change identifies a change in distribution of tokens over places, i.e. removal of tokens from input places and adding them to output places due to firing of transitions.

Enabled Transitions: A transition t is enabled if each input place p_i of t contains at least w_i tokens, where w_i is the weight of the flow relation from place p_i to t.

Firing of Transitions: If a transition t fires, it consumes w_i tokens from each input place p_i and produces w_o tokens to each output place p_o, where w_i is the weight of the flow relation from p_i to t and w_o is the weight of the flow relation from t to p_o.

Figure 3.2 shows the marking of the net after the transition t_1 in figure 3.1 has fired.

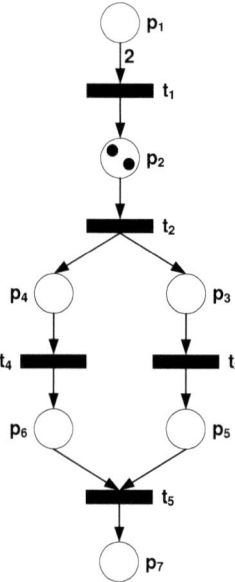

Figure 3.2.: After the transition t_1 in figure 3.1 has fired

The petri-net depicted in figure 3.1 and figure 3.2 contains only a sequence and a parallel structure. Petri-nets are also capable of presenting other control structures like XOR.

3.1.1. Behavioral Properties

In the following some of the most important behavioral properties of petri-nets have been introduced. For a more detailed discussion, its properties and other behaviorial characteristic refer to the references at the beginning of this section.

Definition 3.2: **(Firing Sequence)**
A sequence of place-transitions of the form $\sigma = (p_1)(t_1)(p_2)(t_2)...(p_n-1)(t_n-1)(p_n)(t_n)$ is called a firing sequence if all transitions $t_i : i \in \{1..n\}$ are enabled or fireable.

Definition 3.3: **(Reachability)**

3.2. Workflow-Nets

Let M_1 and M_2 be two markings and σ as defined in Definition 3.2. The marking M_2 is reachable from M_1, if $\exists \sigma : \sigma$ transform M_1 into M_2. $R(M)$ denotes the reachable markings from the marking M.

Definition 3.4: (Liveliness of Transitions)
Let M be a marking and M_0 the initial marking. Further $L(M)$ characterizes the possible firing sequences of M. A transition t is called

L0-live: if t can never fire in $L(M_0)$

L1-live: if t can fire at least once in $L(M_0)$

L2-live: if t can fire at least k times in $L(M_0)$, where $k \in \mathbb{N}$

L3-live: if t fires infinitely in $L(M_0)$

L4-live: if t is L1-live for every M in $R(M_0)$

l_i-liveliness implies L_{i-1}-liveliness

Definition 3.5: (Liveliness of Petri-Nets)
A L4-live petri-net is called a live petri-net. In contrary, a L0-live net is said to be a dead net.

The concept of liveliness correspond to the conflict-free execution of a net and its deadlock-freeness.

Definition 3.6: (Boundedness of Petri-Nets)
Let $N(p_i)$ denote the number of tokens in place p_i, k be a finite integer and $R(M_0)$ as defined in Definition 3.3. A petri-net is bounded if $\forall i \wedge \forall M \in R(M_0) : N(p_i) \preceq k$.

Definition 3.7: (Safeness of Petri-Nets)
A petri-net is safe if it is bounded and $K = 1$.

3.2. Workflow-Nets

Workflow-nets are a subclass of petri-net for modeling workflow process definitions. They are the classical petri-nets with some additional properties. [94, 96, 250, 100]. A WF-net is formally defined as:

Definition 3.8: A WF-net is a Petri-net $N = (P, T, F, W, M_0)$ with the following additional properties:

- N has a special place i whose preset is empty. This place is called *source place*.
- N has a special place o whose postset is empty. This place is called *sink place*.

- Any node $n \in (P \bigcup T)$ is on a path from source place to sink place, Where P is the set of places and T the set of transitions i.e. there is no dangling node and all places and transitions contribute to the processing of cases.

Definition 3.9: A sequence of place-transitions of the form $\rho = (p_1)(t_1)(p_2)(t_2)...(p_n-1)(t_n-1)(p_n)$ is called a path from place p_1 to place p_n if and only if $< p_i, t_i > \in F, 1 \leq i \leq n$, where F is the set of flow relations.

If there is a path ρ for every pair of place p and transition t in N, this net is said to be strongly connected [96].

Chapter 4

Interorganizational Workflows

Interorganizational workflows are an interesting and challenging point for application of workflow management systems. Interorganizational workflows are workflows that belong to a group of several autonomous organizations. These organizations may not be only organizationally autonomous but also geographically separate. The whole process of an interorganizational workflows is spread over the participating organizations, crossing the boundaries of single organizations. Each organization is in charge of implementing parts of the whole process. The overall business goal is defined in the whole interorganizational workflow process. This kind of process definition is very useful and even inevitable in the today world of business. Imagine for example a book shopping scenario at Amazon.com. When a customer orders a book, if the book is not on stock, it will be ordered at the Amazon's supplier's workflow. In another workflow between Amazon and Mater Card the credit card of the customer is charged. This interorganizational workflow is spread over Amazon, Amazon's book supplier and Master card to reach the common business goal of ordering books at Amazon.com. In addition to the need for such interactions and cooperations, availability of Internet that enables a cheap and effective communication medium is an important factor. An essential issue when designing and implementing interorganizational workflows is the balance between privacy and autonomy. The autonomous organizations that participate in an interorganizational workflow want on the one hand cooperate and communicate with other organizations which requires giving others access to the private workflow or at least parts of it. On the other hand they want to prevent others from knowing their know-how which is implemented in their business logic. See chapter 5 for more on the balance between autonomy and privacy.

4.1. Related Works

Interorganizational Workflows: An approach based on Message Sequence Charts and Petri Nets

In this work [98] Van der Aalst after a brief motivation for interorganizational workflows and description of various forms of workflow interoperability, introduces a technique for verification of interorganizational workflows based on the notion of correctness presented in [97]. This works considers loosely coupled interorganizational workflows presented as WF-nets. In this approach, an interorganizational wokrlfow is correct if all of the participating (private) workflows as well as the global workflow, defining the communication among participants, satisfy the correctness criteria. The notion of soundness is used as correctness criteria for private workflows and the IO-soundness for interorganizational workflow. An *unfolding function* connects all the local workflows by a start transition and a termination transition. Further it provides the process with a global source place and a global sink place. Moreover, asynchronous communication elements are mapped onto places and synchronous communication elements are replaced by new transitions. A renaming function maps old transitions into new ones. The application of the unfolding function results in a new unfolded WF-net. The unfolded WF-net is used for correctness verification of interorganizational workflows. An interorganizational workflow is correct if and only if all private workflows are sound and the unfolded global workflow is IO-sound. Furthermore, it defines a notion of consistency, called 1-*consistency* to check if the actual behavior of an interorganizational workflow is consistent with the communication structure between private workflows. A variation of message sequence charts (MSC) [17, 18] is used for description of message exchange among private workflows. For verification of 1-consistency, it must be checked if no firing sequence violates the partial order (of the messages) imposed by the message sequence chart.

Deriving Service Models in Cross-Organizational Workflows

Klingemann et al. in [170] propose an approach to derive models of external services from their visible behavior in an interorganizational setting. They argue that there is a need for service requester to control and monitor the execution of a service. However, service requester has a limited control and a priori knowledge about a service provider. Hence it makes sense to model and predict the service model based on the visible external behavior. The authors only consider the case of *outsourcing* for interoperation of workflows and call a business process cross-organizational if the process provides means for outsourcing to other external organizations or service providers. Hence, an architecture with centralized control of the service requester is proposed. Based on a previous work [169] and by analyzing the logs of external service providers, a technique for deriving the (external) service models as continuous time Markov chain (CTMC)[2] is proposed. However not stated explicitly, the assumption is that the service requester has access to logs of the service provider and services are treated as black box to a service requester. The derived model consists of a set of states, transition between states, transition probability and average amount of time that a service resides in each state. A state is either an start event or an end event. The elapsed time in a state can be calculated by subtracting the time stamps of an end event from its corresponding start event. By analyzing the service logs, CTMC-models are built which help the service requester to compare the actual behavior with intended behavior and derive conclusions such as order of execution. Moreover it allows for predictions such as expected remaining time till end of service or till a state s_j is reached given a state s_i.

Supporting Workflow Cooperation Within and Across Organizations

Asati and Discenza in [71] propose a model for interaction among workflows based on *event nodes*. Synchronization is realized by sending or receiving events to or from other workflows or external non-workflow applications. Hence, an event node is either a send node or a request node. Send nodes are points in a flow where events are produced and are non-blocking activities. Request nodes block until the requested events have been received and correspond to points in a flow where events are consumed. Each event belongs to an event class with a unique name and an optional or mandatory set of parameters. The essential part of the system is a so-called event service [103] for correlation of events, dispatching them between workflow instances as well as data conversion between heterogenous applications. For this, the event service uses a publish-subscribe model. It uses a filtering rule for identification of events in which a request node is interested. A filtering rule is a set of constraints on the names and parameters of events. Filtered events will be sent to the requester by the event service. In addition to filtering rules, capturing rules are used for assignment of values to the parameters in terms of local workflow variables. Authors also introduce an architecture and a prototype called DEPRA [72].

Architectural Issues for Cross-Organisational B2B Interactions

Schulz and Orlowska in [242] introduce an architecture for cross-organizational applications. Their model is two-tiered. The first tier consists of private business processes and the second tier contains shared business processes. The internal logic and structure of a private business process is only known to its owner. A private business process, alone or grouped with other private processes, can be exposed to other partners as a service. In other words, a service is an abstraction or encapsulation of one or more private business process. The shared processes define the interaction between participants and each participant is responsible for parts of the process that belong to him. Contracts are needed for setting up shared business processes. In their model the interaction between private business tasks and shared business tasks is handled through events. An event is defined as a piece of data specifying the sender, recipient, I/O data, description and ID. Moreover an architecture for B2B processes is introduced. This architecture uses a broker for managing the interaction among partners. The partners expose their internal business process as services and the broker is in charge of coordination of interaction and running of the shared business processes. In addition, the broker routes the events to the corresponding partner and can produce audit data for monitoring and logging purposes.

---

[2]A continuous time Markov chain (CTMC) is a stochastic process that proceeds through different states in certain time epochs. The Markov property states that the probability of entering a state depends only on the current state and not on the previous history

Consistency Between Executable and Abstract Processes

Martens in [189] introduces an approach for checking the behavioral consistency between globally defined shared business process and locally defined executable processes. This work uses a Petri-net formalism for process modeling. The mapping from BPEL to Petri-nets can be done automatically by WOMBAT4WS [275]. It uses the notion of simulation as equivalence relation between two workflows. *"A workflow module A simulates a workflow module B if each utilizing environment of module B is an utilizing environment of module A, too"*. Two workflows are equivalent if the simulation relationship is reciprocal. That means if workflow A simulates workflow B and workflow B simulates workflow A. Informally, two workflows have behavioral equivalence if both behave similar and the external observer can not distinguish between their behavior. Note that this notion only considers the behaviorial equivalence and not the structural equivalence. A description of other notions of equivalence can be found in section 8.1 of this book. The notion of communication graphs (c-graphs) [188] is used in this work to formalize the behavior of a web service. A communication graph contains the maximal information that an utilizing environment can derive about a web service. The assumption is that an environment has no explicit knowledge about the internal structure of a web service and derives its information implicitly by observing the communication or communicating with the module. Such implicitly derived information is presented using communication graphs. Two workflows are equivalent if their c-graphs simulate each other.

Business Process Choreography for B2B Collaboration

Authors in [155] present an approach for modeling choreography for B2B applications based on a predefined set of interoperability patterns. Three kinds of processes for realization of a business choreography is defined: contract processes (CP), executable processes (EP) and interface protocols (IP). A contract process is a choreography which defines the collaboration with other business partners and is a sequence of business logic containing elements of data formats, logical end points and security levels. An executable process is the internal realization of the tasks involved in a contract process. Interface protocols are intermediate processes between executable processes and contract processes and define the inter-operations between executable and contract processes. The authors propose a different approach for modeling a shared business process among different partners than some other authors. Whilst e.g. [43, 102, 217, 107] use a shared global choreography that all participants have the same view on, this work suggests a separate contract process for each executable process. The shared business process consists of a set of contract processes that interact which each other. Note that an interface protocol is required for interoperation between an executable process or a group of executable processes and a contract process. The disadvantage of this technique is the more complicated modeling without an obvious advantage compared to the approaches proposed by other authors. Further, based on the proposal of workflow management coalition [15], six basic interoperability patterns for interoperations between processes have been introduced. These basic patterns can be combined together for building more complex patters. The pattern are used for modeling the interactions in the interface protocol. In other words, the interactions in the interface protocol are mapped onto the interoperability patterns. Put it another way, the interaction patterns must cover all possible cases of interactions. The authors provides no proof that six elementary patterns can cover all cases and implicitly leave it to the user for building an optimal and complete set of interaction patterns using the six basic interoperability patterns. A top-down approach is applied for constructing the shared business process. The definition of contract processes is followed by preparing the executable processes of each partner and finally the interface protocols between the two previous processes are defined. This work is silent on the consistency and conformance issues among the suggested patterns.

A Decentralized Services Choreography Approach for Business Collaboration

[278] proposes a technique for inter-enterprize business collaboration based on service choreography. The proposed approach consists of three main steps:

- Building the centralized global business process for collaboration
- Role-based decomposition of the centralized process into a set of subprocesses
- Mediation between decentralized subprocess of internal process of each partner by data dependency analysis

Authors use a state machine formalism proposed by object management group (OMG) for modeling the centralized, shared business process. In the second step the built process in the previous step is decomposed by a role-based decomposition, i.e. each subprocess contains activities that belong to one partner or this partner (role) is in charge of their execution. The abstract activities in such subprocesses are in charge of interaction with other abstract processes as well as mediation of data to and from executable activities. A data-dependency mechanism is used for mediation between subprocess extracted in step 2 and the partner's internal process. Each state in the process, either abstract or executable, has a channel which is used for storage of data. The dependency is defined between the channels of a receiver and a sender by ($channel_s, channel_d.data$), where $channel_s$ is the channel of the source (sender), $channel_d$ is the channel of the destination (receiver) and $data$ is the transmitted message. When a message is received by an abstract process, data is extracted and copied to the channel of the corresponding executable activity. The right executable activity can be decided by the predefined data dependencies. After consumption of data by the executable activity, data is sent back to the channel of the abstract activity. This work does not consider conformance issues between subprocesses and executable process.

E Role-based Decomposition of Business Processes using BPEL

Khalaf and Leymann in [166] present a method for role-based decomposition of BPEL business processes such that each fragment of the process belong to one participant and can be enacted by the owner or executed by the role in charge. A modified version of BPEL, here called BPEL-D, has been used. In BPEL-D scope variables are replaced with data links and each activity possesses input and output containers. Access to the containers is controlled by transition conditions. A data link is a tuple $d(A_1, A_2)$ and assigns (parts of) output container of A_1 to (parts of) input container of A_2. A data link between two given activities can be defined only if a control flow dependency between them exists. The presented approach takes as input a process model described in BPEL-D, the corresponding WSDL-files and a specification of which activities belong to which partners. The output is a BPEL specification and a WSDL-files for each participant and the connection definition of subprocesses of each partner such that the connected subprocesses again builds the initial process. This work uses exchanged messages for passing control if a link after decomposition is broken. After decomposition of the original process, subprocesses are augmented with additional information if necessary e.g. some receive activities must be able to create new instances of the process, new correlation sets must be defined, etc. Finally subprocesses will be wired together such that the original process can again be reached. This approach is advantageous when for example a top-down approach for modeling and execution of a choreography is applied. Its shortcoming is necessity for description of the original process (input) in BPEL-D and not the original BPEL.

Cross-Organizational Workflow Integration using Contracts

Weigand and van den Heuvel in [271] present contracts as a way for modeling interaction in a cross-organizational setting. Such contracts consist of obligations of business partners and are modeled by business contract specification language (XLBC), which is an XML version of formal language for business commitments (FLBC) [168]. The authors consider contracts as a shared purpose comprising the mutual obligations and authorizations in a legally binding manner. In other words a contract contains rights and duties of participants. However, the assertion of "legally binding" is not always necessary. Imagine for example if the participants are two different departments of the same organization. This work considers business interaction as a pyramid with four layers consisting of speech acts (most elementary form), transactions, workflow loops and contracts (highest communication level). The higher level builds upon the lower level. A speech act represents an action like request or promise. A transaction is a pair of speech acts such as request and commit with an effect in the social world of participants. A workflow loop is a group of transactions and finally a contract is represented as two interleaving workflow loops. Note that in this work the concepts, e.g. transactions and workflow loops, have different meaning than in database and workflow literature. This work represents a different approach for contracts. While most other works consider contracts for defining the order of message exchange among participants, this work considers contracts by means of actions and external effects in the social world. Whilst this approach can be suitable for production workflows, it is inappropriate for realm of web services e.g. for definition of choreographies where everything is based on exchange of messages.

4.1. Related Works

[271] describes an inter-organizational workflow as a workflow consisting of two parts: an execution workflow and a control workflow. The execution part is responsible for internal tasks (cf. orchestrations) and the control part, itself comprising an actagenic part and a factagenic part, is in charge of interaction with others (cf. choreographies). An actagenic part controls service providings and a factagenic part is responsible for service requests. Their approach, based on actions rather than messages, is again obvious here. The control workflow, responsible for communications, is divided into two parts: service provision and request. It is mainly taken into account which actions are performed or should be performed instead of which messages are exchanged or should be exchanged.

On the Controlled Evolution of Process Choreographies

Rinderle et al. in [231] deal with the controlled evolution of process choreographies i.e. the problem of change of interaction structure among partners. For instance they study when a change in a private orchestration shall be propagated to the choreography and other orchestrations and how it can be done automatically. This work only considers the structural changes of a process for example insertion and deletion of an activity into or from a process.

Assume two processes P_a and P_b interact. Each with a private process and a public process (cf. process view). If the public process of P_a has been changed, this change must be reflected in its private process. A change can be addition of a message (additive change) or removal of a message (subtractive change). Other types of change, e.g. process reorganization, are not considered in this work. Next, it must be checked if the modified public process of P_a is still consistent with the public process of P_b. If this is the case, there is no need for propagation of change (invariant change), otherwise the pubic process of P_b must be modified as well to cater to the change (variant change). If the performed change in private process of P_a has no effect on its public process, the change can be kept local and no further check or propagation is necessary. Note that consistency here means a deadlock free execution of two processes. This work uses an extension of finite state automaton [145] called annotated finite state automaton (aFSA) for formalizing the consistency and its checking. The authors provide a proof that two automata are deadlock-free and consequently consistent if their intersection is non-empty. In other words two automata are bilaterally consistent if there is a path from the start node to the end node with respect to their execution. For checking the bilateral consistency all transition that do not contribute to the public process are relabeled (cf. silent actions) such that two processes contain only bilateral message sequences. If a change of public process of P_b is necessary, the change must be propagated to the belonging private process such that the newly added or removed messages are taken into account when the process executes. Regions of the private process of P_b that must be changed are to be identified. After performing the appropriate modifications in the private process, these changes are again propagated back to its public process and the consistency with public process of P_a is checked. In case of non-consistency this cycle must be repeated as long as both public processes are consistent. In case of additive change union of public process and added message and in case of subtractive change difference of public process and removed message can be used as basis for adaptation of public processes.

The need for mapping the BPEL from and into aFSA makes the proposed approach rather complex and computationally expensive. In addition, because the required modifications of the private and public processes can be performed in various ways, it is not clear how an effective and optimal method can be achieved. The authors do not mention the complexity of the algorithms.

Matchmaking for Business Processes Based on Choreographies

[274] represents a formal approach for matchmaking of business partners in a choreography in order to decide if processes of two interacting partners are consistent with each other and a deadlock free execution can be guaranteed. This paper uses an annotated deterministic finite state automaton (aDFA) as modeling language. Like [231] the non-emptiness of intersection of two annotated deterministic finite state automata serves as a proof of deadlock-freeness. That means two processes modeled as aDFA match together and are consistent if their intersection is not empty. The emptiness of intersection implies that no final state can be reached.

The proposed formalism and approach can be applied for very simple scenarios but is not suitable for real life applications because deterministic finite state automata (DFA) are incapable of presenting branching conditions and parallel execution which are indispensable for business processes and choreographies. Hence richer formalisms with a higher expressiveness such as Petri-nets are required. In addition the need for mapping from other languages and industry standards such as BPEL onto and from aDFA is another shortcoming of this approach for business processes consisting of some hundred activities.

Compatibility Verification for Web Service Choreography

Foster et al. in [124] represent an approach for testing compatibility of interacting business processes. This paper considers only safety compatibility and liveness compatibility. Safety compatibility concerns checking for deadlock-freeness and liveness compatibility is the progress analysis of a process, i.e. does service exhibit behaviors that do not lead to success e.g. does process eventually terminate?

The proposed approach is based on finite state process (FSP) formalisms and BPEL-processes need to be mapped onto this formalism for safety and liveness compatibility check [122]. The mapping and compatibility check can be done by a tool called LTSA. While not stated explicitly, the assumption here is that there is no predefined choreography that defines the message exchange among partners and only a set of separate orchestrations are available. After identification of all activities involved in all processes the counterparts of activities are identified, for example which receive activity belongs to which invoke activity and so on. Based on the previous analysis step a model of choreography can be built. After mapping of the obtained model onto FSP it can be checked if the process meets the deadlock-freeness and liveliness properties.

The authors do not make clear if only BPEL primitive activities such as receive, reply and invoke are considered or structured activities such as flows as well have to be analyzed and how constructs such as onAlaram or onEvent are handled. On the other side constructing a choreography by analyzing a set of orchestrations is tedious and error-prone.

The Self-Serv Environment for Web Services Composition

[49] introduces a P2P-based orchestration model for discovery, dynamic selection and declarative composition of web services, called self-serv environment. The main component of the system is the so-called service container. It is an aggregation of a set of services with common capabilities. A container is itself a service, that means it can be invoked by other services. Instead of searching and selecting a specific service, the service requester can invoke a service container and the invoked service container selects the service with the highest score from the set of contained services. The highest scored services is chosen based on a multi-attribute selection in the form of sum of weighted scores of attributes, where a scoring function is assigned to each attribute. Attributes' scores may be set a priori or extracted from logs. A Service can be defined as a member of a container at creation time of the container (explicit membership), it can be queried by the container from other registries at invocation time (query membership) or a service can register itself as a member at the container (registration membership). The membership is a n-to-n relationship.

For the interaction of web services the self-serv environment provides two components: a state coordinator and a routing table. A state coordinator is in charge of checking if preconditions for entering a state are fulfilled, receiving notification of completion from predecessor states and sending notification of completion to successor states. An initial coordinator is in charge of service initialization and instantiation. Routing tables store preconditions and post-conditions of each state which is looked up by state coordinators. Further a layered architecture consisting of service layer, conversation layer, directory layer and user layer is presented. Service layer is a collection of services and defines method invocations. Conversation layer supports standardized interaction of services. Directory layer provides meta data information about services and user layer provides access for discovery, building and deployment of services.

The message overhead imposed by state coordinators is a disadvantage of this approach. As one state coordinator is attached to each state and the communication among states and coordinators happens by message exchange, the message exchange overhead is increased.

Managing Virtual Organizations with Contracts

[191] discusses the required features of contracts in B2B virtual organizations and introduces a middleware-based prototype called web-Pilarcos that provides general infrastructure for B2B interactions. The provided functionalities include: business network model repository, where community structures are defined. Service offer repository, service type repository, contract repository, policy repository and monitoring module are other components. The monitoring module is an intermediate module between message senders and receivers. The monitoring module intercepts each message and checks its compliance with context and rules. If a message is compliant, it will be passed otherwise the sender receives an error notification.

This work considers contracts as the governing element of virtual organizations and integrates the exception handling module as a part of the negotiated contract. There is no predefined exception handling mechanisms, rather the corrective actions must be decided by participants in a collaborative manner. This approach has some disadvantages, for example the protocol for group decisions must be again negotiated, communication channels must be reserved in advanced and so on. Furthermore, the ability to react on errors and failures that must be compensated and corrected in a timely manner is severely limited.

Model Driven Distribution of Collaborative Business Processes

Authors in [235] represent a top-down approach for integrated modeling of business processes. The proposed approach consists of seven steps: building a centralized process containing all tasks, building swimlane partitions of the centralized process according to participants, identification of control transfer within and between swimlanes, extraction of distributed process models for each partition, transformation of activities into sender-receiver activities and finally deployment of the process.

The approach presented in [235] is very similar to that presented in [166] where a role based decomposition of business processes is studied.

Summary and comparison of related works

Table 4.1 summarizes the fields of application, used formalisms and consideration of consistency issues of the above discussed papers in the section 4.1

4.1. Related Works

paper	Contribution/ Application	Used Formalism	Consistency
[242]	Architecture for interorganizational applications	-	No
[155]	Architecture for modeling interorganizatioal workflows	-	No
[49]	Architecture for service selection and discovery	-	No
[191]	Architecture for virtual organizations	-	No
[278]	Modeling interorganizational business collaboration	state machines	No
[235]	Modeling business processes	-	No
[170]	Model extraction from log	continuous time Markov chain	Yes
[274]	Consistency of interorganizational workflows	finite state automata	Yes
[124]	Consistency of interorganizational workflows	finite state automata	Yes
[98]	Correctness verification	WF-net and message sequence charts	Yes
[189]	checking behavioral consistency	Petri-nets	Yes
[231]	Propagation of process changes	finite state automata	Yes
[71]	Interaction in interorganizational workflows	-	No
[166]	Partitioning of BPEL-processes	BPEL-D	No
[271]	Contracs for interorganizational workflows	XLBC	No
This work	Architecture for interorganizational workflows	DAG and WF-net	Yes

Table 4.1.: Summary of related works on interorganizational workflows

Chapter 5

Workflow Views

In the always more globalized world of business it is essential for companies to be able to offer their products and services cheaper and become more competitive. For this sake, automation of tasks and processes plays an essential role for providing cheaper services with a better quality. In recent years, workflow management systems have provided an effective and powerful tool for this aim. It is necessary for organizations to build short or long term cooperations with other organizations to reach the overall goal of a business process. Spread of internet, as a mean of communication, provides a powerful infrastructure for interorganizational workflows. Such workflows enable autonomous organizations, which may be geographically distant, to cooperate with each other. A challenging point when constructing such workflows is the balance between autonomy and cooperation. On the one hand, organizations must reveal some information to the business partners which are necessary for communication, monitoring, tracking purposes, etc. and on the other hand they want to hide their internal process logic to protect their know-how and improve their business secrecy. For external partners, as well, it is neither necessary nor desirable to have access to all parts of a provider's internal workflow as they do not want to be overloaded by unnecessary data and uninteresting messages. External partners are interested in those parts of a workflow which address them.

Workflow views provide a mean for this aim. Views define the accessible and visible parts of a process for external partners. A view can be a subset of the (activities of the) original workflow or represent the original workflow in an abstracted or aggregated fashion. External users communicate and interact with the view and not with the private executable workflow. Views are in charge of redirecting the data and messages to the executable workflow as well as forwarding them to external users. In business-to-customer (B2C) applications the external partner is normally a human user and in case of business-to-business (B2B) application the external user is another organization which in turn may interact and take part in the interorganizational workflow through its view. By using views, organizations are able to show as little information as possible but sufficient for the communication and interaction to reach the goals of a business process. By application of views, organizations do not need to change the interaction and communication with other partners or negotiate to set up a new choreography or a shared business process when the internal workflow is changed. As long as changes in a private workflow do not affect its view, this change can be kept local and there is no need for modification of the view and therefore, an organization can be sure that its external partners can still communicate in a conformant and consistent manner. In this work the focus is on business-to-business applications. The assumption is that each organization takes part in the interorganizational workflow through its workflow view, i.e. the shared business process is an integration of the partners' views. The approach presented here can be applied in a straightforward manner to business-to-customer applications where only the organization exposes its private workflow through a view on the process and external (human) users interact with the view. Partners communicate by their views and not with their private workflows. Figure 5.1 depicts this scenario. Three partners take part in the choreography (shared business process), each with its own private workflow. The interaction among partners is defined in the choreography. Each partner provides a view of its private workflow and the choreography is composed of the views of the private workflows. Each view is on the one hand a view on the corresponding private workflow and on the other hand a view on the choreography. For a discussion on correctness of interorganizational workflows refer to section 8.4. It must be ensured that views are conformant with each other and can interact without conflict. Several issues such as structural conformance, data flow conformance, messaging conformance and temporal conformance must be checked in order to ensure the consistency and conformance of an overall interorganizational workflow. This book provides correctness criteria for both views and the interorganizational workflow and besides handles the structural and temporal conformance of view-based interorganizational workflows to ensure that structures of participating processes match and interactions are done in a timely manner with respect to local and global constraints. A temporally conformant interorganizational workflow enables partners to execute the workflow without violating temporal constraints such as explicitly assigned deadlines and also reduces the process costs because fewer temporal exception must be raised and handled accordingly. Such a mechanism is a helpful tool in the hand of process designers and managers to foresee the possible upcoming temporal violations and trigger necessary counter-measures in a proactive manner.

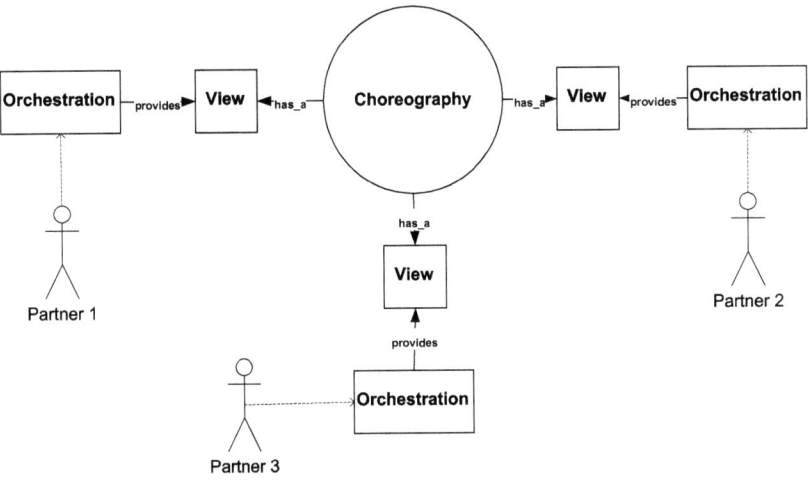

Figure 5.1.: An interorganizational workflow composed of views

5.1. Related Works

Facilitating Cross-Organisational Workflows with a Workflow View Approach

Schulz and Orlowska in [243] propose an application of workflow views as a mean for realizing communication and cooperation between independent and autonomous workflows in an interorganizational setting. In this work, a partner in a business process owns his private workflow which is only visible to its owner. Partners participate in a shared business process, in this work called coalition workflow, through their workflow views. A workflow view is an abstraction of the corresponding private workflow and reflects the communication requirements of the coalition workflow. When running the coalition workflow, the workflow views outsource the execution to the according private workflows. The cross-organizational workflow is composed of the private workflows of the participating partners. Further, an architecture for cross-organizational workflows is proposed. Authors apply a tightly coupled approach between private workflows and its view(s) based on state dependencies and a loosely coupled approach between views in the shared business process or coalition workflow based on control flow dependencies. The state mapping between workflow views and private workflows is realized through a Petri-net based state transition diagram. They also use synchronization tasks for modeling the interaction between two workflow views. This work only discusses the views from a state perspective and is silent on correctness issues of workflow views or how views may be built correctly.

This book uses somehow the same architectural model for view-based interorganizational workflows and in addition proposes two techniques for constructing views. Besides, correctness criteria for views and structural and temporal conformance and temporal execution plans are considered.

Workflow Modeling for Virtual Processes: An Order-Preserving Process-View Approach

Liu and Shen in [180] propose an order preserving approach for constructing views from a given workflow. A workflow view is composed of virtual activities. A virtual activity is an aggregation of base activities of a workflow (cf. complex activity). In this approach, a workflow view is not a subset of the activities of a workflow (e.g. by application of the abstraction operator) rather each virtual activity contains one or more base activities. In other words, a process view contains all activities of the base process but in a new grouping. After a formal definition of elementary and virtual elements such as activity, dependency, loop, etc., a rather simplistic meta-model is introduced. The authors present three rules for construction of process views. An algorithm for automatic construction of possible process views with respect to the above mentioned rules is also presented. It seems that the proposed approach may not be fully sufficient, as the process view is considered as a new ordering of base activities and this may possibly be more effectively implemented by means of complex activities. Note that all activities of the base process must be contained in a process view. On the other hand this work is silent on correctness issues of workflow views in an interorganizational workflow.

In addition to aggregation used in this work, the book proposes application of abstraction operator for constructing views. The approach of this book is complementary in the sense that temporal execution plans of the views and temporal and structural conformance of interacting views are considered.

Business-to-Business Workflow Interoperation Based on Process-Views

[181] can be seen as a combination of [243, 180]. The construction of process views originates from the authors' previous work [180] enriched with the state mapping used in [243]. However the authors use slightly different terminology for naming the states By introducing states for virtual activities, partners might be able to monitor the progress status of a virtual activity. The state of a virtual activity is a function of the states of its member base activities. This work is again silent on correctness issues of workflow views.

The focus of this work is state mapping between a process and its views. However, this book mainly focuses on how views can be correctly built.

The View-Based Approach to Dynamic Inter-Organizational Workflow Cooperation

Chebi, Dustdar and Tata in [74] propose an approach based on software oriented architecture paradigm (SOA) for interconnection and cooperation of workflows. A semantic registry for publishing and discovery of services is proposed, enabling other organizations to build a cross-organizational cooperation by finding and binding to other partners. Participants take part in the interorganizational workflow with their workflow views. In order to minimize a view, it contains only cooperative tasks. i.e. tasks that either send data to external workflows or receive data from external workflows. Workflow views are called cooperative processes in this work. The interorganizational workflow, here called public process, consists of virtual activities. Virtual activities are in charge of transferring data to/from executable activities. A virtual activity is a subset of cooperative activities. The cooperation between partners is handled and modeled by cooperation policies. In contrast to a protocol, cooperation policies describe a set of allowed interaction scenarios and are a set of rules in terms of data flow, access contract and workflow public process definition. A third party is responsible for monitoring the interaction policies. Communication between partners is managed through a trusted third party. The authors claim that their approach is appropriate for a dynamic setting i.e. where partners, their workflows and interconnections are not predefined. However, there is a need for negotiation and a contract for setting up the interaction policy and identification of public virtual activities. The contribution of this work is introducing a semantic service registry, similar to SOA, for searching and identification of partners in a semi-automatic fashion. In other words, the negotiation between partners is shifted after identification of partners from the registry. Note that this step is implicitly done in other approaches. Partners cannot negotiate and set up a contract unless they do not know each other. The assumption that a workflow view consists of only cooperative tasks, may not be sufficient in all scenarios. Imagine for example when a service consumer subcontracts a service to a provider and the consumer requires the monitoring of process progress at provider's workflow. This work is silent on correctness issues of public processes. It is assumed that negotiation between partners results in a correct process.

This work uses views as a mean for cooperation between partners using only communication activities. The approach in this book is more general. Not only communication activities but also other activities which may be necessary for a cooperation between partners can be included in a view. Furthermore, temporal and structural conformance of an interorganizational workflow composed of views is considered.

Workflow View Driven Cross-Organizational Interoperability in a Web-Service Environment

Chiu et al. in [78] propose the application of workflow views for interoperability in cross-organizational workflows. The balance between security and trust is considered to be achieved through views. In other words, views restrict the access on a workflow and conceal the internal, private or unnecessary information. A workflow view is defined as a structurally correct subset of a workflow definition. The authors introduce a meta-model concerning access rights on objects associated with a view. Other aspects like structural or dataflow are not further considered. Moreover, they do not describe how views can be constructed from a workflow and they provide no correctness criteria. An interaction protocol consists of workflow views, communication graphs between these views, and a set of inter-operation parameters. Communication graphs are a container for communication links which in turn, are responsible for sending and receiving messages, i.e. messages are sent through communication links. Inter-operation parameters are a set of attributes describing the necessary information for the business. The authors consider exception rules also as a kind of interoperation parameter. In [78] an integrated view on workflow views in an interorganizational interoperation is missing.

This work focuses on views as a tool for access restriction. This aspect is implicitly considered in the proposed approach of this book. Because such decisions, e.g. which partner can access an activity, depend heavily on the context it is left to the user to decide which activities are included in a view for a partner. The presented approach in this book gives workflow designers tools to design views from a private workflow.

Discovering Role-Relevant Process-Views for Disseminating Process Knowledge

In [182] Shen and Liu based on the framework provided in their previous work [78] present a technique for designing workflow views and identification of relevant tasks included in a workflow view for a specific role. In their approach, workflow views are visible part of a process for a specific role. Hence, the authors argue that defining some metrics for tasks (regarding a given role) in a workflow helps to find the most relevant tasks for the according role. Workflow operations are used as a criteria to evaluate role-task relevance. The provided metrics can be easily altered by considering other factors like cost or the context of a process. These metrics are extracted and calculated by analyzing the workflow logs. Given a threshold and by calculation of the metrics, the authors present three algorithm for construction of a virtual activity set, construction of a virtual activity set whose total relevance degree approximates granular threshold and construction of a legal virtual activity.

This work uses metrics for construction of views. Such metrics are mined from workflow logs which implies that a private workflow must be exposed to specific roles before such data can be mined for construction of views. The approach of this book assumes that workflow owners use views to protect their business know-how encoded in the private workflow and they do not want to expose their private workflow to external users.

Flows and Views for Scalable Scientific Integration

Building upon the notion of workflow views presented in [78], Li et al. in [177] introduce a methodology for decomposition of complex processes in scientific domain and building views based on flows. The authors argue that "the separation of flows results in the increased flexibility and scalability of information services for cross-organizational processes integration". Moreover, this separation yields in a better modifiability of the process for different situations and applications. Note that only predefined exceptions can be handled by exception flows and unknown exception are not considered in this work. The interactions among mentioned flows are triggered by external messages. Each flow can have multiple views. The authors propose to build a view of a flow based on the analysis of the required incoming messages (beginning with the core activities of a process and its sub-processes), its immediate responses and the dependency between data and messages. After all partners have published their views, the overall process can be constructed by integration of all views, whilst other flows such as exception flows and security flows have to be considered in this step.

This work uses views as a tool for decomposition of a complex workflow into some sub-flows. In other words, data flows, control flows, etc. are decomposed and each flow is presented as a view on the workflow. This book applies views mainly for the interaction and cooperation of partners in an interorganizational setting.

Object-Oriented Realization of Workflow Views for Web Services - An Object Deputy Model Based Approach

Shan et al. in [247] introduce an object oriented approach for workflow views called the object deputy model. The definition and concept of workflow views is again taken from [78]. A deputy object has its own persistent identifier and may have additional attributes and methods that are not derived from its source objects. Moreover, there is a bilateral link between objects and one of its deputy objects, which allows not only for inheritance but also for update propagations between them. The authors provide a taxonomy of views and a very simple meta model stating solely a subset-relationship between a workflow and its views. In this work views are used for two main purposes: restriction of access and composition. It is not discussed how workflow views can be constructed for mentioned applications. Similar to a workflow view, a workflow restriction view is defined as a structurally correct subset of a workflow definition. A workflow composition view is a virtual workflow composed of components from different workflows, which may span across organizational boundaries. The authors introduce a deputy algebra for definition of classes and inheritance consisting of six operations. A workflow object model is also introduced in this work. However, this model is mainly based on the model of object management group.

This works sees views as a subset of a flow which can inherit properties from the original flow and is silent on construction of views and its correctness. The focus of this book is on construction and correctness of views.

Summary and comparison of related works

Table 5.1 compares the related works on workflow views. The table summarizes if τ-operator or aggregation are used for construction of view. If any correctness criteria for constructed views are provided and if any other conformance criteria like temporal conformance have been considered and for which purpose views are basically applied. The last row summarizes the contribution of this book. Note that the τ-operator is defined in section 5.3 of this chapter.

This book is complementary to the related works in the sense that it provides two ways for constructing views out of flows and in addition it provides a technique for calculating the temporal execution plans of views based on flows. Furthermore, an approach for checking the temporal and structural conformance of interorganizational workflows composed of views has been proposed.

Paper	Construction of Views		Correctness		Applied for
	τ-operator	Aggregation	Views	Other issues	
[74]	No	Yes	No	No	Cooperation
[78]	No	No	No	No	Interoperability
[177]	No	No	No	No	Flexibility
[180]	No	Yes	Yes	No	N.A.
[181]	No	No	No	No	Monitoring
[182]	No	Yes	Yes	No	N.A.
[243]	No	No	No	No	Cooperation
[247]	No	No	No	No	Access restriction
This book	Yes	Yes	Yes	Yes	Cooperation

Table 5.1.: Summary of related work on workflow views

5.2. Correctness of Views

The assumption is that each partner has a private workflow which is only visible to its owner and external parties have no knowledge about the process structure and internal logic of the private workflow. In order to provide the necessary information for communication and interaction with other partners and/or service requesters, the workflow owner provides views. A workflow can have many views, one for each partner, for each role of a partner or for a group of partners. In this way the workflow is able to interact with external parties whilst protecting private aspects of the process. It is assumed that all workflows are full-blocked, i.e. each split-node has a counterpart join-node and vice versa. In this work workflows are modeled by directed acyclic graphs $G = (N, E)$, where N denotes the set of nodes and E the set of edges. Nodes correspond to activities and control nodes and edges to the dependencies between activities and control nodes. See also subsection 7.2.3. Note that a view on a workflow is again a full-blocked workflow.

In order to construct correct views on workflows it is necessary that activities in a view have the same ordering as in the underlying workflow. In other words a view on a flow can not change the ordering of the activities of the underlying workflow. Such a view is called an order-preserving view.

Definition 5.1: **(Correctness of Views)**

A workflow $G\prime = (N\prime, E\prime)$ is a correct view of a workflow $G = (N, E)$ if and only if the following properties hold:

5.3. Construction of Views

(a) $G\prime$ is a valid full-blocked workflow definition

(b) The nodes contained in $G\prime$ are a subset of the nodes of G or represent a subset of the nodes of G

(c) $\forall$ nodes $a, b \in N \cap N\prime : [a > b]_{G\prime} \Leftrightarrow [a > b]_G$, where $[a > b]_G$ denotes that there is a path from node a to node b in the graph G and $N\prime \subset N$

A view $G\prime$ of a workflow G with the property (c) is called an order preserving view of G. An order preserving view does not change the order of the nodes of the underlying workflow.

5.3. Construction of Views

Here two ways for construction of views are considered:

1. Application of abstraction operator

2. Aggregation

By application of the abstraction operator (called τ-operator in process algebra [51]) it is possible to make parts of a process invisible to external observers. The τ-operator is like a renaming operator that renames the label of an activity into a τ-label. The τ-labeled activities then become internal activities and invisible to an external observer. The abstraction operator provides a mean for construction of views. By application of this operator parts of a process that do not contribute to the interaction with another partner, are not interesting for external partners or are intended to be hidden because of privacy issues can be made unobservable and the rest of the process can be exposed as a view on the process.

Definition 5.2: **(Abstraction operator)**
Let $G = (N, E)$ be a workflow. Application of the abstraction operator on an activity j of a workflow G results in a workflow $G\prime = (N\prime, E\prime)$, denoted by $\tau(G, j) = G\prime$.
$\tau(G, j) = G\prime = (N\prime, E\prime)$ with
$N\prime = N - \{j\}$,
$E\prime = \{(n_s, n_t) \mid [(n_s, n_t) \in E \wedge n_s \neq j \wedge n_t \neq j]\} \cup \{(n_s, n_t) \mid [(n_s, j) \in E \wedge (j, n_t) \in E]\}$

Abstraction of an activity j removes the activity j from the set of nodes N as well as all edges whose source node or target node is the activity j from the set of edges E. An edge from the predecessor of the activity j to its successor is added to the set of edges E. Note that the abstraction operator can only be applied on activities and not on control nodes.

Definition 5.3: **(Silent activity)**
A τ-labeled activity is called a silent activity and is unobservable from outside by an external observer.

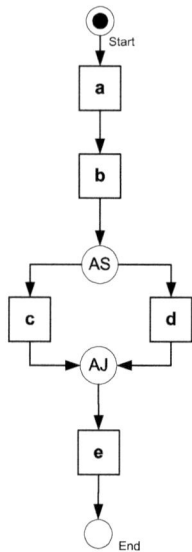

Figure 5.2.: Workflow G modeled as a directed acyclic graph

Let $G = (N, E)$ be the graph depicted in figure 8.39.

The set of nodes of G is $N = \{a, b, c, d, e, AS, AJ\}$ and the the set of its edges is
$E = \{(start, a), (a, b), (b, AS), (AS, c), (AS, d), (c, AJ), (d, AJ), (AJ, e), (e, end)\}$.

After application of the abstraction operator on activity $b \in G$, the graph transforms to a new graph $G\prime$ with $N\prime = \{a, c, d, e, AS, AJ\}$ and
$E\prime = \{(start, a), (a, AS), (AS, c), (AS, d), (c, AJ), (d, AJ), (AJ, e), (e, end)\}$. The new graph $G\prime$ is depicted in figure 5.3.

Proposition 5.1: **(Properties of the abstraction operator)**

(a) Abstraction operator is commutative, i.e.
 Let $G = (N, E), \forall$ activities $a, b \in N$:
 $\tau(\tau(G, a), b) = \tau(\tau(G, b), a)$

(b) Abstraction operator is associative, i.e.
 Let $G = (N, E), \forall$ activities $a, b, c \in N$:
 $\tau(\tau(\tau(G, a), b), c) = \tau(\tau(\tau(G, c), b), a)$

(c) Abstraction is an order preserving operation and does not change the order of remaining activities, i.e. Let $G = (N, E)$ and $G\prime = (N\prime, E\prime)$ be the resulting graph after application of the abstractor operator on an activity of G,

5.3. Construction of Views

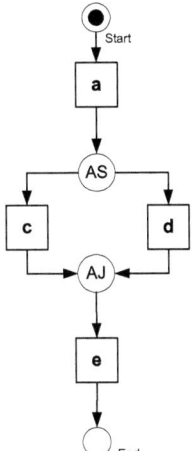

Figure 5.3.: Workflow $G\prime$ after application of abstraction operator on activity b in G

$\forall$ activities $a, b \in N\prime : [a > b]_{G\prime} \Leftrightarrow [a > b]_G$, where $[a > b]_G$ denotes that there is a path from a to b in G

The resulting graph $G\prime$ is a valid full-blocked workflow definition.

The properties (a) and (b) follow directly from definition of the abstraction operator (definition 5.2). The abstraction operator removes an activity from the set of nodes and consequently the ordering of the activities in the resulting graph remains the same as in the underlying workflow. In other words, abstraction is an order-preserving operator and the resulting workflow view is an order-preserving view. Because the abstraction operator can be applied only on activities and not on control nodes and it is assumed that all workflows all full-blocked, the resulting graph after application of the abstraction operator on a workflow is still a full-blocked workflow.

Another way of constructing workflow views is application of aggregation. By aggregation some activities are grouped into a so-called abstract or aggregated activity. Aggregation can be used for hiding the internal structure of a group of activities. The aggregated activity is consequently contained in the workflow view and is in charge of sending and receiving data to and from activities in the underlying workflow.

Definition 5.4: (**Aggregated activity**)

Let $G = (N, E)$ be a workflow. An aggregated activity A_{G_A} represents a graph $G_A = (N_A, E_A)$ with the following properties:

- G_A is a connected subgraph of G

- G_A has a unique first node and a unique last node, i.e. G_A has only one incoming edge and only one outgoing edge

- If a split-node (join-node) is in N_A, its counterpart join-node (split-node) is also in N_A

$N_A \subseteq N$ denotes the set of activities and control nodes in the aggregated activity and E_A the dependencies between activities and control nodes, where $E_A = \{(n_s, n_t) \in E \mid n_s, n_t \in N_A\}$.

Note that G_A is the graph representing internal structure of the aggregated activity and A_{G_A} identifies the aggregated activity.

Definition 5.5: (**Aggregation**)

Aggregation is an operator that groups a subset of nodes of a workflow into an aggregated activity. Let $G = (N, E)$ be a workflow and $G\prime = (N\prime, E\prime)$ the resulting graph after application of aggregation on some activities of G. Application of the aggregation operator on a workflow G results in a new workflow $G\prime$, denoted by $AG(G, N_A) = G\prime$.

$AG(G, N_A) = G\prime(N\prime, E\prime)$ with

$N\prime = N - N_A \cup \{A_{G_A}\}$,

$E\prime = \{(n_s, n_t) \in E \mid n_s \notin N_A \wedge n_t \notin N_A\} \cup \{(n_s, A_{G_A}), (A_{G_A}, n_t) \mid \exists (n_s, n_f), (n_l, n_t) \in E, n_f, n_l \in N_A\}$, where n_f denotes the first node of G_A and n_l its last node respectively.

All nodes $n \in N_A$ are removed from N and the aggregated activity A_{G_A} is added. All edges of the nodes contained in G_A are as well removed from the set of edges E and two edges are added. One edge from the predecessor of the first node of the aggregated activity to the aggregated activity and another from aggregated activity to the successor of the last node of the aggregated activity.

The above properties for N_A are required to ensure that the workflow after application of aggregation is still a valid full-blocked workflow definition. The following figures demonstrate that by lack of any of these properties in definition 5.4 the resulting graph is not a valid full-blocked workflow definition anymore.

Figure 5.4 clarifies why it is required that an aggregated activity be a connected subgraph of the underlying workflow. The aggregated activity in figure 5.4 is not a connected subgraph and it can be seen that after aggregation the resulting workflow is not a valid workflow definition anymore.

5.3. Construction of Views

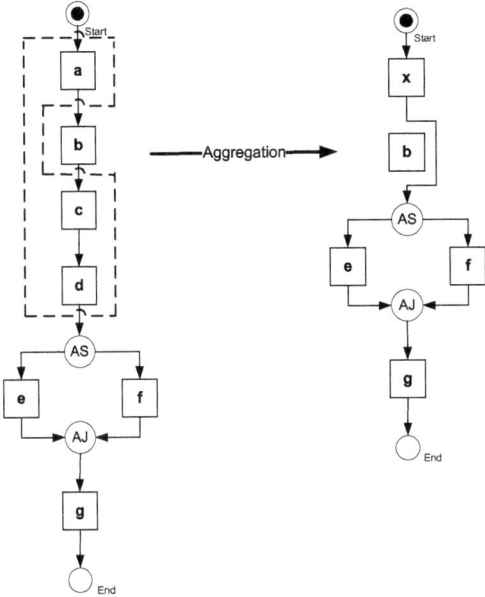

Figure 5.4.: Aggregated activity is not a connected subgraph

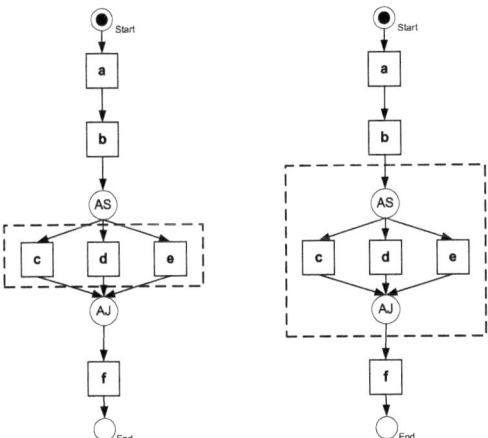

Figure 5.5.: Left: A wrongly aggregated activity, Right: A correctly aggregated activity

The left part of the figure 5.5 illustrates a wrongly aggregated activity. As it can be seen the aggregated activity has three incoming edges and three outgoing edges. In such a case it is not clear which activity is the first and the last activity of the aggregated activity. The right part of the figure shows a correctly aggregated activity with only one incoming and outgoing edge.

Figure 5.6 illustrates the need to include the counterpart of control nodes in aggregation. If it is not the case, the resulting graph is not a valid workflow definition as it can be seen in figure 5.6.

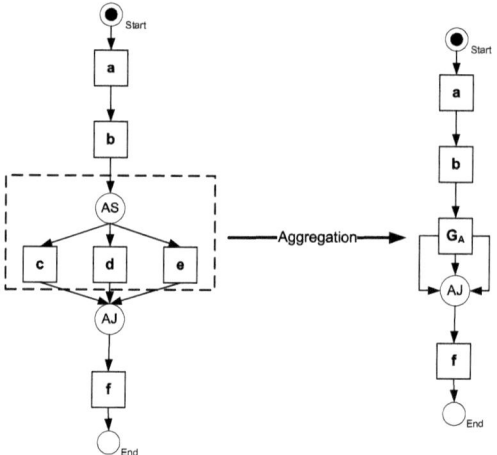

Figure 5.6.: The counterpart of control nodes must be included in aggregation

Figure 5.7 demonstrates an application of aggregation. The workflow G on the left part of the figure 5.7 has $N = \{a, b, c, d, e, f, g, AS, AJ\}$ and
$E = \{(start, a), (a, b), (b, c), (c, d), (d, AS), (AS, e), (AS, f), (e, AJ), (f, AJ), (AJ, g), (g, end)\}$.
The resulting graph $G\prime$ has $N\prime = \{a, x, e, f, g, AS, AJ\}$ and
$E\prime = \{(start, a), (a, x), (x, AS), (AS, e), (AS, f), (e, AJ), (f, AJ), (AJ, g), (g, end)\}$.

5.3. Construction of Views

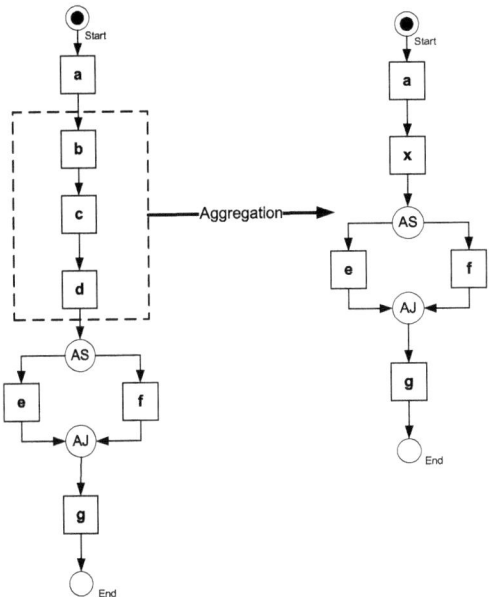

Figure 5.7.: Application of aggregation

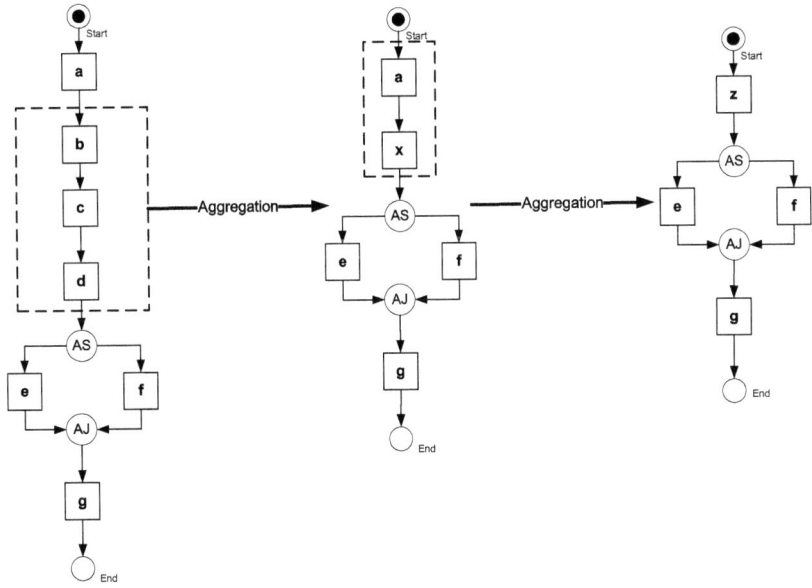

Figure 5.8.: Recursive application of aggregation

The activities contained in an aggregated activity are not necessarily executable activities. Aggregated activities can again be aggregated into a new aggregated activity. In other words aggregation can be applied in a recursive fashion. Aggregation is transitive in the sense that if an activity j is contained in an aggregated activity x and the aggregated activity x is itself contained in another aggregated activity y, then the activity j is contained in the aggregated activity y, $j \in x \wedge x \in y \Rightarrow j \in y$.

Figure 5.8 demonstrates a recursive application of aggregation.

Proposition 5.2: **(Properties of aggregation)**

(a) Let $G = (N, E)$ be a workflow and $G\prime = (N\prime, E\prime)$ the resulting workflow after application of aggregation on some activities of G and N_A the set of nodes of the aggregated activity A_{G_A}:

$\forall a, b \in N$:
$[a > b]_G \wedge a, b \notin N_A \Rightarrow [a > b]_{G\prime}$
$[a > b]_G \wedge a \notin N_A \wedge b \in N_A \Rightarrow [a > A_{G_A}]_{G\prime}$
$[a > b]_G \wedge a \in N_A \wedge b \notin N_A \Rightarrow [A_{G_A} > b]_{G\prime}$

(b) $\forall a, b \in N\prime$:
$[a > b]_{G\prime} \wedge a, b \neq G_A \Rightarrow [a > b]_G$
$[a > A_{G_A}]_{G\prime} \Rightarrow \forall i \in N_A : [a > i]_G$

(c) $G\prime$ is a valid full-blocked workflow definition

The above properties of the aggregation operator follow directly from the definition of the aggregation operator (definition 5.5).

It is clear that if two nodes are not member of an aggregated activity, the path between these two nodes remains the same and hence the ordering between these nodes remains also the same. $([a > b]_G \wedge a, b \notin N_A \Rightarrow [a > b]_{G\prime})$ is true because aggregation only affects members of an aggregated activity and all other nodes remains unaffected. If a node a precedes a node of an aggregated activity, aggregation removes all edges of the aggregated activity and adds one incoming edge to the aggregated activity, i.e. the node a precedes the aggregated activity and $([a > b]_G \wedge a \notin N_A \wedge b \in N_A \Rightarrow [a > A_{G_A}]_{G\prime})$ is true.

If a node b follows a node of an aggregated activity, aggregation removes all edges of the aggregated activity and adds one outgoing edge from the aggregated activity, i.e. the node b follows the aggregated activity and $([a > b]_G \wedge a \in N_A \wedge b \notin N_A \Rightarrow [A_{G_A} > b]_{G\prime})$ is true. With the same argumentation the reverse direction can also be proved. The above properties show that aggregation is an order-preserving operator.

Also directly from definition of the aggregation operator follows that the resulting graph after aggregation is a valid full-blocked workflow. Definition 5.5 requires that the counterpart of each join-node or split-node must also be contained in an aggregated activity. Because the underlying workflow is a full-blocked workflow, the resulting graph remains also a valid full-blocked workflow definition.

5.3. Construction of Views

Definition 5.6: **(Event Correspondence)**
An aggregated activity begins when its first activity begins and terminates when its last activity has terminated. The start of an aggregated activity corresponds to the start of its first activity and its end corresponds to the end of its last activity

Proposition 5.3: **(Property of views)**
Let $N = (G, E)$ be a workflow. Construction of views by application of abstraction operator or aggregation as defined in definitions 5.2 and 5.5 on N results in a graph $N\prime = (G\prime, E\prime)$ which is again a workflow.

The proof follows directly from the definition and properties of abstraction operator and aggregation.

Theorem 5.1: **(Aggregation and abstraction construct correct views)**
Let $N = (G, E)$ be a workflow. Application of abstraction operator or aggregation as defined in definitions 5.2 and 5.5 on N results in a graph $N\prime = (G\prime, E\prime)$ which is a correct view on N

In the properties of the abstraction operator (proposition 5.1) and properties of the aggregation (proposition 5.2) it has been shown that the abstraction operator and aggregation are order-preserving operators and the resulting graph after application of the abstraction operator and aggregation is a valid full-blocked workflow definition. From the definition of the abstraction operator (definition 5.2) follows that the set of nodes in the resulting graph is a subset of the nodes of the underlying workflow and from the definition of aggregation (definition 5.5) follows that only one node representing a subset of nodes of the underlying workflow is added to the set of nodes of the resulting graph and the other nodes are a subset of the nodes of the underlying workflow. Hence, workflow views constructed by application of abstraction operator and aggregation satisfy all the correctness criteria in definition 5.1 and such views are correct workflow views.

5.3.1. Concatenation of Operators

After application of abstraction or aggregation operators on a workflow, the resulting workflow is again a valid full-blocked workflow definition on which abstraction or aggregation operators can again be applied. Operators can be applied consecutively on a workflow to construct a view.

Definition 5.7: **(View Constructor)**
Let $G = (N, E)$ be a workflow and $G\prime = (N\prime, E\prime)$ a view on G. The view constructor operator, $VC(G) = G\prime$, is a sequence of abstraction or aggregation operators, denoted by $G \xrightarrow{\alpha} .. \xrightarrow{\alpha} .. \xrightarrow{\alpha} G\prime$, where α is either the abstraction operator or the aggregation operator.

After each application of α the workflow transforms to a new workflow. Note that the sequence is finite and can be empty. Obviously there is no unique way of constructing views rather the same view can be constructed by different sequence of operators. The view constructor is transitive in the sense that if $G\prime$ is a view on G and $G\prime\prime$ a view on $G\prime$ then $G\prime\prime$ is a view on G. However, the commutativity is not valid because different sequence of operators, produce different views.

Figures 5.9 and 5.10 show how the same view on the same workflow can be constructed by two different sequences of operators.

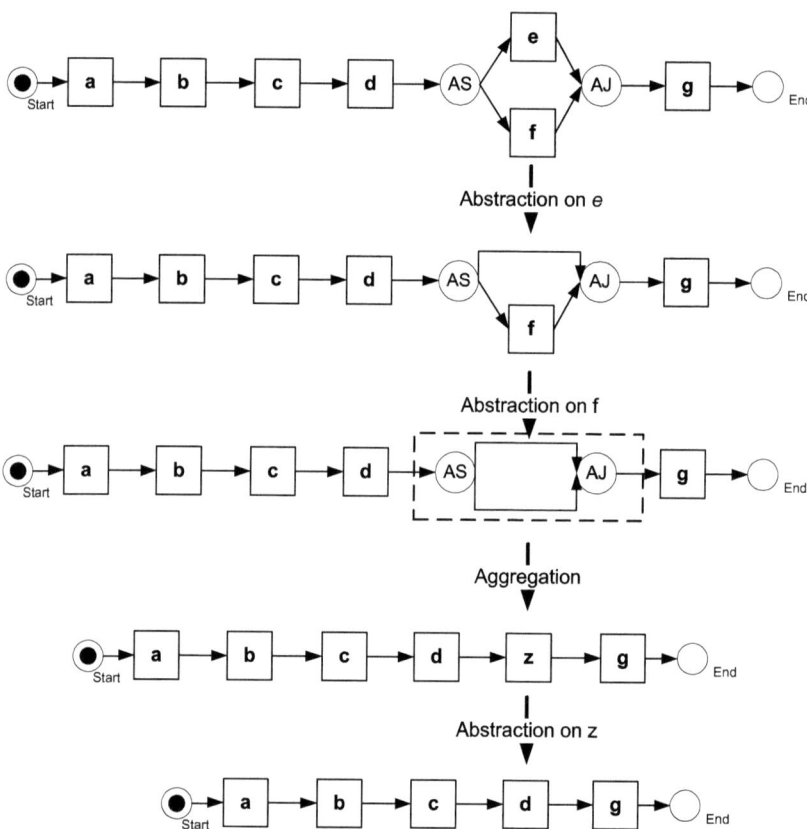

Figure 5.9.: Constructing a view by a sequence of operators

5.3. Construction of Views

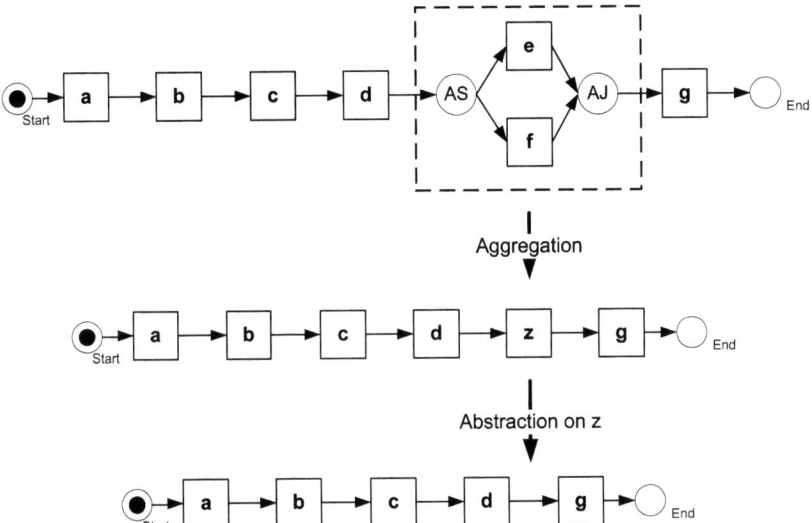

Figure 5.10.: Constructing the same view as in Figures 5.9 by a different sequence of operators

Chapter 6

Web Services and Web Service Standards

This chapter provides an overview on web services and the state of the art of its most important related standards.

6.1. Web Services

A web service is a piece of code that executes a task. Web services are published on the internet by service providers. A service provider can develop a web service with defined interfaces and publish it. A service requester can search for services that he is interested in, find them, bind to available web services and use the published services. This paradigm remembers very strong of remote procedure calls (RPC). In the recent years web services and web service technology have become popular in both industry and academia. This is mainly because of useful and handy characteristics of web services that make them a suitable technology for many application areas such as business process management and distributed information systems. On the other hand, availability of internet as a medium plays also an important role. Another reason for acceptance of web services is the fact that it is standardized. The big plus of web services that makes them specially interesting is their capability of being integrated into more complex systems, the so-called web service composition. In other words web services are autonomous, stand-alone systems that can be used as building blocks of other systems. Web services are autonomous in the sense that they are operational in isolation as stand-alone systems and besides, they can be part of a bigger, more complex, composed system.

The world wide web consortium defines a web service as "a software application identified by an URI, whose interfaces and bindings are capable of being defined, described, and discovered as XML artifacts. A Web service supports direct interactions with other software agents using XML based messages exchanged via Internet-based protocols". This definition points out the important characteristics of web services. First of all web services should be defined and published (by service providers) such that they can be discovered by others (service requesters). It describes the main underlying standard of web service technology: XML. All web service standards are XML-based. Web service technology is

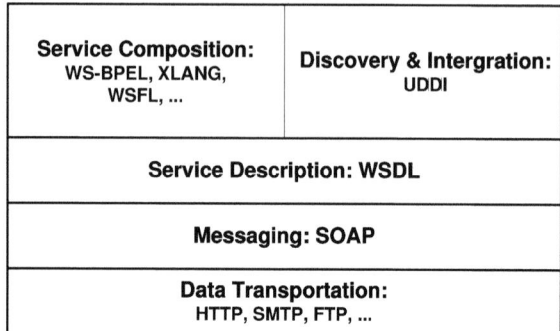

Figure 6.1.: Web serive standards

based on a set of standards as depicted in figure 6.1. In the following subsections the web service standards are briefly introduced and discussed. Because the data transportation layer is not web service specific, it is omitted and is out of scope of this work.

6.2. SOAP

Simple Object Access Protocol (SOAP) is a language and platform independent transport protocol for data transportation which enables interoperability between services, systems and remote machines over the Internet. SOAP has been specified by Microsoft in late nineties with the primary goal of enabling remote procedure calls in decentralized, non-homogeneous, distributed environments like Internet. Later other international big players such as IBM , Sun Micro Systems , Developmentor and Userland have joined. SOAP is an XML-based specification and builds upon existing transport protocols such as Hypertext Transfer Protocol (HTTP), Simple Mail Transfer Protocol (SMTP) or File Transfer Protocol (FTP). SOAP does not force any specific transport protocol. However, till now only HTTP has been specified as underlying transport protocol and seems to become the standard. SOAP is an XML-based language and it uses XML as intermediary representation when messages are exchanged among heterogenous systems like java-based and C-based systems. In such a case the messages are transformed from the source representation into an XML-representation and after the transport, again, to the data format of the destination system.

A SOAP-message consists of three Parts:

1. An obligatory envelope

2. An optional header

3. An obligatory body

All three parts are XML-messages. Body and header are child-elements of the envelope. The envelope covers the message and provides a description of the message content. The SOAP specification enforces how messages should be processed and who should process them (the so-called actors). The optional header may contain additional information such as comments, usernames, etc. that are not contained in the actual message. The actual message is presented in the body of a message. It provides a mechanism for remote procedure calls (RPC) and responses to such calls. The actual message may contain variables for RPCs, responses to RPCs or possible failures. Note that only failures resulted by message processings will be contained in the body of a message. Other failures resulted by the message transportation are handled directly by the HTTP mechanisms. The SOAP-specification can be found at [1].

For specification, discussion, applications and detailed information on SOAP, refer to [245, 249, 244, 151, 234, 116, 28].

6.3. WSDL

Web Services Description Language (WSDL) is an XML-based specification for description of web services' interfaces, interactions among web services as well as specification of their locations. In the view of WSDL, a web service is a collection of ports. A WSDL-document is basically comprised of two parts:

1. Abstract definition

2. Concrete definition

The separation of abstract and concrete definitions of ports or endpoints in WSDL enables reusability, in the sense that concrete endpoint can reuse and deploy the definition of abstract endpoints. The abstract part contains the following elements:

Types : defines the used data types for message exchange.

Messages : consist of one or more parts and are abstract definitions of exchanged data (compare with function parameters).

PortTypes : are an aggregation of operations together with the involved messages (input and output parameters).

WSDL supports all type systems such as XML schema definition and provides the possibility for importing other data types defined in external schemas. An operation refers to the communication style supported by an endpoint. WSDL Provides four types of operations:

1. **Notification**: an endpoint sends a message

2. **One-way**: an endpoint receives a message

3. **Solicit-response**: an endpoint sends a message and then receives its response

4. **Request-response**: an endpoint receives a message and then sends its response

Figure 6.2 illustrates the possible message transmission primitives, called operations, in WSDL.

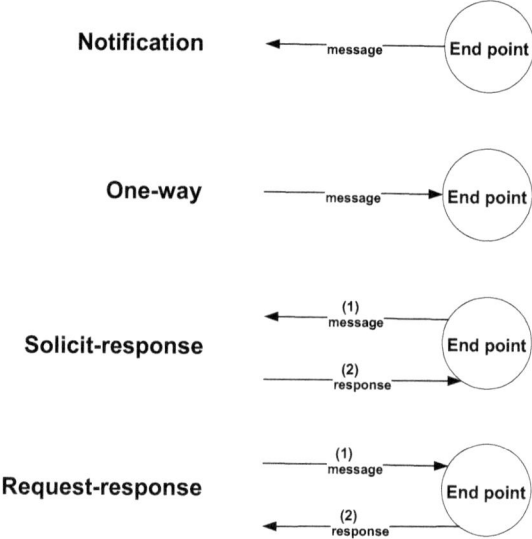

Figure 6.2.: Possible operations in WSDL

The concrete part definition provides possibility for actual network deployment of the abstract parts and consists of:

Bindings : define the binding information (message format, protocol details) for each of the operations defined in the PortTypes part.

Services : are collection of ports. Each port is a communication endpoint for bindings.

Figure 6.3 shows schematically the relationship among different elements of a WSDL specification.

6.3. WSDL

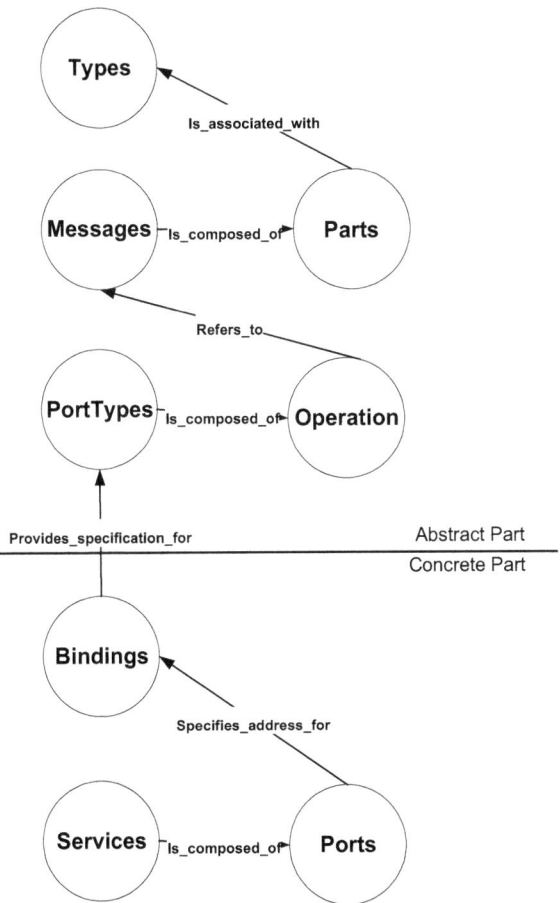

Figure 6.3.: The relationship among different elements of WSDL

For specification, application, extensions, relationship with other web service standards and discussion on WSDL, please refer to [77, 53, 27, 31, 84]

6.4. UDDI

Universal Description, Discovery and integration (UDDI) [2] is an specification based on standards such as XML and SOAP that does the almost similar thing for business services and web services as search engines like Google do for the web. As its name implies, by UDDI one can publish web services (description), search for web services (discovery) and bind to the discovered web services (integration). A collaboration of IBM, Microsoft and Ariba released the first version of the UDDI specification by the year 2000. The second version has followed in the year 2001. The latest released version of UDDI is UDDI Version 3.0.2. An organization consisting of several hundred firms [2] is responsible for management, development and specification of UDDI.

As the numbers of available web services rapidly increases and almost explodes, there is a need for a kind of search engine through which available web services can be explored according to some user defined criteria and parameters. In addition, after finding the appropriate web service or web services that match the user's criteria, the user must know where to find the service and how to bind to it. On the other hand, service providers also need a mechanism for publishing their services. Building a bridge between service providers and service requesters is the core idea of UDDI. This has obvious advantages for business-to-business applications and facilitates the use of international marketplaces over the Internet for enterprizes of any size on the globe.

Figure 6.4 shows how a UDDI registry works. The numbers beside the arrows, show the order of execution.

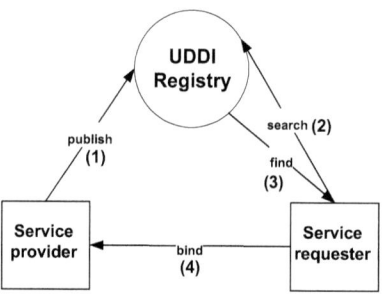

Figure 6.4.: The idea of UDDI

A service provider publishes its services on a UDDI registry (1), a service requester queries the registry (2), receives the result list (3) and finally binds to the chosen service (4). In the following, it is explained in more detail how each step is performed. Although an UDDI-registry may seems to be a singular database to the user, it is in fact a distributed database. For publishing data in a UDDI-registry, it is imperative to use taxonomies and

6.4. UDDI

data has to be published within taxonomies. Taxonomies provide a structure for data presentation and information can be published in a coherent and consistent way. In addition to standard taxonomies such as the United Nations Standard Products and Services Code System (UNSPSC) [14] or the North American Industry Classification System (NAICS) [12], UDDI allows users to define their own taxonomy. Note that simultaneously more than one taxonomy can be used. In addition to the requirement of using taxonomy for publication of data into registries, it is required that UDDI implementations provide a way for querying registries based on different taxonomies.

Analogous to a telephone directory, an UDDI-registry is composed of three different categories:

1. White pages
2. Yellow pages
3. Green pages

White pages and yellow pages provide information for locating a service provider (service discovery) while green pages provide technical information (service integration). On white pages, general information about a provider such as name, contact information e.g. address, telephone number, fax number, e-mail and URL can be found. Other optional identifiers of a service provider may also be contained in white pages. Yellow pages are classification of providers into different business categories. Service providers are categorized on yellow pages and can be searched based on their business field. Finally, the required technical information on how to bind to specific services can be found on green pages. Green pages include references to web service implementations.

6.4.1. UDDI Architecture

The UDDI main architecture is composed of the following parts, which are briefly described:

1. Data
2. Services and API sets
3. Nodes
4. Registries

UDDI Data Model

Data represents the stored information in nodes. The UDDI data model consists of six different entities. Each entity is an XML-based, persistent piece of data.

1. **businessEntity:** a description of a service provider

2. **businessService:** a description of provided services by a service provider

3. **bindingTemplate:** a description of the required information for binding to the provided services

4. **tModel:** a description of the technical model of a web service such as the used protocol

5. **publisherAssertion:** a description of the relationships between different service providers

6. **subscription:** by which a subscriber can be informed of possible changes in entities. A change can be a new entry, deletion or update of data

UDDI Services and API sets

Application Programming Interfaces (APIs) and services are used for manipulation of stored data and a standardized behavior and communication. By offered APIs, nodes and clients are able to perform required actions such as data publication and data replication.

UDDI Nodes

An UDDI node is a web service or a set of web services supporting at least one of the APIs. Each node can belong to at most one registry. The communication and manipulation of data is realized through APIs.

UDDI Registries

An UDDI registry is a collection of (at least one) UDDI nodes. The stored data and entities in a registry are managed by all of the constructing nodes of the registry. Stored data in a registry can be accessed and manipulated by SOAP-messages through available APIs. In addition, UDDI-registries may provide a web interface for accessing the stored data in the registries. Some implementations of UDDI registry include the implementation of IBM, accessible at [3] and the public test version of SAP which can be found at [4]. Microsoft has discontinued to operate its public UDDI registry.

6.4.2. Comparison of UDDI

In addition to UDDI, other somehow similar specifications such as ebXML [5] and microsoft's BizTalk [6] are available.

ebXML working groups encompass more than one thousand companies and have been started by the United Nations Center for Trade Facilitation and Electronic Business (UN/CEFACT) [7] and Organization for the Advancement of Structured Information Standards (OASIS). The aim of ebXML is to manage business processes between the partners in a specific business field. It describes the business processes and data exchanges in an operational and functional view. The former describes the semantics and the latter the services respectively. ebXML shows many parallels to UDDI. Shared data and services are stored in a registry which is tightly coupled with a repository. The repository serves as back-end. ebXML-based systems and UDDI-based systems can be integrated into each other in the sense that ebXML based systems can contain UDDI registries and UDDI registries may have references to ebXML registries. Despite their similarities, the main ideas for developing both specifications are different. While UDDI helps firms to integrate to Internet-based market places, ebXML is thought for facilitation of business-to-business applications [270]. In addition, ebXML provides a richer description data than UDDI. It seems that UDDI is more suitable for large sized firms and ebXML for small and middle sized companies.

BizTalk [184] is an initiative of Microsoft to enable secure exchange of documents and is again an XML-based language. BizTalk enables organizations to exchange documents through a Biztalk server [184]. Like ebXML, BizTalk can use and can be used by UDDI, however it does not offer any possibilities for web service integration. Therefore UDDI is more suitable for implementation of business processes through web services.

For specification, applications and discussions on UDDI refer to [8, 213, 159, 257]

6.5. WS-BPEL

Business Process Execution Language for Web Services (WS-BPEL) is a specification of Microsoft, IBM, Siebel Systems, BEA and SAP aimed at providing interoperability among business processes. WS-BPEL is a successor of IBM's Web Services Flow Language (WSFL) [176] and Microsoft's XLANG (Web Services for Business Process Design) [255]. XLANG is a hierarchical block structured language with common control flow constructs (sequence, parallel, etc) while WSFL offers graph based constructs with specific control flow structures. WS-BPEL combines possibilities of both languages and provides both block structured and graph-based constructs. WS-BPEL is an XML-based language and lies on top of WSDL. WS-BPEL uses common web services and XML standards such as WSDL [79], XML schema [16], XPATH [82], WS-Addressing [62] and WS-Policy [39]. It should be noted that WSDL introduces basically a stateless model of interaction while long running business processes modeled by WS-BPEL are essentially stateful. For example when a requester sends requests to some service providers, the requester must know which reply belongs to which request.

WS-BPEL provides a formalism for modeling business processes, their (data dependent) behavior and interactions among involved partners. It also provides an exception handling mechanism including compensation activities. Every functionality is realized thorough web services. Interactions, represented as abstract WSDL definitions, are performed via web service interfaces and all partners are presented as services described in

WSDL. The business process itself is again a web service which can be used and invoked by other business processes.

WS-BPEL provides possibilities for two kinds of business processes:

1. Executable processes (orchestrations)

2. Abstract processes (choreographies)

An executable process is owned by one service provider and models the actual work performed by a service including data transformations, data manipulations, etc. and is only visible to its owner. An abstract process is owned by no partner and models the message exchange protocol among involved partners. All involved partners are of equal importance and the involved messages are visible to all of them. For the reasons of data visibility, the data associated with an executable process is referred to as *opaque data* and the associated data with an abstract process as *transparent data*. This distinction has obvious advantages. The service provider dose not need to reveal its internal process logic and can protect its business know-how while still able to communicate with other partners. In addition, as long as an abstract process remains the same, the executable process can be changed and modified with no external effect. In other words, interacting partners need just to conform to the abstract process and do not care about the executable processes of other partners. (compare workflow views, introduced in chapter 5). Despite the distinction between executable and abstract processes, these two have an implicit relationship with each other, e.g. the executed paths and decisions made at choice nodes may depend on exchanged messages in the abstract process. For example in a web shopping scenario, the quantity of purchased items by the buyer decides if the buyer receives a discount on his purchase or no. Figure 6.5 illustrates such a scenario in graph representation. The left side of the figure represents the abstract process between the buyer and the seller and the right side the executable process of the seller. Note that this scenario is very simplistic and does not represent a real life application. In the abstract process: the buyer first selects the items (from a possible set of items), selects the quantity, finalize the order and puts it in the basket and requests an invoice for his order. The seller receives the request for invoice, calculates the final price and sends the invoice back to the buyer. The buyer receives the invoice for his order and the interaction terminates. In the seller's executable process: the seller calculates the invoice. If the quantity of the ordered items is greater or equal to 5, the buyer receives 10% discount on his order, otherwise the original price is calculated. This example shows that how message exchange in the abstract process may influence the behavior of the executable process. In this example the quantity of the ordered items implicitly decides which branch of the decision node in the seller's executable process must be taken and executed. For a more detailed discussion on abstract and executable processes please refer to section 7.1.

6.5. WS-BPEL

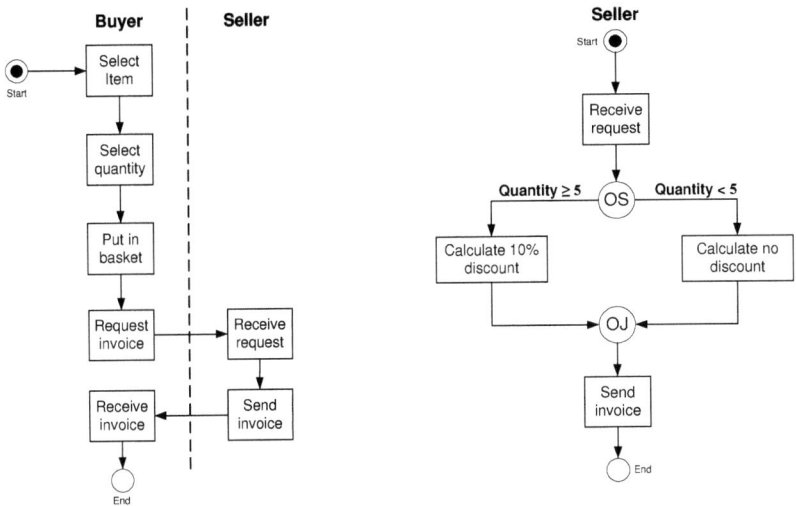

Figure 6.5.: Left: the abstract process between buyer and seller, Right: seller's executable process

6.5.1. Business Processes in WS-BPEL

Definition of business processes in WS-BPEL contains the following parts, which are shortly described in this subsection:

- Partner Links
- Partners
- Variables
- Correlation and Correlation Sets
- Fault Handlers
- Compensation handlers
- Event Handlers
- Activities

6.5.1.1. Partner Links

A *PartnerLink* defines the interaction model between two business partners, where port types and messages are defined. The interaction is modeled as a peer-to-peer (P2P) conversation. In other words, a PartnerLink identifies the interacting partner on the other side of the communication and defines the static behavior of the process. Each PartnerLink is characterized by a *PartnerLinkType* and must have a unique name. In a PartnerLinkType the roles of the interacting partners are provided, where *myRole* and *partnerRole* identify the defined roles for the business process and its interacting partner respectively. Roles and WSDL ports have a one-to-one relationship. Note that it is also possible to define only one role (myRole) in partnerLinkType definition. In this case the business process can bind to any partner without constraints. WS-BPEL uses the notion of endpoint references [62] for dynamic binding to other partners. Each role has a unique end point reference and business processes can dynamically bind to providers of specific services.

6.5.1.2. Partners

The optional definition of *partner* is simply a disjoint subset of partnerLink definitions. The relationship between a partnerLink and a partner definition is one-to-one.

6.5.1.3. Variables

in WS-BPEL variables are used for three purposes:

1. Data expression
2. Data manipulation
3. Management of process states

WS-BPEL assumes that the main work, including data manipulation, is performed externally by web services and hence only basic, general purpose data expression and manipulation possibilities are provided. WS-BPEL provides four types of variable expressions:

- **Boolean expressions** are used for evaluation. E.g. decision nodes or exit conditions of loops.
- **Deadline expressions**: identify reaching of a specific deadline (date and time).
- **Duration expressions**: identify that a period has passed.
- **General expressions**: such as alphanumeric values.

6.5. WS-BPEL

In addition to common operators such as $\geq, \leq$, the activity *assignment* is used for copying and insertion of values from a source variable to a target variable. *assignment* can also be used for copying of endpoint references.

6.5.1.4. Correlation and Correlation Sets

As stated earlier, in contrast to stateless nature of WSDL messages, WS-BPEL processes are long running and stateful business processes which send and receive many messages during execution of a process. It must be clear which reply belongs to which request and also it must be ensured that messages are sent to the right WSDL port of the receiver in course of the execution. In addition to the assurance of delivery to the right WSDL port, it must be guaranteed that the message is also delivered to the right instance of a process definition, as a process may have many simultaneously running process instances. WS-BPEL as a platform and implementation independent specification, realizes these goals by "business data and communication protocol headers". Correlation tokens are in charge of handling the automatic instance routing. Correlation tokens or correlation set is referred to the shared properties by all messages in a correlated set of operations within a single instance. A correlation token may by for example a reference number that uniquely identifies this communication. The relationship between messages and correlation tokens is one to many, in the sense that one message can carry many correlation tokens. Correlation sets can be declared and are valid within scopes. correlation sets declared within a local scope, are called local correlation sets. They loose their validity outside of the associated scope or after completion of the scope. The correlation sets defined for the entire business process are called global correlation sets (cf. variable declaration in object oriented programming). Within the validity scope, the property values of the correlation set, carried by different messages of different operations, are not allowed to be changed and must remain the same. A scope provides the execution context for activities in WS-BPEL. A scope, in addition to its normal activities, correlation sets and variables, may have fault, compensation and event handlers. Each scope is only visible and valid up to its next immediate scope that directly encloses it.

6.5.1.5. Fault Handlers

During the execution of a WS-BPEL process several kinds of faults may occur. Occurrence of faults means that the normal behavior of the scope is interrupted and the scope is in faulty mode. Similar to the object-oriented paradigm, WS-BPEL provides a throw-catch mechanism for fault handling where faults have associated fault handlers. WS-BPEL provides two types of fault handlers:

1. Explicit fault handlers

2. Implicit fault handlers

Explicit fault handlers are basically user defined activities that will be executed when a certain fault or a set of faults are caught. Explicit fault handlers may contain an empty set of activities and simply do nothing about the caught faults. They can be seen as a wrapper for the defined set of fault handling activities. An optional *catchAll* can catch all faults that are not caught by more specific fault handlers. The semantic of a fault handler in WS-BPEL is in fact reversal and undoing the faulty parts of the associated scope. Note that fault handler itself does not always complete successfully and may rethrow the fault. If a fault handler itself ends up faulty or if the fault is not caught by the scope within a fault handler, it will be delivered to the scope that immediately encloses the current scope.

A fault is uniquely identifiable by its name and may have associated fault data and an optional internal fault variable. By absence of fault data, faults are caught by their matching fault names. If no such catch activity is present, they will be caught by the *catchAll* activity. If again, no *catchAll* statement is given, the fault is delivered to the parent scope, i.e. the scope that directly encloses the current scope. If fault data is present, a fault handler whose catch activity has the matching fault name and fault variable is in charge of catching and handling the fault. If there is no fault handler with both matching fault name and fault variable, a fault handler with just a matching fault is responsible for catching and handling the fault. Else, as before, a *catchAll* and the parent scope respectively are in charge of catching and handling the fault. In addition to the fault handler associated to the scope in which an activity executes, it is possible to define inline fault handlers for each activity.

In case no explicit fault handler has caught a specific fault, this fault is handled implicitly in the sense that all compensation handlers of the scope in which the fault has occurred are executed in the reverse order for the parent scope and the fault is delivered to the parent scope and rethrown there.

6.5.1.6. Compensation Handlers

Another possibility of WS-BPEL is compensation handlers. Compensation means reversal and undoing the done work. Compensation can be performed for a single activity, a scope or an entire business process instance. Note that there is an important difference between compensation and cancel activity. A cancel activity is usually has no side effects, the canceled activity terminates and the state of the world is the same as before the execution of the activity. On the other hand, compensation is usually associated with additional costs or side effects. In many scenarios, compensation does not bring the state of the world back to the original state of the world (the state of the world before the execution of the activity). Imagine for example buying a book from Amazon. When a buyer orders a book, he can cancels his order before the book is shipped and his credit card is not charged.

6.5. WS-BPEL

But when the ordered book is shipped and the buyer wants to compensate his order, he has to send the book back to Amazon, which is coupled with shipping costs and also he may not receive the whole purchase price.

Based on Sagas [126, 41] providing semantic atomicity and open nested transaction [256, 273], WS-BPEL provides a mechanism for execution of compensation activities. In the domain of business processes, compensation handlers are more important and play a bigger role than fault handlers. Due to the long running nature of business processes, the ACID properties- atomicity, consistency, isolation, durability- are not available for the entire business process and hence it is impossible to lock the the resources for a long period.

Like faults handlers, compensation handlers are a group of defined activities, which again can be empty. These activities will be executed in case of invocation of the associated compensation handler. A compensation handler can be defined for a scope, inline for single activities or for an entire business process instance. In contrast to fault handlers which can be invoked if their scope terminates unsuccessfully and abnormally, compensation handlers can only be invoked if the scope, for which they are defined, has completed successfully. It means also that a faulty scope never has an installed compensation handler. The semantic of compensation handlers says that compensation handlers after completion of their associated scopes see a snapshot of variables (state of the world) i.e. live data of a business process cannot be updated by compensation handlers. A compensation handler can be explicitly invoked by the activity *compensate*. Note that the activity compensate can be used only in a fault handler of a compensation handler of the parent scope. If no compensation handler is present, WS-BPEL provides an implicit compensation handling mechanism by running all compensation handlers of the parent scope in the reverse order of completion of the current scope.

6.5.1.7. Event Handlers

Another type of handlers in WS-BPEL are event handlers. Event handlers define a group of activities that will be executed in case of occurrence of the corresponding event. In WS-BPEL, an event is either an incoming message or an alarm event that indicates a timeout. Except for explicit invocation of compensation activities, activity *compensate*, an event handler can contain all activities. Event handlers are parallel constructs to the associated scope and are considered as normal behavior of the scope. It means that faulty behavior of an event handler is considered as faulty behavior of the scope. Event handlers can be enabled as long as the scope is active and the whole scope, itself, remains active as long as the event handlers are enabled.

A message event handler, identified with the tag *onMessage*, defines the activities that have to be performed if a message arrives. Its semantics is very similar to that of the reply activity (see subsection 6.5.1.8 for the semantics of the reply activity). Note that the incoming message may correspond to a synchronous or asynchronous pattern. In the former pattern, the event handler is in charge of sending the reply. It is obvious that multiple messages may arrive during the lifetime of a scope and hence message event handlers remains active as long as the scope is active and can be enabled multiple times.

An alarm event handler, identified by *onAlarm* tag, executes a set of defined activities when a predefined time point has been reached. This can be a deadline (a point in time) a period in time (a duration). The clock starts when the scope becomes active. Unlike message event handlers, alarm event handlers can be enabled only once during the lifetime of a scope.

6.5.1.8. Activities

Activities are basic units of work that are performed in the course of a business process. They include control flow activities, web service invocations and activities for interaction and messaging. WS-BPEL does not provide sophisticated activities for data manipulation or alpha-numerical operations. The assumption is that data manipulations and computations are basically carried out externally by web services. For concurrency and synchronization purposes, two activities can be connected through a link. A link is identified by a unique name and defines the order of execution of activities. The target activity of a link can not execute until the source activity has terminated successfully. In addition to structural requirements of a business process, links, as well, impose restrictions on execution order of activities. There may be an optional transition condition for a link. A link with a transition condition is followed if its transition condition evaluates to true.

Figure 6.6 illustrates parts of a business process in graph notation. The dotted line demonstrates a link between activities X and D. The activity X is the source activity and the activity D the target activity. In this example, the activity D must wait for its predecessor, activity B (structural constraint) and also for the the source activity of the link, activity X (link constraints) before it can start execution. As this example shows, a link can cross the boundaries of structured activities such as sequence and parallel constructs. However it must bo noted that links are not allowed to cross the boundaries of while, event and compensation handlers and serializable scopes[1].

---

[1]Similar to serializability in database systems [54, 214], a serializable scope provides concurrency and access control for shared resources and variables. The fault handler of a serializable scope share its serializability while its compensation handlers do not.

6.5. WS-BPEL

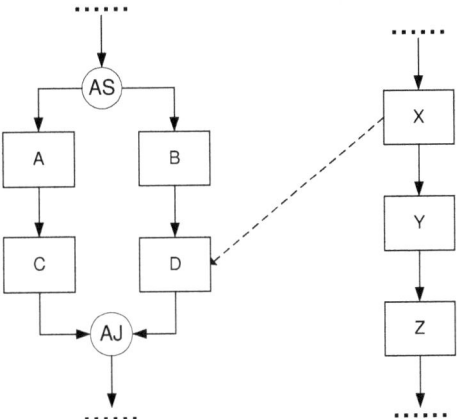

Figure 6.6.: A link between two activities

An activity has two standard boolean-valued attributes: *join condition* and *suppresseJoin-Failure*. The join condition specifies when the target activity of other activities can execute i.e. it evaluates the status of incoming links and the corresponding activity is executed if the join condition evaluates to true. If an explicit join condition is absent, WS-BPEL assumes an implicit join condition which evaluates to true when status of at least one incoming link is positive. suppresseJoinFailure whose default value is no, determines if an occurred join failure should be suppressed or no. A value of yes for suppresseJoinFailure means that the failure has been caught by an inline fault handler for this activity. However, the inline fault handler has an empty list of fault handling activities and actually does nothing about the caught fault. If a join condition of an activity whose suppresseJoin-Failure value is set to yes evaluates to false, the activity will be skipped and consequently all of its outgoing links will be assigned a negative status.

WS-BPEL provides following activities which are briefly discussed:

- invoke
- receive
- reply
- throw
- wait
- empty
- sequence

- switch

- while

- pick

- flow

Invoke provides the possibility of invoking exposed services of other web services. This can be done in a synchronous (request-response) or asynchronous (one-way) fashion. The difference between these two communication patterns is that in a synchronous communication the requester after sending the request, blocks and waits until the corresponding reply is arrived and then the execution of the rest of business process can be continued. The advantage of this pattern is its rather simple implementation and its obvious disadvantage is longer execution time because the requester blocks and waits for the response. In an asynchronous communication the requester after sending the request does not block and continues with the business process. In a later time point when the reply has arrived, it will be processed. The advantage of this pattern is the shorter execution time of the whole business process but on the other hand the implementation is more complex than synchronous pattern. In WS-BPEL, synchronous communications require variables for both input and output while an asynchronous communication requires variables only for input.

Through *receive* activity web services expose their services which can be invoked by other web services. The invoking partner must know which operation via which partner link and port type can be invoked. Note that the same port type, operation, partner link and correlation set can be assigned to only one receive activity. In addition, a receive activity can be creator of a new process instance. The activity receive can be used in synchronous communications i.e. it is a blocking activity that blocks and waits for the corresponding message to arrive at its specified ports through the specified link.

After a message has been received through a receive activity its response can be sent through a *reply* activity. A reply activity must always come after a receive activity. It is obvious that it is impossible to reply as long as no request or message is present.

The *throw* activity is used when faults need to be thrown and consequently handled. Faults must have unique names. However, there is no need to predefine them before they are thrown by a throw activity.

Activity *wait* can be applied in scenarios when delays need to be inserted in a business process. In such a case the business process simply waits and delays the execution of subsequent activities. This activity can be used for time management purposes. E.g. invocation of a partner's service can be performed only at a certain time point or time interval.

empty is a basic activity that does nothing and has no effect. See for example suppressing join failures described above for an application of this activity.

sequence is a control flow activity that defines in which order a group of activities will be performed. The activity sequence describes a chain of activities that are executed one after another in the exact order that are listed between the sequence tags. Figure 6.7 illustrates a sequence of activities *A, B* and *C*. The activities will be executed exactly in this order. Note that each activity can executes as soon as its predecessor has finished execution. E.g. activity *B* must wait for activity *A* to finish in order to start execution. A sequence starts when its first activity starts execution and finishes when its last activity finishes execution.

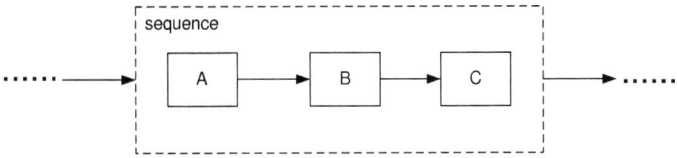

Figure 6.7.: A sequence of activities

The conditional behavior (XOR-split) can be modeled by activity *switch*. This activity has several branches and an optional otherwise branch. If the condition for a branch is fulfilled (characterized by the *case* statement), this branch will be taken and executed. If condition of no branch evaluates to true, the otherwise branch is taken. By absence of an explicit otherwise branch, WS-BPEL assumes an implicit otherwise-branch that does nothing. In other words, a switch terminates always even if condition of no branch evaluates to true. A switch activity starts when a branch is taken and completes when the taken branch completes.

Similar to other programming languages, the activity *while* models loops. The loop is iterated as long as the while condition remains true.

The activity *pick* is used for event handling. It waits for the occurrence of a set of events and handles the event accordingly. An event can be either an alarm or a message. In the latter case, the pick activity can be used as an alternative to a receive activity which also provides possibility of creation of a new process instance (createInstance=yes). The pick handles the first arriving event and discards the subsequent events. If two events arrive almost simultaneously, the accepted event is chosen based on temporal and implementation issues.

Parallelism and concurrency can be modeled by the activity *flow*. It provides several branches that are executed in parallel. A flow construct terminates when all of its branches have terminated. In other words, a flow construct always waits for its longest branch to complete and the execution duration of a flow construct is equal to the length of its longest branch. In addition to parallelism, flow enables expression of concurrency for its nested activities.

For a whole specification of WS-BPEL [32], syntax of activities, examples and extensions for executable and abstract processes please refer to WS-BPEL specification which can be found at [9].

Chapter 7

An Architecture for Interorganizational Workflows

In this chapter an architecture for interorganizational workflows is presented. Such workflows cross the boundaries of single organizations and inter-connect several partners that belong to different organizations. Partners communicate and cooperate with each other in the context of the interorganizational workflow to reach the over all goals of a business process. It is assumed that partners and organizations use web services and web service related technologies to define the communication protocol and implement the tasks. One of the biggest advantages of web services is their capability of being composed into more complex systems. Web services can be seen as autonomous, stand-alone entities that can be integrated in a modular fashion into bigger systems with web services as their building blocks. The composed system is greater than the sum of their components. Composition of web services is recursive, in the sense that the composed system can itself be published as a web service and be integrated in an even more complex system. By composition, there is no need to develop web services for specific tasks from scratch rather the system can be built using available web services. In this chapter, in addition to presentation of a nouvelle architecture that offers some advantages compared with available proposals, the concepts used in web service composition and state of the art are discussed and introduced.

7.1. Choreographies and Orchestrations

Two mostly used concepts in the realm of web service composition are choreographies and orchestrations. Web service composition refers to building more complex and sophisticated systems out of the basic building blocks. The composed system is in turn a web service that can be invoked by other web services.

An orchestration, also called an executable process in WS-BPEL, belongs to and is controlled by one partner and describes an executable process which is run by its owner. A partner's internal logic and business know-how are contained in his orchestration. Another tasks such as data transformations, data handling, arithmetic operations, the actual performed work and communication tasks (send and receive of messages) are as well contained in an orchestration. An orchestration is solely visible to its owner and other external partners have no view on and knowledge about this orchestration. An orchestration is a process viewed only from the perspective of its owner. An orchestration is a recursive composition of web services, in the sense that it is composed of web services and the orchestration, itself, can be exposed as a service and reused by other orchestrations. An orchestration engine is in charge of running and execution of orchestrations. Different languages such as WS-BPEL executable process or business process modeling language (BPML) [34] can be used for definition of Orchestrations.

On the other hand, a choreography, called abstract process in WS-BPEL, is a non-executable, abstract process that defines the message exchange protocol between (at least two) partners. A choreography defines a collaboration among involved partners for reaching an overall business goal. A choreography contains only the visible messages that are exchanged between partners in course of a business process. The exchanged messages are visible to all participants of a choreography. External parties who are not part of a choreography are not able to view and monitor the messages and have no view on the choreography. A choreography has no owner or a super user in charge of control and all involved partners are treated equally. A choreography is a process definition from a global perspective shared among all involved partners [217]. A choreography can be seen as a contract among partners where duties and rights of each partner are defined. In other words, it is defined which operations a partner has to execute and provide for other partners (duties) and to which operations a partner has access (rights). The tasks contained in a choreography are divided between its participants i.e. each task is assigned to a partner for execution. Partners execute their tasks in their orchestrations. Because of the abstract nature of a choreography definition, there is no engine needed for execution of a choreography. Choreographies are called collaboration protocol profiles in ebXML. Choreographies can be modeled amongst other by WS-BPEL abstract process or web services choreography description language (WS-CDL) [158]. A discussion and critique on WS-CDL can be found at [90, 42].

Figure 7.1 illustrates the difference between choreographies and orchestrations. On both left and right sides there are two orchestrations composed of web services. The choreography defines the message exchange and communication protocol between these two orchestrations.

7.1. Choreographies and Orchestrations

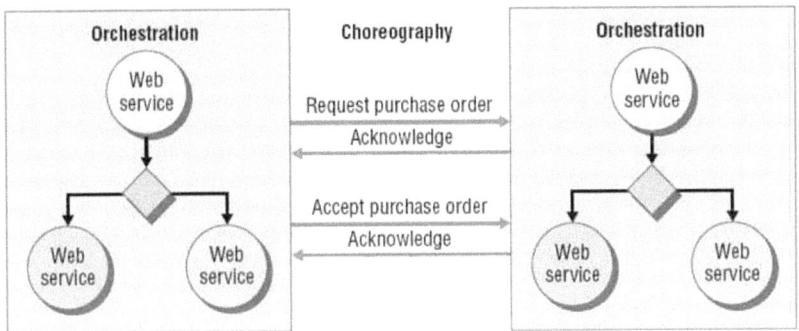

Figure 7.1.: The difference between choreography and orchestration (Image from [217])

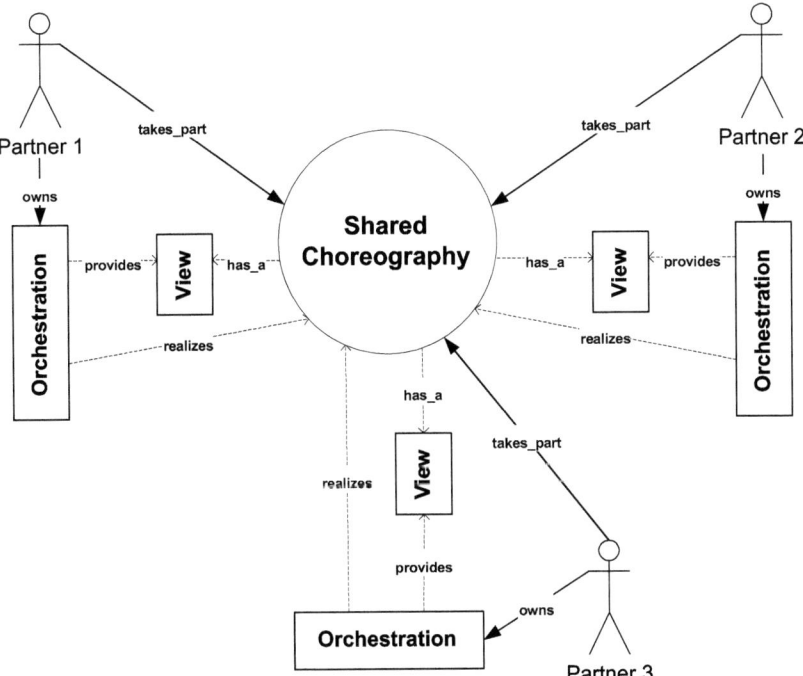

Figure 7.2.: A typical scenario of web service composition

A typical scenario [90, 42, 102] of web service composition assumes one choreography shared among several partners where each partner realizes and executes its parts of the choreography in its private orchestration. Each orchestration provides a view which is used for interaction and communication with other partners. The shared choreography defines and coordinates the communication and interaction among orchestrations and is an integration of the views on the orchestrations. A view is not only a view on an orchestration bur also a view on the shared choreography. For a more detailed discussion on views and its correctness criteria refer to chapter 5. Figure 7.2 illustrates this scenario consisting of three partners each with his own orchestration. The *realize* relationship between orchestrations and the shared choreography describes a partial realization of the shared choreography by an orchestration. An orchestration realizes only those parts of the shared choreography that belong to its owner, i.e. the provided view on this orchestration. In other words, the realization of the shared choreography is divided among the three orchestrations. The parts that belong to each partner is defined in its view.

Imagine a procurement scenario, which is a well understood scenario in the literature, whose participants are a buyer, a seller and a shipper. Figure 7.3 shows a choreography between them. In this choreography, the seller after receipt of the *Request quote* from buyer, processes it and decides if to accept or reject the request and then informs the buyer about his decision. After buyer has received the result, if seller has rejected the request the process goes to the end states and terminates, otherwise the buyer places an order. The seller processes the order and sends the details, such as recipient's name and address to the shipper which are needed for the shipment of the ordered item. The shipper receives the results and processes it. The shipper then in parallel ships the goods to the seller and informs the seller about the shipment. After the seller has been notified that the ordered item is shipped, sends the bill to the buyer. The buyer after receipt of both bill and the ordered item, makes the payment. The process terminates when the seller has received the payment. This process represents a simple scenario. A real life business process is more complex including exception handling mechanisms or for example the shipper may be chosen dynamically from a possible list of available shippers based on some criteria by the seller. The partners' orchestrations have additional activities which are not contained in the shared choreography. The buyer's orchestration is depicted in figure 7.4. The buyer before making a request for quote to the seller, searches for available sellers for his requested item and based on his internal criteria selects a seller. Figure 7.5 depicts the view on the buyer's orchestration. As noted earlier, a view on an orchestration is in addition a view on the shared choreography and identifies the parts that belong to a specific partner of the shared choreography and this partner is in charge of its realization. By realization of the activities that belong to a partner, the partner has a conformant behavior with respect to the agreed upon choreography. A view shows a single partner's perspective on the choreography and can be used as a skeleton for designing the partner's orchestrations by adding other internal tasks. In other words they show the minimum amount of task as

7.1. Choreographies and Orchestrations

well as the structure of the tasks that a partner's orchestration must contain in order to be conformant with the shared choreography.

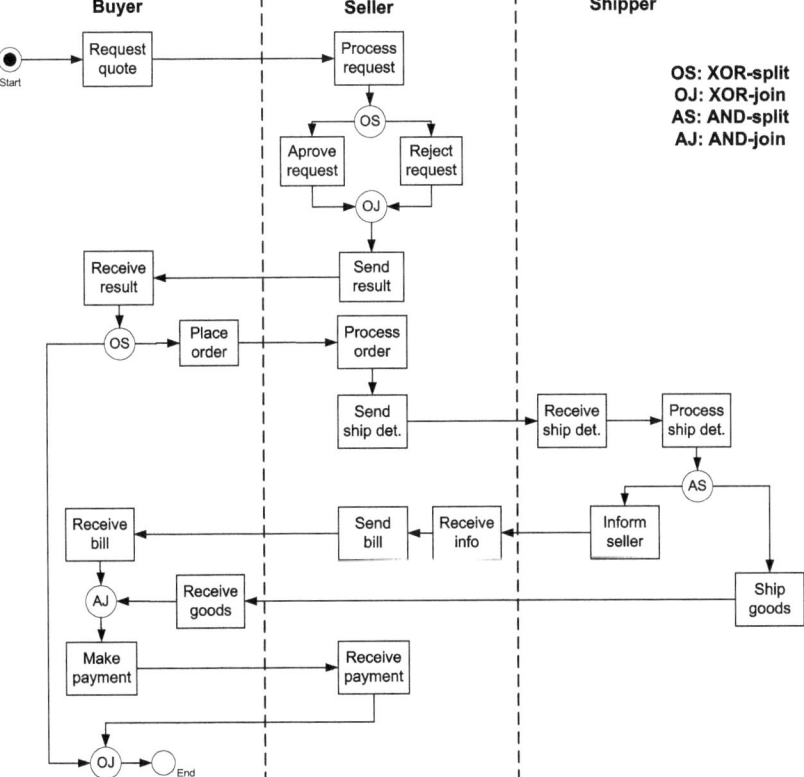

Figure 7.3.: The shared choreography between buyer, seller and shipper

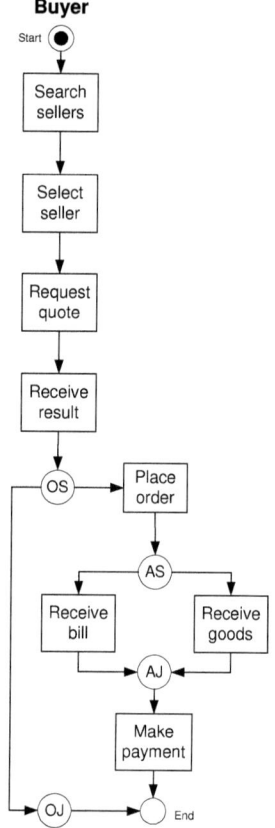

Figure 7.4.: The buyer's orchestration

7.1. Choreographies and Orchestrations

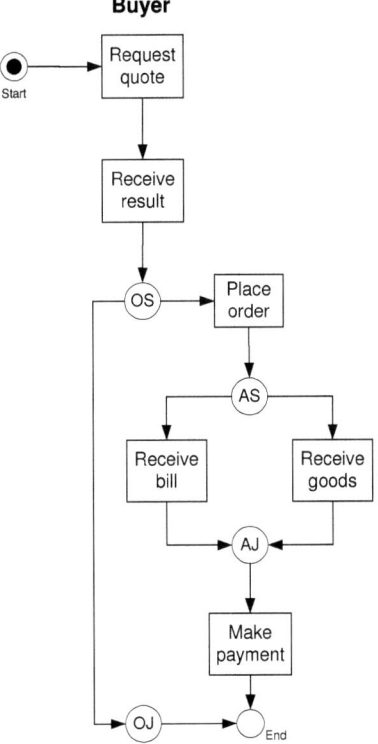

Figure 7.5.: The view on the buyer's orchestration

The seller's orchestration is presented in figure 7.6. The seller in parallel to preparing the shipment (this includes also payment of the shipment costs to the shipper), evaluates the history of the buyer and based on the buyer's previous purchase history considers possible discounts. In addition, the seller calculates the total cost based on the original price, possible discounts and shipment costs. After receiving the payment from the buyer, the seller's orchestration is finalized by updating buyer's history. The view on the seller's orchestration is presented in figure 7.7.

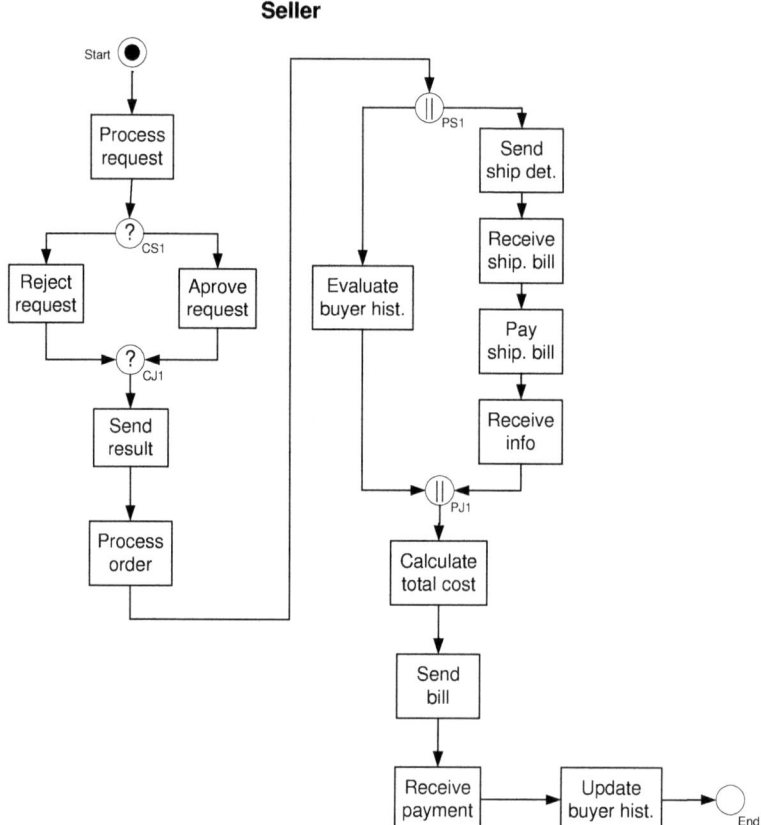

Figure 7.6.: The seller's orchestration

7.1. Choreographies and Orchestrations

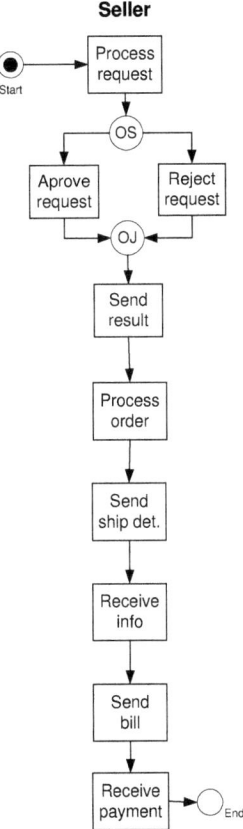

Figure 7.7.: The view on the seller's orchestration

The shipper's orchestration, as illustrated in figure 7.8, has as well additional activities compared to his part in the choreography. This includes sending the shipment bills to the seller, activity *Send Ship bill*, and receiving a confirmation from bank indicating the payment of the bill by the seller, activity *Receive confirm*. After the goods are sent to the buyer and the seller has been informed about the shipment details, the seller's history is being updated in shipper's database. The view on the shipper's orchestration is presented in figure 7.9.

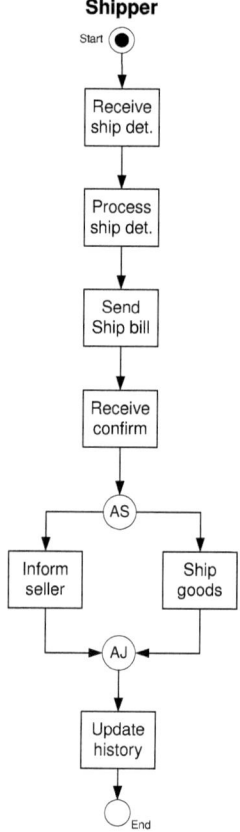

Figure 7.8.: The shipper's orchestration

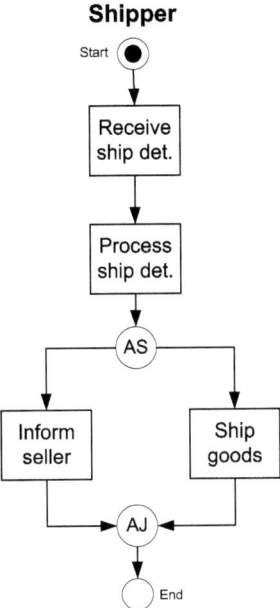

Figure 7.9.: The shipper's part in the shared choreography

7.2. Federated Choreographies

The typical scenario explained above, one shared choreography and a set of private orchestrations, misses an important facet. This scenario, presence of only one choreography, is not fully adequate for all real life applications. Imagine a web shopping scenario. When shopping online a buyer takes part in a choreography whose partners are the buyer, a seller company like Amazon , a credit card provider like Visa or Master Card and a shipper company like DHL or FedEx. The buyer knows the following partners and steps: the buyer orders something at the seller, pays by a credit card and expects to receive the items from a shipper. At the same time the seller takes part in several other choreographies which are not visible to the buyer, e.g. the seller and the credit card company are involved in a process for handling payment through a bank. Furthermore, the seller and the shipper realize another protocol they agreed upon containing other actions such as money transfer from the seller's bank to the shipper for balancing shipment charges (see seller's and shipper's orchestrations represented in figures 7.6 and 7.8). As this example shows, more than one choreography may be needed for reaching the goals of a business process.

Besides, two partners involved in one choreography may also take part in another choreography that is not visible to other partners of the choreography, however essential for the realization of business goals. All these choreographies overlap in some parts but cannot be composed into a single global choreography. Moreover, such choreographies must be realized by orchestrations of partners that take part in them. In the above example the seller implements an orchestration enacting the different interaction protocols with the buyer, the shipper and the credit card company. Even if the combination of all choreographies into one choreography would be possible, the separation offers obvious advantages. To overcome these restriction, a new architecture and a nouvelle approach for interorganizational workflows, called *federated choreographies*, is proposed. The main idea of the federated choreographies is presented in figure 7.10. It consists of two layers. The upper layer consists of the federated choreographies shared between different partners, e.g. in figure 7.10 *choreography 1* is shared between partner 2, partner 3 and partner 4. A choreography is composed of views of the orchestrations by which the choreography is (partially) realized. In other words, the activities contained in a choreography are only those in the views. A choreography may support another choreography. This means the former, the supporting choreography, contributes to the latter, the supported choreography, and partially elaborates it. E.g. *choreography 1* is the supporting choreography and *global choreography* is the supported choreography. The set of activities contained in a supporting choreography is an extended subset of the activities of the supported choreography. The supporting choreography describes parts of the supported choreography in more detail. The choreography which supports no other choreography and is only supported by other choreographies is called the *global choreography*. Informally, the global choreography captures the core of a business process and other choreographies which support the global choreography describe parts of the global choreography in the needed detail for implementation. In order to clarify the concept, the general architecture is applied to the web shop example and is depicted in figure 7.11. The bottom layer consists of orchestrations that realize the choreographies in the upper layer. Each orchestration provides several views for different interactions with other partners. The interactions with other partners are reflected in the choreographies. Hence, an orchestration needs to provide as many views as the number of choreographies this orchestration (partially) realizes. Each partner provides its own internal realization of relevant parts of the according choreographies, e.g. seller has an orchestration which realizes its part in all three choreographies. The seller's orchestration is presented in figure 7.6.

7.2. Federated Choreographies

Figure 7.10.: The idea of the federated choreographies

In order to clarify the concept the general architecture is applied to the web shop example and is depicted in figure 7.11. In figure 7.11 the global choreography, *Purchase processing choreography*, describes how an item is sold and shipped to the buyer. It contains the activities and steps which are interesting for the buyer and the buyer needs to know them in order to take part in or initiate the business process. How shipping of the items and debiting the buyer's credit card is handled in reality are described in the *Shipment processing choreography* and the *Payment processing choreography* respectively. Let the purchase processing choreography be the choreography depicted in figure 7.3, the *Shipment processing choreography*, the supporting choreography, is represented in figure 7.12.

7. An Architecture for Interorganizational Workflows

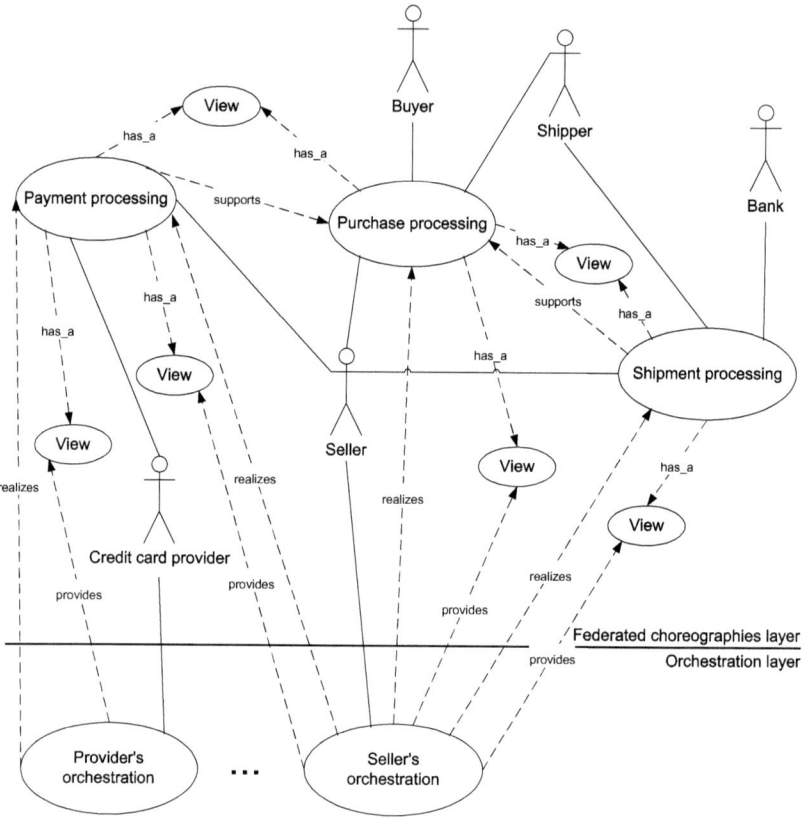

Figure 7.11.: A web shopping example modeled by the federated choreographies

The bottom layer consists of orchestrations that realize the choreographies in the upper layer. Each orchestration provides several views for different interactions with other partners. The interactions with other partners are reflected in the choreographies. Hence, an orchestration needs to provide as many views as the number of choreographies this orchestration (partially) realizes. Each partner provides its own internal realization of relevant parts of the according choreographies, e.g. seller has an orchestration which realizes its part in all three choreographies. The seller's orchestration is presented in figure 7.6.

The presented approach is fully distributed and there is no need for a centralized coordination. Each partner has local models of all choreographies in which it participates. All local models of the same choreography are identical. By having the identical local models

7.2. Federated Choreographies

of choreographies, partners know to which activities they have access, which activities they have to execute and in which order. In addition, partners are aware when to expect messages and in which interval they can send messages. In other words, the knowledge about execution of the model is distributed among involved partners and each partner is aware of its duties in the course of process execution. Hence, there is no need for a super-user or a central role that possesses the whole knowledge about execution of the process. Rather this knowledge is distributed among participants and each partner knows what he needs to know. Additionally, each partner holds and runs its own model of the orchestration. Note that if there is a link between two choreographies and/or orchestrations, either a support link between two choreographies or a realize link between a choreography and an orchestration, it implies that these two choreographies and orchestrations have at least one activity in common. That means that the greatest common divisor of these two choreographies and/or orchestrations is not empty. Greatest common divisor is defined in definition 8.38.

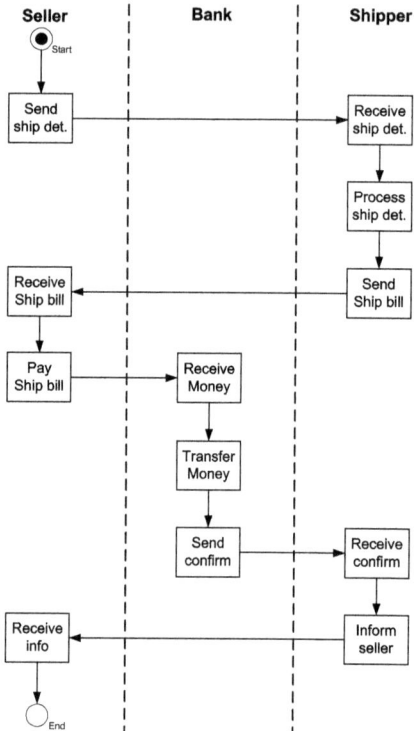

Figure 7.12.: The shipment processing choreography

In fact, one can argue that supporting choreographies may be combined by the means of composition as described in [158, 70] where existing choreography definitions can be reused and recursively combined into more complex choreographies. But, in fact, the relationship between choreographies can be more sophisticated than merely a composition. In our example the relationship between the seller and the shipper includes not only the passing of shipment details from the seller to the shipper but it also involves payment of shipment charges through the seller's bank. This is described by a separate choreography between seller, shipper and the bank. This choreography, shown in figure 7.12, has additional activities and partners which are not visible in its supported choreography. This choreography contributes to the *Purchase processing choreography* (see figure 7.3) and elaborates the interaction between the seller and the shipper.

7.2. Federated Choreographies

7.2.1. Advantages of the Federated Choreographies

Federated choreographies are more flexible than typical compositional approaches used in proposals like WS-CDL and it closes the gap between choreographies and orchestrations by providing a coherent and integrated view on both choreographies and orchestrations. Federated choreographies offer obvious advantages such as:

Protection of busienss know-how: Federated choreographies improve business secrecy and protect business know-how. If the whole business process including all involved partners are modeled as one single choreography, all message exchanges are visible to all partners. For example a customer or a provider can view how the seller handles the shipment with the shipper. But if the interactions between the seller and the shipper are separated into a different choreography, other external observers has no view on and knowledge about the message exchanges and the actual handling of business. In other words, the seller can keep how he does business with the shipper private .

Avoidance of unnecessary information: Federated choreographies avoid unnecessary information. Even if there is no need for protection of business know-how, it is desirable to separate choreographies and limit them only to the interested parties. Imagine a customer intending to buy a book from Amazon. As long as he receives the orderer book, the customer is not interested to be aware of how the shipment is handled between Amazon and the shipper and he/she has no interest to receive messages regarding the detail of shipment process between Amazon and the shipper.

Extendability: Federated choreographies are extendable, when such a need arises. See figure 7.11 where a web shopping example is illustrated. If the bank needs to check the credit-worthiness of the buyer, it can initiate a new choreography and extend the model without interfering with other choreographies or interactions. This scenario is depicted in figure 7.13. As it can be seen, a *Credit-check processing* choreography whose participants are the bank and a credit-check firm and supports the *Payment processing choreography* is added to the model. In other words as long as the conformance conditions are satisfied, the model can be extended and there is no need to interfere with the running process and notifying the partners for setting up new choreographies. The conformance issues are discussed in chapter 8.

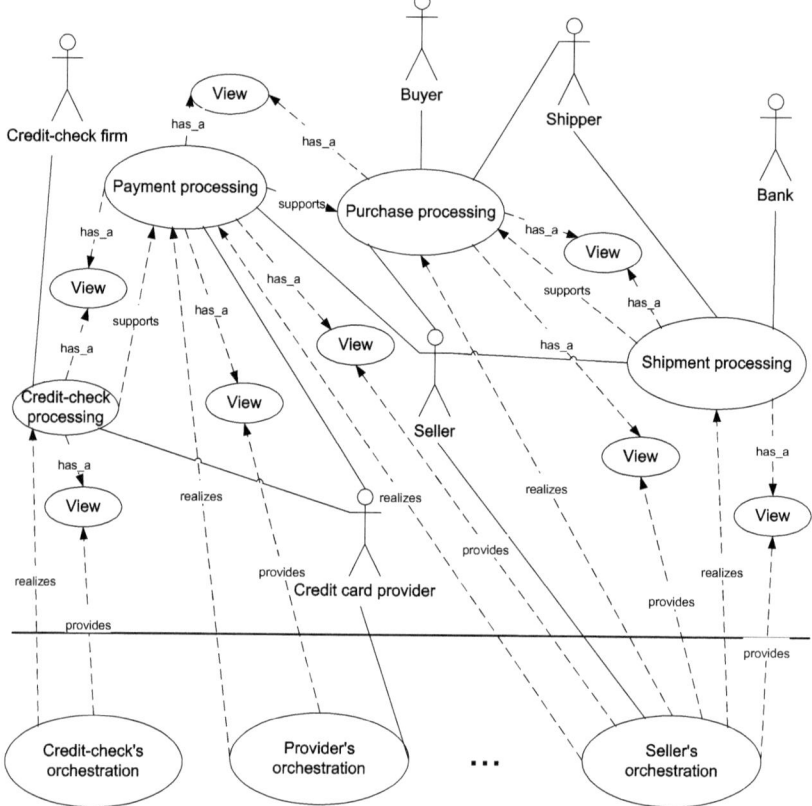

Figure 7.13.: Federated choreographies are extendable

Uniform modeling: Finally, federated choreographies use a coherent and uniform modeling for both choreographies and orchestrations and eliminates the need for different modeling languages and techniques for choreographies and orchestrations. The uniform modeling technique reduces the cost of process at design phase.

7.2.2. Metamodel of the Federated Choreographies

Choreographies, orchestrations and workflow views are treated as workflows. Thus a workflow is either a choreography, an orchestration or a workflow view. A choreography coordinates several orchestrations owned by different partners and a single orchestration

7.2. Federated Choreographies

may realize parts of several choreographies. An orchestration provides several views. Choreographies can be federated into more complex ones. Choreographies are composed of views. Moreover, as all choreographies are workflows, they can be composed out of other choreographies by means of complex activities and control structures available in the workflow models. The same applies for orchestrations. The metamodel enables the representation of choreographies, orchestrations and workflow views which are described as workflow models. Therefore, choreographies, orchestrations and workflow views can be modeled using typical workflow control flow structures. Moreover, it provides a coherent view on both choreographies and orchestrations and their mutual relationships, thus bridging the gap between abstract and executable processes. The metamodel allows to describe several choreographies on different levels of detail and orchestrations responsible for a private implementation of these choreographies. Choreographies and orchestrations can share the same activities. These activities are contained in a view that is provided by the orchestration and is also a view on the choreography. Such a view identifies which activities of the choreography must be realized in the orchestration. An activity visible in one choreography can be extended by its relationships with other activities in a federated choreography. On the other hand, an activity visible in a choreography can have a complex implementation described in an orchestration. Thus, choreographies and orchestrations together with their activities can be viewed on different levels of detail and in context of different relationships. The metamodel of the federated choreographies is represented in figure 7.14.

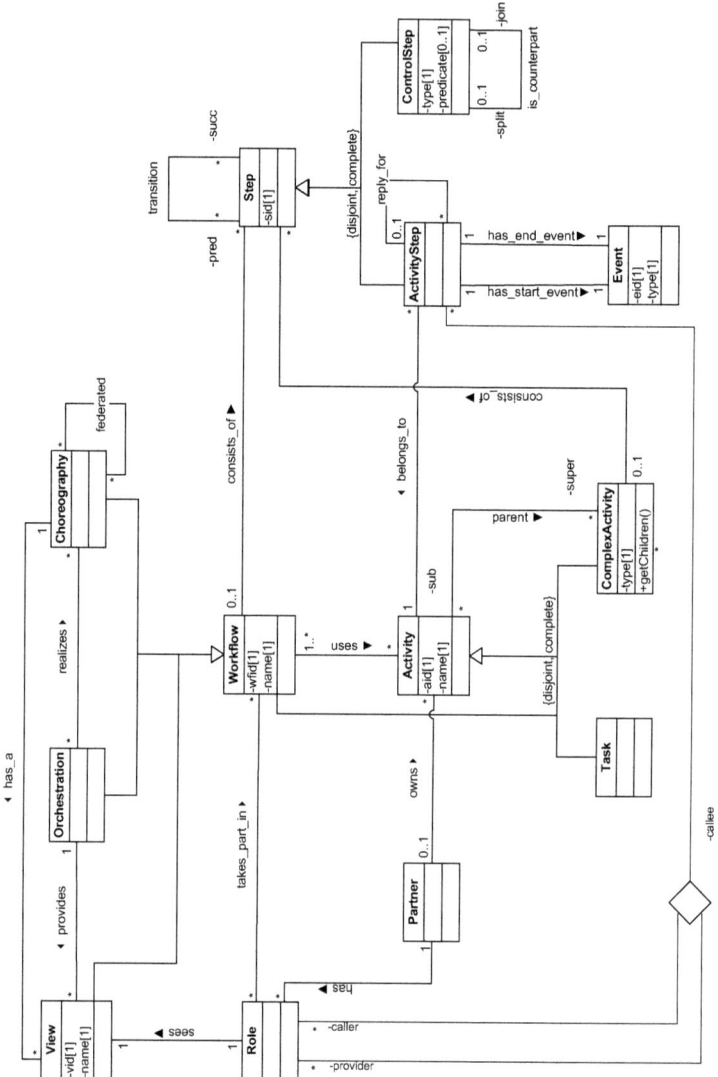

Figure 7.14.: Metamodel of the Federated Choreographies

7.2. Federated Choreographies

A workflow is either a *choreography*, an *orchestration* or a *workflow view*. A workflow can have many *views*. A workflow define views for different roles (of partners). Each role sees and accesses the workflow through the view. A workflow uses *activities*. An activity is either a *task*, a *complex activity* or a *(sub-)workflow*. An activity can be used to compose complex activities and workflows. An activity occurrence in such a composition is represented by an *activity step*. One activity can be represented by several activity steps in one or several workflows or complex activities and each activity step belongs to exactly one activity. In other words, activity steps are placeholders for reusable activities. The same activity can occur in different workflows (choreographies, orchestrations or workflow views). The control structure of a complex activity is described by its *type* (*seq* for sequence, *par* for parallel and *cond* for conditional).

An activity may be owned by a *partner*. Orchestrations and tasks must have an owner, whereas choreographies must not have an owner. A partner may have several *roles* and one role can be played by several partners. A role may take part in a workflow and call an activity step in this workflow. An activity step is provided by another role. Thus a single parter can use different roles to participate in a workflow and provide or call activity steps. A role sees and accesses a defined view on the workflow.

The notion of a *step* is very important for the presented metamodel. Both workflows and complex activities consist of steps. Between the subsequent steps there can be a *transition* from a predecessor to a successor which represents control flow dependencies between steps.

A complex activity may be decomposed in a given workflow into steps that constitute this complex activity only if all of the activities corresponding to these steps are also used and visible in this workflow. Therefore, a workflow can be decomposed and analyzed on different levels of detail with complex activities disclosing their content, but without revealing protected information on the implementation of these complex activities. To allow a correct decomposition, a complex activity must have only one activity without any predecessors and only one activity without any successors. The same applies to workflows.

A step can be either an *activity step* or a *control step*. As mentioned above, activity steps are placeholders for reusable activities and each activity step belongs to exactly one activity. Activity steps can be called in a workflow definition. An activity step may be used as a reply for a previous activity step. A single activity step may have several alternative replies.

A control step represents a control flow element such as a split or a join. Conditional and parallel structures are allowed, i.e. the type of a control step is one of the followings: *par-split*, *par-join*, *cond-split* or *cond-join*. An attribute *predicate* is specified only for steps corresponding to a conditional split and represents a conditional predicate. Conditional splits have XOR-semantics. A split control step may have a corresponding join control step what is represented by the recursive relation *is_counterpart*. This relation is used to represent well structured workflows [104] where each split node has a corresponding join node of the same type and vice versa.

7.2.3. Graph Representation of the Control Flow

A control flow of a workflow model can be represented as a directed graph with two kinds of nodes corresponding to activity steps and control steps. The edges correspond to transitions between steps and determine the execution sequence of nodes, i.e. a successor can start if its predecessor(s) is(are) completed. A complex activity can be decomposed into a subgraph with one input node and one output node. In the graphical notation additionally two control nodes are used: start node and end node, before the start activity and after the end activity of the workflow, respectively. Figures 7.3- 7.8 are examples of the graph representations.

7.2.4. Mapping onto WF-nets

A graph representing the control flow of a workflow model, described in terms of the metamodel, can be mapped onto a workflow-net (WF-net) [95, 261] in a similar manner as described in [264]. Workflow-nets are an extension of classical Petri-nets [198, 218]. A WF-net contains exactly one place without any predecessors (source place) and exactly one place without any successors (sink place). Moreover, the net extended with an additional transition from the sink place to the source place is strongly connected, i.e. for each node n there exists a path from the source place to n and from n to the sink place. A formal definition of WF-nets is presented in section 3.2. WF-nets are used with a set of special transitions added to express branching decisions in a more human readable form: AND-split, AND-join, XOR-split and XOR-join.

A workflow model transformed onto a WF-net can be analyzed with all the techniques developed for Petri-nets and important properties of such a model can be checked. WF-nets are used to test structural conformance as described in section 8.2. On the other hand, models described with Petri-nets are usually much larger than traditional workflow graphs (because they contain both transitions and places) and therefore difficult to understand by humans.

The mapping from a workflow graph onto a WF-net is as follows:

- Each activity step is mapped onto a transition with a single input and output place, the label of the transition is the same as the name of the activity

- Each cond-split is mapped onto a XOR-split transition with a single input place and at least two output places

- Each cond-join is mapped onto a XOR-join transition with at least two input places and exactly one output place

- Each par-split is mapped onto an AND-split transition with a single input place and at least two output places

7.2. Federated Choreographies

- Each par-join is mapped onto an AND-join transition with at least two input places and exactly one output place
- A start node is mapped onto a single source place
- An end node is mapped onto a single sink place
- Edges in the original graph are mapped onto dummy transitions connecting subsequent transformed nodes

After the mapping completes, the dummy transitions introduced in the last step can be reduced by fusion of series places (FSP) [198] to improve readability. Mapping of the workflow graph in figure 7.3 onto a WF-net is presented in figure 7.15.

The concept of federated choreographies and the metamodel has been also presented separately in [107]. The metamodel presented in this book reflects only the control flow aspects of workflows and do not consider data flow aspects. For a variation of the metamodel that also considers data flow aspects please refer to [107].

98 7. An Architecture for Interorganizational Workflows

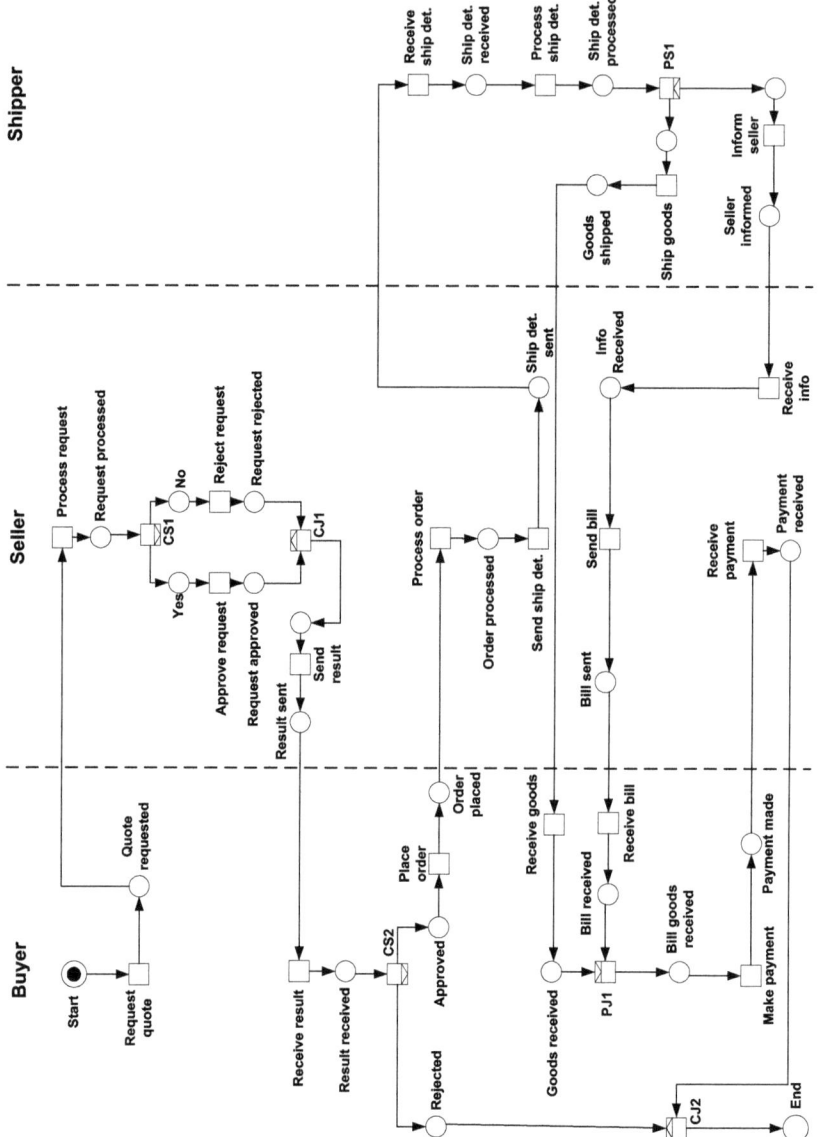

Figure 7.15.: The WF-net of workflow graph in figure 7.3

Chapter 8

Conformance of the Federated Choreographies

The key requirement of the federated choreographies is the inter-layer and intra-layer conformance and consistency. This requires conformance of orchestrations with the choreographies, as well as conformance of choreographies with each other in the choreography layer. The execution of the model should not lead to any conflicts. Several issues have to be considered: the structure of the business processes must match, i.e. supporting choreographies and realizing orchestrations must have no conflicts regarding the structure of the process with the choreography they support or realize (structural conformance). The sent messages between two business processes must be received and understood (messaging conformance). The exchanged data follow a common and known format and can be interpreted correctly (data flow conformance) and finally messaging is done in a timely manner and data is delivered at the right time (temporal conformance).

In the following sections two techniques for checking the structural and temporal conformance of the federated choreographies are presented. Using these techniques, one can check at design-time if the model is structurally and temporally conformant and if not, necessary modifications can be done to ensure the compatibility of the model. Checking the model for conflict-freeness reduces the cost of a process because on the one hand detected errors at runtime cause more costs than those detected at design-time and on the other hand less exception handling mechanisms need to be triggered. Exception handling mechanisms are as well associated with additional costs during the process execution. In addition, a conflict-free and conformant process model increases the quality of service (QoS) as organizations in the competitive world of business strive for the highest possible quality.

8.1. Differrent Notions of Process Equivalence

8.1.1. Bisimulation

Branching bisimulation is an important equivalence when studying the behavior of concurrent systems. In contrast to *linear time* equivalences (cf. trace equivalence in [140]) branching time semantics consider the branching structure of a process. Such semantics are independent of precise nature of observability (of process) and allow for a proper modeling of deadlock behavior [129, 130]. The branching bisimulation as a generalization of the theory of bisimulation has become popular in the computer sciences community e.g. for studying the concurrent systems. Other equivalences have also been introduced by other authors [203, 204, 262, 263, 36, 56, 65, 201, 202, 142] and also see [220, 222, 223, 38, 55, 76, 89, 209]. Note that the other introduced equivalences lie between linear time and branching time equivalence semantics and can be seen as a subset of the branching time semantics. In other words, the verified equivalence in branching time semantics is valid in all of the proposed equivalence relations but the converse is not true.

Central to the definition of branching bisimulation is the concept of silent action. In process algebra the notion of abstraction [51] provides a mean for making actions unobservable or hiding them. The abstraction operator renames the label of actions to the label τ. A τ-labeled action is called a *silent action* or synonymously *hidden action* or *internal action*. The abstraction operator is like a renaming operator and changes the label of an action into τ. Multiple τ-labels have no additional effect since only one τ-label makes the relabeled action invisible. A silent action is invisible from outside and cannot be recognized since it is hidden from the external observer and has no external effect. All other actions are external actions and visible. The branching bisimulation as introduced in [129, 130] extends the observation equivalence [192, 215], also known as weak bisimulation, and makes more processes distinguishable than the weak bisimulation. The difference between ordinary bisimulation and weak bisimulation is that weak bisimulation allows for arbitrary τ-steps proceeding and succeeding actions. Consequently, it can not be guaranteed that all intermediate states of computations of two bisimilar processes correspond to each other. In other words, weak bisimulation lacks this central property of ordinary bisimulation equivalence. Another notion of bisimulation is also presented in [193]. A weaker form of bisimulation, also called η-bisimulation, can be found in [37].

Weak bisimulation, synonymously observation equivalence or τ-bisimulation equivalence, as the basis for bisimulation equivalence can be formalized as follows. Note that in the provided definitions the following notations are used:

- Let $\{A\}$ be the set of action a system may perform, i.e. the set of executable actions, $A_\tau = A \bigcup \{\tau\}$, where τ is the silent action

- $\wp$ is the set of processes

- $r \xrightarrow{\alpha} r\prime$ denotes the existence of an edge from a node r to a node $r\prime$ with label α. In other words, It says that the system evolves from a state r to another state $r\prime$ by performing the action $\alpha \in A_\tau$

- $r \Rightarrow r\prime$ denotes a path from a node r to a node $r\prime$ with at least 0 τ-steps

- A process graph is a connected, directed graph whose edges are labeled with $\alpha \in A_\tau$. G denotes the domain of process graphs

8.1. Different Notions of Process Equivalence

- $g.r$ denotes the root of a graph g

Definition 8.1: (Weak Bisimulation)

The graphs g and h are weakly bisimilar, denoted $g \simeq_w h$, if there exists a symmetric relation $\Re$ satisfying:

- $(g.r \Re h.r)$
- $[(r \Re s) \land (r \xrightarrow{\alpha} r\prime)] \Rightarrow \{[(\alpha = \tau) \land (r\prime \Re s)] \lor [\exists (s \Rightarrow s_1 \xrightarrow{\alpha} s_2 \Rightarrow s\prime) : r\prime \Re s\prime]\}$

The notation $(r \Re s)$ denotes that a node r is related by the relation $\Re$ to a node s.

Figure 8.1 depicts the weak bisimilarity. Left part of the figure illustrates the first case, $[(r \Re s) \land (r \xrightarrow{\alpha} r\prime)] \Rightarrow [(\alpha = \tau) \land (r\prime \Re s)]$, and the right part of the figure illustrates the second case, $[(r \Re s) \land (r \xrightarrow{\alpha} r\prime)] \Rightarrow [\exists (s \Rightarrow s_1 \xrightarrow{\alpha} s_2 \Rightarrow s\prime) : r\prime \Re s\prime]$. Note that the dotted line represents the weak bisimulation and the double arrow represents a path consisting of at least 0 τ-steps, denoted by $\Rightarrow$ in the definition.

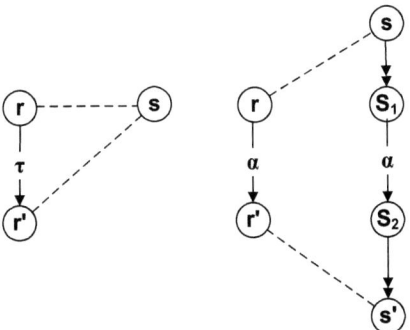

Figure 8.1.: Weak bisimulation

Alternatively, by considering only the external action steps and extraction of the internal actions (τ-steps), weak bisimulation can be defined as follows:

Definition 8.2: (Weak Bisimulation)

Let $p \Uparrow p\prime$ denote a path from p to $p\prime$ containing only external actions, two graphs g and h are weakly bisimilar, denoted $g \simeq_w h$, if there exists a symmetric relation $\Re$ satisfying

- $(g.r \Re h.r)$
- $[(r \Re s) \land (r \Uparrow r\prime)] \Rightarrow [\exists (s \Uparrow s\prime) : (r\prime \Re s\prime)]$

$r \Uparrow r\prime$ is similarly $(r \Rightarrow \xrightarrow{\alpha_1} \Rightarrow \xrightarrow{\alpha_2} \Rightarrow ... \xrightarrow{\alpha_{n-1}} \Rightarrow \xrightarrow{\alpha_n} \Rightarrow r\prime)$. Remember that internal actions are removed.

Another variant of observation equivalence has been also introduced by [193], which in [129] is called *delay bisimulation*.

Definition 8.3: **(Delay Bisimulation)**

Two graphs g and h are delay bisimilar, denoted $g \simeq_d h$, if there exists a symmetric relation $\Re$ satisfying

- $(g.r\Re h.r)$

- $[(r\Re s) \wedge (r \xrightarrow{\alpha} r\prime)] \Rightarrow \{[(\alpha = \tau) \wedge (r\prime \Re s)] \vee [\exists (s \Rightarrow s_1 \xrightarrow{\alpha} s_2 \Rightarrow s\prime) : ((r\prime \Re s_2) \wedge (r\prime \Re s\prime))]\}$

Figure 8.2 shows the concept of delay bisimulation. Again here, the left part corresponds to the first case, $[(r\Re s) \wedge (r \xrightarrow{\alpha} r\prime)] \Rightarrow [(\alpha = \tau) \wedge (r\prime \Re s)]$, and the right part corresponds to the second case, $[(r\Re s) \wedge (r \xrightarrow{\alpha} r\prime)] \Rightarrow [\exists (s \Rightarrow s_1 \xrightarrow{\alpha} s_2 \Rightarrow s\prime) : ((r\prime \Re s_2) \wedge (r\prime \Re s\prime))]$.

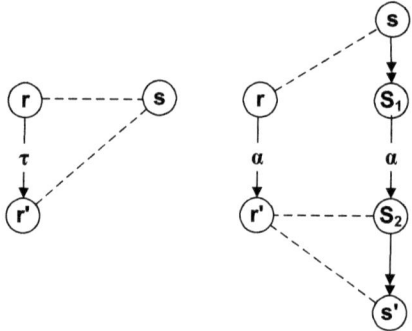

Figure 8.2.: Delay bisimulation

Above figures makes the difference between weak and delay bisimulation visible. Note the additional horizontal line between $r\prime$ and s_2 which corresponds to $((r\prime \Re s_2))$ and shows a delay bisimulation between these two nodes.

Another variant by Baeten and van Glabbee has been also introduced in [37], the so-called η-bisimulation.

Definition 8.4: **(η-Bisimulation)**

Two graphs g and h are η-bisimilar, denoted $g \simeq_\eta h$, if there exists a symmetric relation $\Re$ satisfying

- $(g.r\Re h.r)$

8.1. Different Notions of Process Equivalence

- $[(r\Re s) \wedge (r \xrightarrow{\alpha} r\prime)] \Rightarrow \{[(\alpha = \tau) \wedge (r\prime\Re s)] \vee [\exists (s \Rightarrow s_1 \xrightarrow{\alpha} s_2 \Rightarrow s\prime) : ((r\Re s_1) \wedge (r\prime\Re s\prime))]\}$

Figure 8.3 illustrates the η-bisimulation graphically. In this figure, again, the left part corresponds to the first case and the right part corresponds to the second case. The difference between η-bisimulation and other two notions is clear. Consider the horizontal lines. While in the delay bisimulation, there is a bisimulation relationship between $r\prime$ and s_2, in η-bisimulation the bisimulation relationship exists between r and s_1.

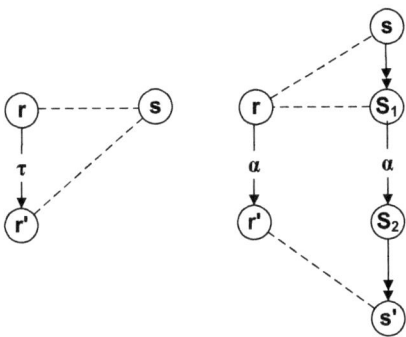

Figure 8.3.: η-bisimulation

Based on [215, 192, 194, 195, 196] the bisimulation equivalence on G can be formalized as follows:

Definition 8.5: (Bisimulation Equivalence)
Let g and h be graphs. Bisimulation equivalence is a relation $R \subseteq nodes(g) \times nodes(h)$, satisfying

- $(g.r\Re h.r)$
- $[(r\Re s) \wedge (r \xrightarrow{\alpha} r\prime)] \Rightarrow [\exists s\prime : (s \xrightarrow{\alpha} s\prime) \wedge (r\prime\Re s\prime)]$
- $[(r\Re s) \wedge (s \xrightarrow{\alpha} s\prime)] \Rightarrow [\exists r\prime : (r \xrightarrow{\alpha} r\prime) \wedge (r\prime\Re s\prime)]$

It is obvious that the bisimulation equivalence in the Definition. 8.5 is a symmetric relations. Hence, bisimulation equivalence can be equivalently defined as follows:

Definition 8.6: (Bisimulation Equivalence)
Two graphs g and h are bisimilar, denoted $g \simeq_h h$, if there exists a symmetric relation $\Re$ satisfying

- $(g.r\Re h.r)$

- $[(r\Re s) \wedge (r \xrightarrow{\alpha} r\prime)] \Rightarrow [\exists s\prime : (s \xrightarrow{\alpha} s\prime) \wedge (r\prime\Re s\prime)]$

Figure 8.4 illustrates the bisimulation equivalence graphically.

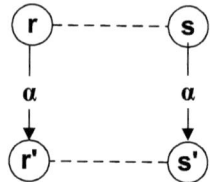

Figure 8.4.: Bisimulation equivalence

Finally, the branching bisimulation is formalized as follows according to [129, 130]

Definition 8.7: **(Branching Bisimulation)**

Two graphs g and h are branching bisimilar, denoted $g \simeq_b h$, if there exists a symmetric relation $\Re$, called branching bisimulation, between the nodes of g and h satisfying

- $(g.r\Re h.r)$

- $[(r\Re s) \wedge (r \xrightarrow{\alpha} r\prime)] \Rightarrow \{[(a = \tau) \wedge (r\prime\Re s)] \vee [\exists (s \Rightarrow s_1 \xrightarrow{\alpha} s_2 \Rightarrow s\prime) : (r\prime\Re s_1), (r\prime\Re s_2), (r\prime\Re s\prime)]\}$

Figure 8.5 illustrates the substantial nature of branching bisimulation.

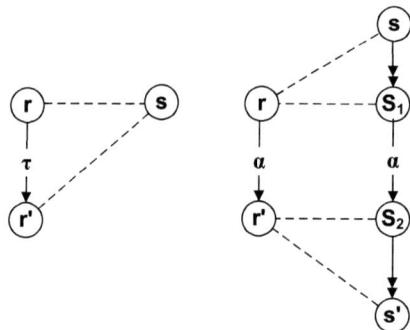

Figure 8.5.: Branching bisimulation

Branching bisimulation is closed under arbitrary union, i.e. existence of branching bisimulation means existence of largest branching bisimulation and union of two branching bisimulations is again a branching bisimulation [272].

8.1. Different Notions of Process Equivalence

In addition to above mentioned notions of bisimulation, Van Glabbeek and Weijland defined a slightly different notion of bisimulation which can be used to prove branching bisimulation is an equivalence relationship. This notion, called semi-branching bisimulation, is formalized as follows and is referred to in this work for the sake of completeness.

Definition 8.8: **(Semi-branching Bisimulation)**

Two graphs g and h are semi-branching bisimilar if there exists a symmetric relation $\Re$, called semi-branching bisimulation, between the nodes of g and h satisfying

- $(g.r\Re h.r)$
- $[(r\Re s) \wedge (r \xrightarrow{\alpha} r\prime)] \Rightarrow \{[(a = \tau) \wedge (\exists(s \Rightarrow s\prime) : ((r\Re s\prime) \wedge (r\prime\Re s\prime)))] \vee [\exists(s \Rightarrow s_1 \xrightarrow{\alpha} s_2 \Rightarrow s\prime) : ((r\Re s_1) \wedge (r\prime\Re s_2) \wedge (r\prime\Re s\prime))]\}$

Figure 8.6 illustrates this relationship. The left part corresponds to $[(r\Re s) \wedge (r \xrightarrow{\alpha} r\prime)] \Rightarrow [(a = \tau) \wedge (\exists(s \Rightarrow s\prime) : ((r\Re s\prime) \wedge (r\prime\Re s\prime)))]$ and the right part corresponds to $[(r\Re s) \wedge (r \xrightarrow{\alpha} r\prime)] \Rightarrow [\exists(s \Rightarrow s_1 \xrightarrow{\alpha} s_2 \Rightarrow s\prime) : ((r\Re s_1) \wedge (r\prime\Re s_2) \wedge (r\prime\Re s\prime))]$ respectively.

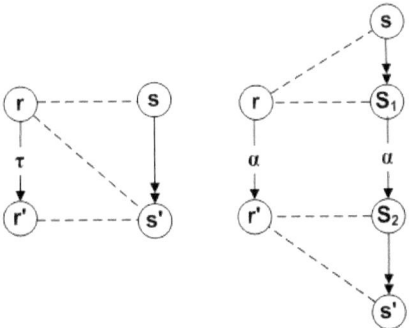

Figure 8.6.: Semi-branching bisimulation

Figure 8.7 clarifies the difference between both notions of branching and semi-branching bisimulation. It can be observed that any branching bisimulation is a semi-branching bisimulation but the converse is not true. Besides, a compositional relation of two semi-branching bisimulations is again a semi-branching bisimulation, which is not valid for branching bisimulation. Therefore, a semi-branching bisimulation is an equivalence relationship [44]. Note that This property only shows the transitivity of semi-branching bisimulation. Other two properties needed for an equivalence relationship, reflexivity and symmetry, are obvious from definition. Let $\Re$ be the semi-branching bisimulation, $\forall$ process $r, r\Re r$ (reflexivity) and symmetry follows immediately from the definition of semi-branching bisimulation, i.e. the inverse of $\Re$ is again a semi-branching bisimulation, $r\Re s \Rightarrow s\Re r$.

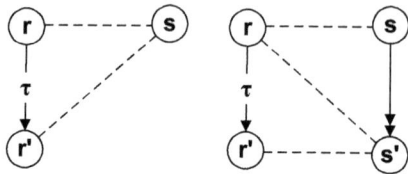

Figure 8.7.: Left: Branching bisimulation, Right: Semi-branching bisimulation

Although, Van Glabbeek and Weijland do not explicitly prove that branching bisimulation is an equivalence relationship but provide the required material for the proof which is done by Basten [44]. However Basten uses a slightly different and more intuitive definition of branching and semi-branching bisimulation. Whatever definitions, both notions as defined in [129, 130] and [44] induce the same concept of bisimilarity, i.e. the defined process equivalence relation is the same.

Before formalizing the definitions of bisimilarity according to [44] some auxiliary and supporting definitions are needed.

Definition 8.9: **(Process Space)**

A process space over A_τ is a pair $(\wp, \rightarrow)$, where $\wp$ and A_τ as defined before and $\_ \rightarrow \_ \subseteq \wp \times A_\tau \times \wp$ a ternary transition relation.

Definition 8.10: The relation $\_ \twoheadrightarrow \_ \subseteq \wp \times \wp$ is the smallest relation $\forall r, r\prime, r\prime\prime \in \wp$, satisfying:

- $r \twoheadrightarrow r$

- $[(r \twoheadrightarrow r\prime) \wedge (r\prime \xrightarrow{\tau} r\prime\prime)] \Rightarrow (r \twoheadrightarrow r\prime\prime)$

Definition 8.10 states that a process evolves to another process by performing a sequence of zero or more silent actions. Now the semi-branching and branching bisimulation according to Basten can be formalized. In the following definition the notation $(r \xrightarrow{(\alpha)} r\prime)$ is used as an abbreviation for $(r \xrightarrow{\alpha} r\prime) \vee (\alpha = \tau \wedge r = r\prime)$. That is either the system evolves from r to $r\prime$ by performing an action $\alpha \in A_\tau$ or the action τ is a sequence of zero or more silent steps and both r and $r\prime$ overlap.

Definition 8.11: **(Semi-branching Bisimulation)**

$\forall r, r\prime, s, s\prime \in \wp, \alpha \in A_\tau$, a binary relation $\Re \subseteq \wp \times \wp$ satisfying the following properties is called a semi-branching bisimulation

- $[(r \Re s) \wedge (r \xrightarrow{\alpha} r\prime)] \Rightarrow [(\exists s\prime, s\prime\prime : (s \twoheadrightarrow s\prime\prime \xrightarrow{(\alpha)} s\prime) \wedge (r \Re s\prime\prime) \wedge (r\prime \Re s\prime)]$

- $[(r \Re s) \wedge (s \xrightarrow{\alpha} s\prime)] \Rightarrow [(\exists r\prime, r\prime\prime : (r \twoheadrightarrow r\prime\prime \xrightarrow{(\alpha)} r\prime) \wedge (r\prime\prime \Re s) \wedge (r\prime \Re s\prime)]$

8.1. Different Notions of Process Equivalence

The first condition can be decomposed to
$$\{[(r\Re s) \wedge (r \xrightarrow{\alpha} r\prime)] \Rightarrow [(\exists s\prime, s\prime\prime : (s \twoheadrightarrow s\prime\prime \xrightarrow{\alpha} s\prime) \wedge (r\Re s\prime\prime) \wedge (r\prime\Re s\prime)] \vee$$
$$[(r\Re s) \wedge (r \xrightarrow{\tau} r\prime)] \Rightarrow [(\exists s\prime, s\prime\prime : (s \twoheadrightarrow (s\prime\prime = s\prime)) \wedge (r\Re s\prime\prime) \wedge (r\prime\Re s\prime)]\}$$
and the second condition can be decomposed to:
$$\{[(r\Re s) \wedge (s \xrightarrow{\alpha} s\prime)] \Rightarrow [(\exists r\prime, r\prime\prime : (r \twoheadrightarrow r\prime\prime \xrightarrow{\alpha} r\prime) \wedge (r\prime\prime\Re s) \wedge (r\prime\Re s\prime)] \vee$$
$$[(r\Re s) \wedge (s \xrightarrow{\tau} s\prime)] \Rightarrow [(\exists r\prime, r\prime\prime : (r \twoheadrightarrow (r\prime\prime = r\prime)) \wedge (r\prime\prime\Re s) \wedge (r\prime\Re s\prime)]\}$$

Whilst the semi-branching bisimulation is a symmetric relationship, it can also be defined using the symmetry property which yields in a more compact definition and the transfer property needs to be defined only for one direction.

Definition 8.12: (Semi-branching Bisimulation)

$\forall r, r\prime, s, s\prime \in \wp, \alpha \in A_\tau$, a symmetric binary relation $\Re \subseteq \wp \times \wp$ satisfying the following property is called a semi-branching bisimulation

- $[(r\Re s) \wedge (r \xrightarrow{\alpha} r\prime)] \Rightarrow [(\exists s\prime, s\prime\prime : (s \twoheadrightarrow s\prime\prime \xrightarrow{(\alpha)} s\prime) \wedge (r\Re s\prime\prime) \wedge (r\prime\Re s\prime)]$

Figure 8.8 illustrates the concept of semi-branching bisimulation according to Basten.

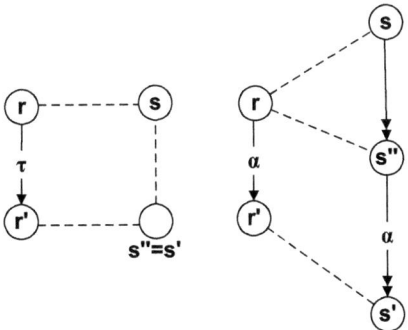

Figure 8.8.: Semi-branching bisimulation

The Basten's definition of branching bisimulation is also slightly different but more intuitive than that defined by Van Glabbeek and Weijland.

Definition 8.13: (Branching Bisimulation)

$\forall r, r\prime, s, s\prime \in \wp, \alpha \in A_\tau$, a binary relation $\Re \subseteq \wp \times \wp$ satisfying the following properties is called a branching bisimulation

- $[(r\Re s) \wedge (r \xrightarrow{\alpha} r\prime)] \Rightarrow \{[(\alpha = \tau) \wedge (r\prime\Re s)] \vee [\exists s\prime, s\prime\prime : (s \twoheadrightarrow s\prime\prime \xrightarrow{\alpha} s\prime) \wedge (r\Re s\prime\prime) \wedge (r\prime\Re s\prime)]\}$

- $[(r\Re s) \wedge (s \xrightarrow{\alpha} s\prime)] \Rightarrow \{[(\alpha = \tau) \wedge (r\Re s\prime)] \vee [\exists r\prime, r\prime\prime : (r \twoheadrightarrow r\prime\prime \xrightarrow{\alpha} r\prime) \wedge (r\prime\prime \Re s) \wedge (r\prime \Re s\prime)]\}$

Using the symmetry property of branching bisimulation as required in [129, 130], branching bisimulation can be defined more concisely as follows:

Definition 8.14: **(Branching Bisimulation)**

$\forall r, r\prime, s, s\prime \in \wp, \alpha \in A_\tau$, a symmetric binary relation $\Re \subseteq \wp \times \wp$ satisfying the following property is called a branching bisimulation

- $[(r\Re s) \wedge (r \xrightarrow{\alpha} r\prime)] \Rightarrow \{[(\alpha = \tau) \wedge (r\prime \Re s)] \vee [\exists s\prime, s\prime\prime : (s \twoheadrightarrow s\prime\prime \xrightarrow{\alpha} s\prime) \wedge (r\Re s\prime\prime) \wedge (r\prime \Re s\prime)]\}$

If two processes $r_1, r_2 \in \wp$ are branching bisimilar, denoted $r_1 \approx_b r_2$, one process must be able to simulate an arbitrary action of its equivalent(i.e. $\forall \alpha : \alpha \in A_\tau$) process after execution an arbitrary number of τ-steps. Figure 8.9 shows the definition of branching bisimulation (Definitions 8.13 and 8.14) graphically. In the above definitions of branching bisimulation, the internal actions at the beginning of a process can be removed and do not contribute to the external behavior of the process.

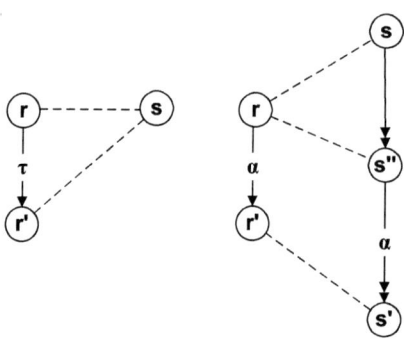

Figure 8.9.: Branching bisimulation

Figure 8.10 clarifies the difference between branching and semi-branching bisimulation according to Basten.

8.1. Different Notions of Process Equivalence

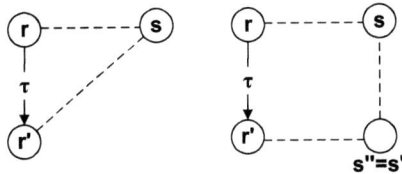

Figure 8.10.: Left: Branching bisimulation, Right: Semi-branching bisimulation

Basten suggests several ways to prove that branching bisimulation is an equivalence relation and uses semi-branching bisimulation for the proof. He concludes that "*Branching bisimlarity is an equivalence relation, which coincides with semi-branching bisimilarity*". For a detailed proof, discussion and definitions please refer to [44].

In a later work [47] Basten and van der Aalst extend the branching bisimulation by considering the termination predicate of processes and introduce a variant of branching bisimulation called *rooted branching bisimulation*. In contrast to branching bisimulation, rooted branching bisimulation does not allow for removal of τ-actions at the beginning of a process. Rooted branching bisimulation is again an equivalence relationship.

Definition 8.15: **(Branching Bisimulation)**

$\forall r, r\prime, s, s\prime \in \wp, \alpha \in A_\tau$, a binary relation $\Re \subseteq \wp \times \wp$ satisfying the following properties is called a branching bisimulation

- $[(r\Re s) \wedge (r \xrightarrow{\alpha} r\prime)] \Rightarrow \{[\exists s\prime, s\prime\prime : (s \twoheadrightarrow s\prime\prime \xrightarrow{(\alpha)} s\prime) \wedge (r\Re s\prime\prime) \wedge (r\prime \Re s\prime)]\}$
- $[(r\Re s) \wedge (s \xrightarrow{\alpha} s\prime)] \Rightarrow \{[\exists r\prime, r\prime\prime : (r \twoheadrightarrow r\prime\prime \xrightarrow{(\alpha)} r\prime) \wedge (r\prime\prime \Re s) \wedge (r\prime \Re s\prime)]\}$
- $(r\Re s) \Rightarrow [(\downarrow r \Rightarrow \Downarrow s) \wedge (\downarrow s \Rightarrow \Downarrow r)]$

where $\downarrow r$ is the termination predicate of process r and $\Downarrow r$ as defined in definition 8.16.

Definition 8.16: $\forall r, r\prime \in \wp, \Downarrow \_ \subseteq \wp$ is the smallest set of processes satisfying following properties:

- $(\downarrow r \Rightarrow \Downarrow r)$
- $[\Downarrow r \wedge (r\prime \xrightarrow{\tau} r)] \Rightarrow \Downarrow r\prime$

where $\downarrow r$ is the termination predicate of process r

Note that in definition 8.15 the notation $(r \xrightarrow{(\alpha)} r\prime)$ is a placeholder for $(r \xrightarrow{\alpha} r\prime) \vee (\alpha = \tau \wedge r = r\prime)$ and hence it can be equivalently rewritten as

Definition 8.17: **(Branching Bisimulation)**

$\forall r, r\prime, s, s\prime \in \wp, \alpha \in A_\tau$, a binary relation $\Re \subseteq \wp \times \wp$ satisfying the following properties is called a branching bisimulation

- $[(r\Re s) \wedge (r \xrightarrow{\alpha} r\prime)] \Rightarrow \{[(\alpha = \tau) \wedge (r\prime \Re s)] \vee [\exists s\prime, s\prime\prime : (s \twoheadrightarrow s\prime\prime \xrightarrow{\alpha} s\prime) \wedge (r\Re s\prime\prime) \wedge (r\prime \Re s\prime)]\}$

- $[(r\Re s) \wedge (s \xrightarrow{\alpha} s\prime)] \Rightarrow \{[(\alpha = \tau) \wedge (r \Re s\prime)] \vee [\exists r\prime, r\prime\prime : (r \twoheadrightarrow r\prime\prime \xrightarrow{\alpha} r\prime) \wedge (r\prime\prime \Re s) \wedge (r\prime \Re s\prime)]\}$

- $(r\Re s) \Rightarrow [(\downarrow r \Rightarrow \Downarrow s) \wedge (\downarrow s \Rightarrow \Downarrow r)]$

8.1.2. Trace Equivalence

Trace Equivalence, also known as string equivalence [141] is the weakest equivalence presented here, in the sense that it discriminates less processes than all other equivalence relationships. The main idea behind the trace equivalence is that two processes are equivalent and possess the same behavior if they perform the same sequence of observable actions (here called trace) or engage in the same sequence of observable transitions. Let T^* denote the set of all possible traces i.e. all possible transition in which a process may engage in or alternatively all visible action that a process may perform.

Definition 8.18: (Trace)
Let p_1, p_2 be two processes and T^* as defined above.
$tr(p_1) = \{t \in T^* \mid \exists p_2 : p_1 \xrightarrow{t} p_2\}$
the set $tr(p_1)$ contains all possible traces of a process p_1.

Definition 8.19: (Trace Equivalence)
Two processes are trace equivalent, denoted $p_1 \sim_{tr} p_2$ if and only if they have exactly the same traces.
$tr(p1) = tr(p_2) \Leftrightarrow p_1 \sim_{tr} p_2$

Figure 8.11 shows an example of two trace equivalent processes. These two processes produce the same sequence of visible actions and their traces are the same.

For a more detailed discussion on trace equivalence, concepts, model and its application for other domains refer to [223, 118, 60, 138, 146, 268, 205, 123, 185, 30].

8.1.3. Testing Equivalence

Testing equivalence [200, 201, 202] deals with the external observable behavior of processes and considers two processes as equivalent if their external behaviors are equivalent. Testing of processes is considered as the measure for evaluation of interaction of processes with the environment. Let P be a set of processes and O a set of observers. In this setting the tests are performed by the observers. Performing a test t by an observer o on a precess p results in a computation c at process p. $c \in C(o,p)$, where $C(o,p)$ denotes the set of computations resulted by the tests performed by an observer o on a process p. The result of a computation c decides if a process p has passed a test t or not. If the result of the computation c is successful, a process p has passed the test, otherwise p has failed.

8.1. Different Notions of Process Equivalence

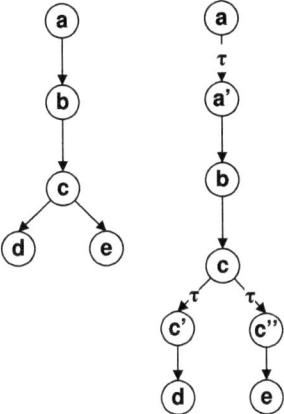

Figure 8.11.: Two Processes are trace equivalent

Let S be the set of states, the set of successful states is a subset of S, denoted by $succ$, i.e. $\{succ\} \subseteq \{S\}$. Further let $R(o,p)$ be the result of the test performed by o on p. The result set is defined as follows:

Definition 8.20: (**Result Set**)
$R(o,p) \subseteq \{\top, \bot\}$, where

- $\exists c \in C(o,p) : c \in \{succ\} \Rightarrow \top \in R(o,p)$
- $\exists c \in C(o,p) : c \notin \{succ\} \Rightarrow \bot \in R(o,p)$

Note that deadlocks and divergent states are also contained in the unsuccessful states. A divergent state denotes an infinite computation without the possibility of reaching a successful state. Whereas a deadlock denotes a finite computation that can not terminate successfully.

The testing equivalence can be formalized as follows

Definition 8.21: (**Testing Equivalence**)
Two processes $p_1, p_2 \in P$ are testing equivalent, denoted $p_1 \approx_t p_2$, if the result set of the tests performed by all observers on these two processes are the same. Formally:
$\forall o \in O : R(o,p_1) = R(o,p_2) \Rightarrow p_1 \approx_t p_2$

If all computations end in a successful state, the process p *must* satisfy the observer o. However if only a subset of computations ends in a successful state, we say p *may* satisfy o. If all computations are unsuccessful, process p cannot satisfy o.

For a detailed discussion, the model, testing equivalence for asynchronous processes, its applications and relationship with other equivalence notions, refer to [143, 164, 192, 233, 60, 25, 83, 59, 148, 172].

8.1.4. Failure Equivalence

Failure equivalence [65, 143] is another equivalence relationship that studies the behavior of a process in terms of its interaction with the environment. The important difference between failure equivalence and other notions of equivalence, e.g. observational equivalence and trace equivalence, is that failure equivalence deals with the negative behavior of a process, i.e. what must not happen whereas other notions of equivalence consider the positive aspects of the behavior, i.e. what may happen. Failure equivalence has been first proposed by Hoare, Brookes and Roscoe in [143, 65]. In the failure equivalence, failure sets of a process describe its behavior. These sets are of the form (s, X), where s is a sequence of visible events or transitions, also called trace, in which a process has engaged up to a specific moment in time and X denotes the set of future transitions that a process may not be able to perform. The inability of a process to perform transitions X comes from the indeterministic nature of a process. Let p_1, p_2 be two processes and $p_1 \xrightarrow{s} p_2$ denotes that a process p_1 has been engaged in the sequence s and has transformed to the process p_2. The failure set can be formalized as:

Definition 8.22: **(Failure set)**
$$\text{failures}(p_1) = \{(s, X) \mid \exists p_2 : p_1 \xrightarrow{s} p_2 \land \forall x \in X : \nexists p_2 : p_1 \xrightarrow{x} p_2\}$$

After the process p_1 has been engaged in the sequence of events s and has transformed to the process p_2, p_1 refuses to perform any more, i.e. all the transitions of the set x. However the transitions $x \in X$ are offered by the environment. The Set X is called the *refusal set* of the process p_1 and identifies all the transition that the process p_1 may not be able to perform. The failure set can be formalized in terms of the refusal set.

Definition 8.23: **(Refusal set)**
$$\text{refusal}(p_1) = \{X \mid X\text{finite} \land \exists p_2 : p_1 \xrightarrow{()} p_2 \land X \cap in(p_2) = \varnothing\}$$

In the above definition, X *finite* describes an environment which is able of performing a finite number of events. $p_1 \xrightarrow{()} p_2$ denotes that a process p_1 transforms into and behave like p_2 after performing an empty sequence. This can be the case if p_1 has only performed internal steps and transitions which are externally not observable. The set $in(p_2)$ identifies those events that can be performed by p_2 at its first step and is called the *initial set* of p_2. Let X denote all the possible events offered by the environment. $X \cap in(p_2) = \varnothing$ means that the events that can trigger a process are not offered by the environment and the process can not continue. The refusal set, $refusal(p_1)$, describes those events that a process p_1 can not perform. This set together with the previous sequence of a process define a failure set of a process.

8.1. Different Notions of Process Equivalence

Definition 8.24: (Failure set)
$$\text{failures}(p_1) = \{(s, X) \mid \exists p_2 : p_1 \xrightarrow{s} p_2 \wedge X \in \text{refusal}(p_2)\}$$

The failure sets of process are externally visible and its behavior is distinguishable in terms of its failure sets. Moreover, failure sets uniquely identify a process. i.e. if two processes have the same failure set they are equivalent.

Definition 8.25: (Failure Equivalence)
Two processes p_1 and p_2 are failure equivalent, denoted $p_1 \sim_f p_2$ if they have the same failure set.
$$\text{failure}(p_1) = \text{failure}(p_2) \Rightarrow p_1 \sim_f p_2$$

The failure equivalence is a PSPACE-complete problem [156, 157, 67], which makes it slower for verification that observation equivalence which can be verified in cubic time. However, [259] claims that despite of theoretical worst case complexity results of the failure equivalence and observational equivalence, in typical practical situations it is not clear and there are no supporting evidences that failure-based equivalences are slower for verification than observational-based equivalences.

For a more detailed introduction and discussion, proofs and applications refer to [207, 64, 52, 154, 66, 211, 232, 228, 266, 149].

8.1.5. Observation Equivalence

Observation equivalence [192] has been presented by Milner and as its name implies, it deals with the external observable behavior of processes. The set of actions is divided into a set of observable actions and the unobservable action τ. Let A be the set of observable actions. A_τ is defined as $A_\tau = A \cup \{\tau\}$. If two processes p_1 and p_2 are equivalent, then p_1 must be substitutable with p_2 (or vice versa) in a larger environment without any observable effect on the environment. Bearing this mind, it implies that intermediate states of two equivalent processes p_1 and p_2 must also be taken into account. Two processes whose intermediate states do not corresponding may expose different behaviors and substitution of one with another may lead to deadlock. Let P be a set of processes and $p_1, p_2 \in P$. Moreover, Let O denote the set of possible observation types. Observations are captured through the interaction of processes with the environment. Note that an observation changes the process state. In other words, after observation the process transforms into a new process because of a change in its process state. Observational equivalence can be formalized as a series of relations over P.

Definition 8.26: (Observation Equivalence)
Let R_o denote a binary relation over P, where o is an observation, i.e. $\{R_o \subseteq P \times P \mid o \in O\}$. p and q are n-observational equivalent if and only if

- $p, q \in P \Rightarrow p \sim_o q$

- $\{[\forall o \in O : (p,p\prime) \in R_o \Rightarrow \exists q\prime : (q,q\prime) \in R_o \wedge p\prime \sim_n q\prime] \wedge [\forall o \in O : (q,q\prime) \in R_o \Rightarrow \exists p\prime : (p,p\prime) \in R_o \wedge p\prime \sim_n q\prime]\} \Rightarrow p \sim_{n+1} q$

p and q are observationally equivalent, denoted $p \sim_o q$ if $\forall n : p \sim_n q$.

In the above definition the set R_o includes the observation instances. Note the difference between the sets R_o and O. The observational equivalence is decidable in cubic time [156, 157]. The advantages of observational equivalence include its intuitive notion, mathematical models and properties and several algorithms developed for it.

Milner in [192] uses the notion of synchronization trees over which the observational equivalence is defined. Synchronization trees are used to model the behavior of processes.

Definition 8.27: **(Synchronization Tree)**

A synchronization tree is a rooted, unordered, finitely branching tree whose arcs are labeled with elements of A_τ.

Let $S \xrightarrow{\alpha} T$ denote that S accepts α or performs an action α and transforms to T. When we consider a sequence of atomic actions, it is possible that arbitrary τ-actions occur in between, i.e. $S \xrightarrow{\beta} T$, where β is of form $\tau^i \alpha_1 \tau^j \alpha_2 \tau^k \alpha_3 ...., i,j,k,... \geq 0$. $S \xrightarrow{\tau} T$ means that S performs an internal action and transforms into T. However, This transformation is not observable. Because the observer cannot see the τ-actions, we can remove these internal actions and define an S-experiment which contains only visible actions.

Definition 8.28: **(S-experiment)**

Let $\beta = \tau^i \alpha_1 \tau^j \alpha_2 \tau^k \alpha_3 ...., i,j,k,... \geq 0$ be a sequence of atomic experiments. An S-experiment is defined by removal of all τ-actions. i.e. $s = \alpha_1 \alpha_2 \alpha_3, ...$

$S \xRightarrow{s} T$ denotes that S accepts or performs an S-experiment and transforms to T and this transformation is fully observable. Now observation equivalence can be formalized in terms of synchronization trees and S-experiment as follows: Let A denote a finite alphabet and A^* the set of finite strings over the alphabet A.

Definition 8.29: **(Observation Equivalence)**

Let S, T be synchronization tress

- $S \sim_0 T$ always true

- $S \sim_{n+1} T \Leftrightarrow \forall s \in A^* :$
  - $S \xRightarrow{s} S\prime \Rightarrow \exists T\prime : (T \xRightarrow{s} T\prime) \wedge (S\prime \sim_n T\prime)$
  - $T \xRightarrow{s} T\prime \Rightarrow \exists S\prime : (S \xRightarrow{s} S\prime) \wedge (S\prime \sim_n T\prime)$

S is observation equivalent to T, denoted $S \sim_o T$ if any only if $\forall n \geq 0 : S \sim_n T$

8.1. Different Notions of Process Equivalence

By induction on n it can be proved that $\sim_n$ is an equivalence relation and $\sim_{n-1}\subseteq\sim_n$, i.e. $S \sim_n T \Rightarrow S \sim_{n-1} T$. The observation equivalence is defined as intersection of all $\sim_n$. With increasing n, one obtains a finer equivalence relationship $\sim_n$ to depth n. The trees S and T are observationally equivalent if none of the $\sim_i, 0 \leq i \leq n$ can distinguish their external behavior.

Figure 8.12 depicts an example. The left part illustrates the original process and the right part its visible parts for the external observer. Remember that edges with a label τ are internal actions and therefore not externally visible. For a more detailed introduction, discussion, proofs and the relationship of the observational equivalence with other notions of equivalence refer to [135, 136, 25, 118, 120, 117, 57, 238, 58, 227].

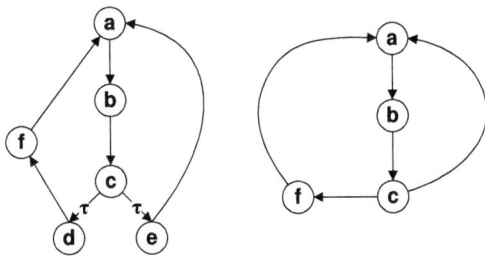

Figure 8.12.: Left: The original process, Right: Visible parts of the process

8.1.6. Weak Observation Equivalence

The weak observational equivalence is a special form of the observation equivalence with the exception that at each iteration external actions can be constructed (not τ-labeled) whose lengths are at most one. This equivalence relation can be formalized as follows, where ε denotes the empty word and the rest as defined in the subsection 8.1.5.

Definition 8.30: **(Weak Observation Equivalence)**

- $S \sim_0 T$ always true

- $S \sim_{n+1} T \Leftrightarrow \forall s \in A \cup \{\varepsilon\}$:
  - $\square\ S \stackrel{s}{\Rightarrow} S' \Rightarrow \exists T' : (T \stackrel{s}{\Rightarrow} T') \wedge (S' \sim_n T')$
  - $\square\ T \stackrel{s}{\Rightarrow} T' \Rightarrow \exists S' : (S \stackrel{s}{\Rightarrow} S') \wedge (S' \sim_n T')$

$p_1 \sim_{wo} p_2$ denotes that p_1 and p_2 are weak observational equivalent. As the name implies, this relationship is weaker than general observational equivalence relation (cf. subsection 8.1.5). However, in case of image-finiteness both observational and weak observational equivalences overlap [192].

8.1.7. Logical Equivalence

In addition to above described equivalence relations, it is possible to formalize and describe the behavior of processes through logical formulas. Two processes are then equivalent if they accept the same set of formulas. Regular trace logic [208, 284], propositional dynamic logic [121, 133, 252], Hennessy-Milner logic [136, 174, 144] belong to this group. The relationship between these three logics has been studied in [67].

8.1.8. Classification of the Equivalence Relationships

In the previous subsections following equivalence relationships have been introduced and defined:

- Bisimulation
- Trace Equivalence
- Testing Equivalence
- Failure Equivalence
- Observation Equivalence
- Weak Observation Equivalence
- Logical Equivalences

It is important to note that the above mentioned equivalence relationships posses different discrimination power, i.e. they do not discriminate exactly the same set of processes. Two processes that are trace equivalent may not be observational or failure equivalent as well. Based on the discrimination power of the equivalence relations, the notion of equivalence weakness (strength) can be defined. In the sense that weakest equivalence relation is the least discriminating equivalence and identifies the biggest set of equivalent processes under this equivalence notion. Consequently, the strongest relationship is the most discriminating equivalence relation and identifies the smallest set of equivalent processes under this equivalence relation.

Definition 8.31: **(Weakness of Equivalence Relations)**
Let $\Re_a$ and $\Re_b$ be two equivalence relations and p, p' two processes. $p\Re_a p'$ denotes that p and p' are equivalent under the equivalence relation $\Re_a$. Equivalence relation $\Re_a$ is weaker than $\Re_b$, i.e. $\Re_a$ is less discriminating than $\Re_b$, if and only if $\Re_b \subseteq \Re_a$, i.e. $p\Re_b p' \Rightarrow p\Re_a p'$

Note that the weakness or strength of an equivalence says nothing about how good this equivalence relationship is. The choice of the equivalence relationship is more based on the application and environment. Figure 8.13 Show the relationship among equivalence notions. The following abbreviations are used: trace equivalence (*TR*), failure equivalence

8.1. Differrent Notions of Process Equivalence

(*FA*), Logical Equivalence (*LO*), observation equivalence (*OB*), weak observation equivalence (*WO*), bisimulation (*BI*), Regular trace logic (*RTL*), propositional dynamic logic (*PDL*), Hennessy-Milner logic (*HML*) and testing equivalence (*TE*).

As one can see in the figure 8.13, the observation equivalence is the weakest equivalence relationship, followed by failure equivalence, logical equivalence, observation equivalence and finally the strongest equivalence relation, bisimulation. Note that weakest equivalence implies that this equivalence is the least discriminating equivalence among processes.

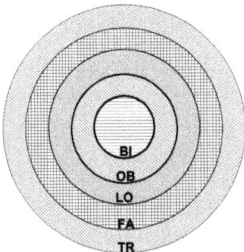

Figure 8.13.: Classification of equivalence relationships

The logical equivalence itself can be divided into three equivalence relations, which are RTL, PDL and HML. Figure 8.14 shows classification of these logical equivalences.

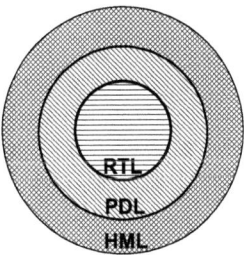

Figure 8.14.: Classification of Logical equivalences

With consideration of the weak observational equivalence, the relationship among equivalence relationships are depicted in figure 8.15.

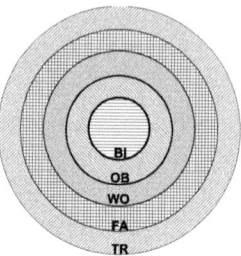

Figure 8.15.: Classification of Equivalence relationships

The testing equivalence and other equivalence relationships, except trace equivalence, are not comparable and it can only be concluded that testing equivalence is stronger that trace equivalence, which is depicted in Figure 8.16.

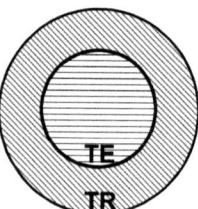

Figure 8.16.: $TE \subseteq TR$

Note that in case of image-finiteness, we have $BI = OB = WO = HML$. [135, 136]. For a formal proof of discriminating power of equivalence notions refer to [67, 224]. In addition to introduced equivalence relations, there are other equivalences, Kennaway equivalence and Darondeau equivalence, which can be seen as an extension to the previously presented equivalence relations and are briefly discussed in the following subsections for the sake of completeness.

8.1.9. Kennaway Equivalence

Kennaway and Hoare in [165] have presented an equivalence relationship very similar to testing equivalence as described in subsection 8.1.3. The main idea of the kennaway equivalence is that if two different sets of non-deterministic machines M_1 and M_2 pass exactly the same set of tests, it is impossible for an external observer to distinguish them and hence they are equivalent with respect to the exposed behavior to the external observer. In this equivalence, a test is a finite set of actions or observations performed on the machines.

8.1. Different Notions of Process Equivalence

Let M be a set of non-deterministic machines and T a set of tests. $P \subseteq M \times T$ identifies the tests T passed by the machines M. $P(m, t)$ denotes if a machine m can pass a test t.

Definition 8.32: (Tests passed by a machine)
$\forall m \in M : t(m) = \{t \in T \mid P(m, t)\}$
The set $t(m)$ includes all the tests t that can be passed by a machine m.

Definition 8.33: (Machine capable of passing a test)
$\forall t \in T : m(t) = \{m \in M \mid P(m, t)\}$
The set $m(t)$ includes all the machines m that can pass a test t.

The above defined sets, $t(m)$ and $m(t)$ are maximal sets. That means $t(m)$ includes the largest set of tests t_i that can be passed by a machine m and $m(t)$ includes the largest set of machines m_j that are capable of passing a test t.

Definition 8.34: (Kennaway Equivalence)
Let M_1 and M_2 be sets of non-deterministic machines. $d(t(M_1))$ is the largest set of non-deterministic machines equivalent to M_1 containing all deterministic machines with the property $t(M_1)$, i.e. capable of passing the same set of test as M_1.
M_1 and M_2 are kennaway equivalent, denoted $M_1 \approx_k M_2$ if and only if $d(t(M_1)) = d(t(M_2))$. i.e:
$$M_1 \approx_k M_2 \Leftrightarrow d(t(M_1)) = d(t(M_2))$$

The kennaway equivalence considers the partial or total correctness of machines for expressing M *may satisfy* T or M *must satisfy* T. If only a subset $M\prime \subseteq M$ pass the tests $t_i \in T$ we can say M may satisfy T. Whereas all $m_j \in M$ pass the test $t_i \in T$ one can say M must satisfy T.

8.1.10. Darondeau Equivalence

Darondeau in [88] presents an equivalence relationship for finite state processes with full synchronization. The daroundeau equivalence is based on Milner's observational equivalence and can be seen as its extension. However, the used algebraic notations are different. As in observational equivalence the interactions of processes with the environment decide equivalence of processes. Imagine that an observer sends a request r to a process and receives an answer a. If two processes p_1 and p_2 have exactly the same answers to a sequence of requests r_i, then p_1 and p_2 are equivalent. Note that exactly the same answers includes also lack of answers. It means that if a process p_1 sends no answer to a request r_j, then the equivalent process p_2 lacks also an answer for this request.

Definition 8.35: (Possible experiment with a process)
Let $(r_i \rightarrow a_i)$ be a pair of corresponding request-answer, where r_i and a_i is a request sent to a process by an observer and the received answer from the process respectively. A possible experiment is a sequence of request-answer pairs.
$S = (r_1 \rightarrow a_1)(r_2 \rightarrow a_2), ...(r_i \rightarrow a_i) i \in n$

The darondeau-equivalence is formalized as follows:

Definition 8.36: **(Darondeau Equivalence)**
Two processes p_1 and p_2 are equivalent if and only if:

- If S is a possible experiment in p_1 then it is a possible experiment in p_2

- For any possible experiments: after experiment S, two processes p_1 and p_2 send exactly the same answers to the same experiment

8.2. Structural Conformance of the Federated Choreographies

Intuitively, the notion of structural conformance indicates that supporting choreographies and realizing orchestrations must violate none of the requirements of the choreographies they support or realize. Such choreographies and orchestrations are an extended subset of the supported choreography. This means supporting choreographies and realizing orchestrations can not change the order of execution of the activities defined in a supported and/or realized choreography nor define any alternative for activities. The reason is that at run-time the alternative activity and not the originally defined activity can be executed which is an obvious violation of the requirements of the supported choreography. For example, as depicted in figure 7.11, the *Shipment processing choreography* supports the choreography responsible for *Purchase processing*. As illustrated in figure 7.3 (*Purchase processing choreography*), the seller orders the shipment after the buyer has placed an order. The choreography between the buyer and the shipper in the *Shipment processing choreography* (figure 7.12) and their orchestrations must be designed in such a way that their executions do not lead to skip of any of the tasks defined in the *Purchase processing choreography* e.g. no shipment order or shipment details are sent to the shipper after receipt of the order by the seller. In the following subsection the notion of conformance using projection inheritance [101, 45] based on branching bisimulation as equivalence relation has been formalized. Branching Bisimulation has been explained in subsection 8.1.1.

In order to check the structural conformance of federated choreograhies, the choreographies and orchestrations need to be translated into WF-nets (section 3.2). The reason for this translation is availability of tools for checking the branching bisimulation of WF-nets, e.g. [99, 265]. Thus WF-nets are used as modeling language throughout this section for the aim of structural conformance checking. How graph representations can be translated into WF-nets is explained in subsection 7.2.4. The WF-nets of *Purchase processing choreography* and *Shipment processing choreography* are presented in figures 7.15 and 8.17 respectively.

Essentially, the participating partners are autonomous organizations that may have existing workflows for their orchestrations as well as for their interactions with other organizations. Therefore, they favor to use the existing workflows instead of designing new ones from scratch and integrate them in the organization. It is pivotal to ensure that utilization of these orchestrations and choreographies lead to no conflict with other choreographies

8.2. Structural Conformance of the Federated Choreographies

and orchestrations. In order to check if two workflows, choreographies or orchestrations, are conformant the notion of projection inheritance is used. This concept and other notions of inheritance and the relationship among them as well as the relationship with branching bisimulation have been defined in [101, 45].

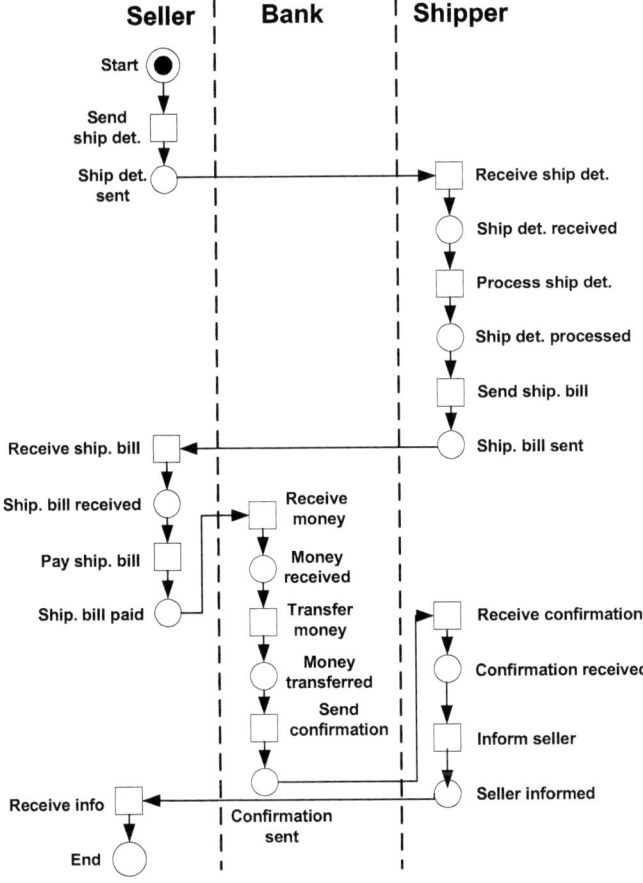

Figure 8.17.: The WF-net of the workflow graph in figure 7.12

Definition 8.37: **(Projection inheritance)**

"If it is not possible to distinguish the behaviors of x and y when arbitrary tasks of x are executed, but when only the effects of tasks that are also present in y are considered, then x is a subclass of y."

Assume W_a and W_b are two choreographies or orchestrations, modeled as WF-nets, and W_b has a link to W_a i.e. W_b supports or realizes W_a. This scenario is depicted in figure 8.18.

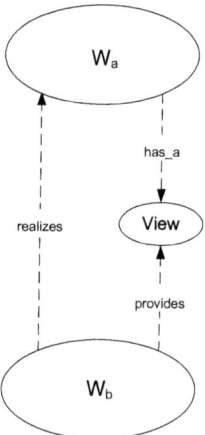

Figure 8.18.: W_b supports or realizes W_a

W_b comprises a set of tasks some of which are internal and not included in W_a and W_a includes activities that are not interesting for W_b. These activities can be made invisible using the abstraction operator. In order to decide which activities of W_a shall be made invisible, the greatest common divisor of W_a and W_b needs to be defined.

Definition 8.38: **(Greatest Common Divisor)** The greatest common divisor of two WF-nets are parts of the nets that two nets have in common, denoted GCD_{W_a,W_b}.

The greatest common divisor of W_a and W_b is the shared view between them. Note that the view is a view on both W_b and W_a. W_b is conformant with W_a, if and only if its visible behavior has a branching bisimulation relation to the shared view. Note that a view can be extracted by abstraction of all non-common activities of two graphs, i.e. those that are not members of the GCD. For instance for the running example let $W/_a = W_a - GCD_{W_a,W_b}$, these are the nodes of W_a that are not included in GCD_{W_a,W_b}. Let $\tau_1(W/_a)$ be the corresponding net after application of the abstraction operator on $W/_a$. $\tau_1(W/_a)$ is the view between W_a and W_b.

8.2. Structural Conformance of the Federated Choreographies

Groote and Vaandrager in [131] have introduced an algorithm by which in polynomial time is decidable if two processes are branching bisimilar. This algorithm has time complexity $O(n.(n+m))$ and space complexity $O(n+m)$, where n is the number of states and m the number of transitions.

8.2.1. Conformance Algorithm

Let W_a, W_b be two WF-nets such that there is a link between W_a, W_b and W_b supports or realizes W_a. Further let $V_{a,b}$ be the view between W_a and W_b. In order to decide if the federated choreographies are conformant it must be checked if all choreographies and orchestrations that are linked to another choreography are conformant.

The Structural conformance algorithm

---

1 conformance := true;
2 **repeat**
3   select randomly a link s.t. W_b supports or realizes W_a and $V_{a,b}$ is the view between W_b and W_a;
4   **if** W_b *is not a subclass of* $V_{a,b}$ *under projection inheritance* **then**
5   conformance :=false;
6   **endif**
7   mark the selected link;
8 **until** *all links are marked* $\lor$ *conformance = false* ;

The algorithm iteratively takes two supporting and supported choreographies (intra-layer conformance) or realizing orchestration and realized choreography (inter-layer conformance). It then checks if W_b, the supporting choreography or the realizing orchestration, has a subclass relationship with the shared view. If such a relationship does not exist, the federated choreographies are not structurally conformant and the boolean variable *conformance* is set to false which stops the loop. Otherwise if this subclass relationship for all links of the model exists, the federated choreographies are structurally conformant. If two choreographies and/or orchestrations has no link they are structurally conformant. In other words two independent choreographies and/or orchestrations are always conformant. This is also reflected in the algorithm. Only choreographies and orchestrations with a link are checked for structural conformance. There are some tools that based on the algorithm in [131] by an enumerative approach can decide if a WF-net is a subclass of another WF-net under projection inheritance among other inheritance definitions. For example Woflan [99, 265] can be used for deciding the subclass relationship between two WF-nets.

Figure 7.15 depicts the *Purchase processing* choreography and figure 8.17 the *Shipment processing* choreography. As illustrated in figure 7.11, the *Shipment processing* choreography supports the *Purchase processing* choreography. In order to check if the *Shipment processing* choreography is conformant with the *Purchase processing* choreography it must be checked if the *Shipment processing* choreography (the supporting choreography) is subclass of the shared view between the *Shipment processing* choreography and the *Purchase processing* choreography under projection inheritance. Figure 8.19 illustrates the shared view between these two choreographies. It can be checked, and in fact is true, that in this case a subclass relationship exists and two choreographies are structurally conformant.

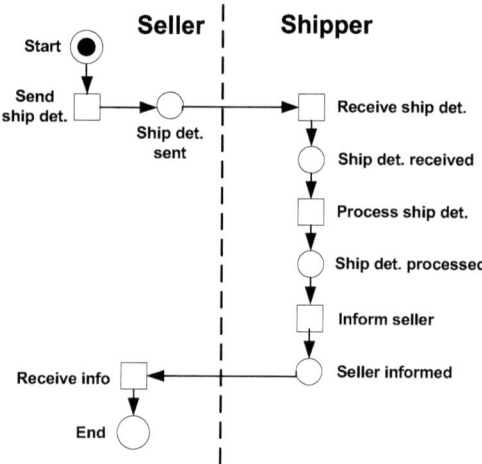

Figure 8.19.: The shared view between the Purchase processing choreography and the Shipment processing choreography

Checking of the structural conformance of an orchestration with the choreography that is realizes can be done in a similar way. The inter-layer conformance of the model, e.g. between the *Purchase processing choreography* and the *seller's orchestration* can be done in the same manner. For this, again it can be checked if the subclass relationship under projection inheritance between the shared view and the realizing orchestration exists. Note that this algorithm checks only the structural conformance of the model and not other consistency issues. Figure 8.20 represents the seller's orchestration in WF-net notation. The shared view between the choreography and the orchestration is presented in figure 8.21.

8.2. Structural Conformance of the Federated Choreographies

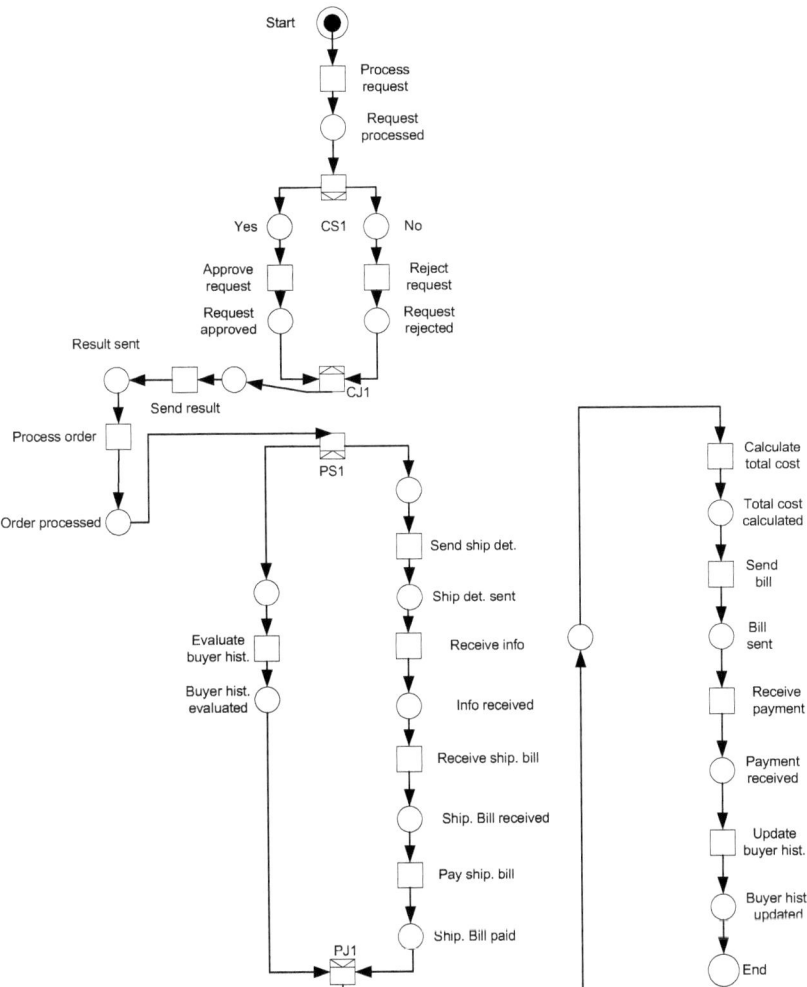

Figure 8.20.: Seller's orchestration in WF-net

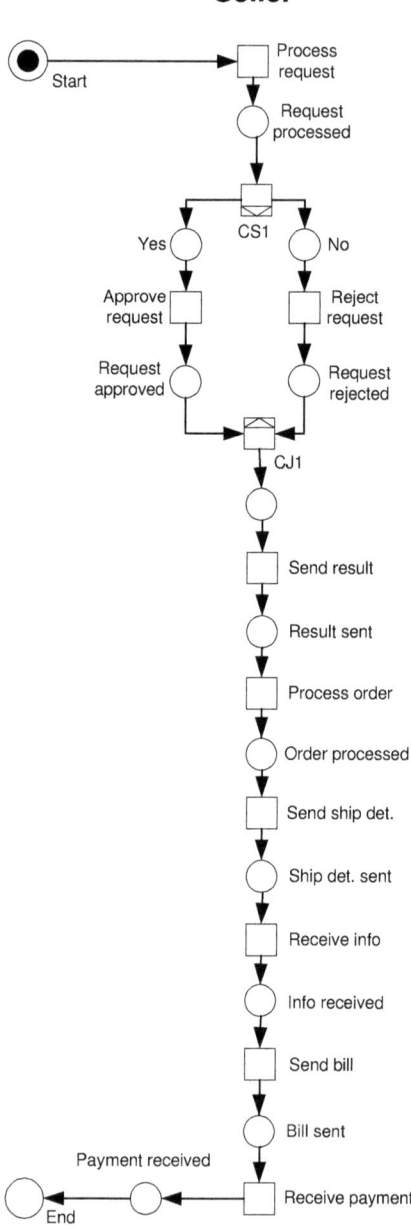

Figure 8.21.: The shared view between the Purchase processing choreography and the Seller's orchestration

8.2. Structural Conformance of the Federated Choreographies

If in the seller's orchestration (figure 8.20) the AND-split be changed to a XOR-split, the seller's orchestration will not be structurally conformant with the *Purchase processing choreography*. The reason is that at run-time only the path containing the evaluation of the buyer's history may be executed and the activities on the other path which are sending of shipment details, receiving info, receiving shipment bill and paying the shipment bill will be omitted. This means that the activities of choreography will not be realized in the orchestration. This variation of the seller's orchestration is depicted in figure 8.22.

Structural conformance of federated choreographies is also presented separately in [108]. However, the algorithm presented in [108] does not consider workflow views.

128   8. Conformance of the Federated Choreographies

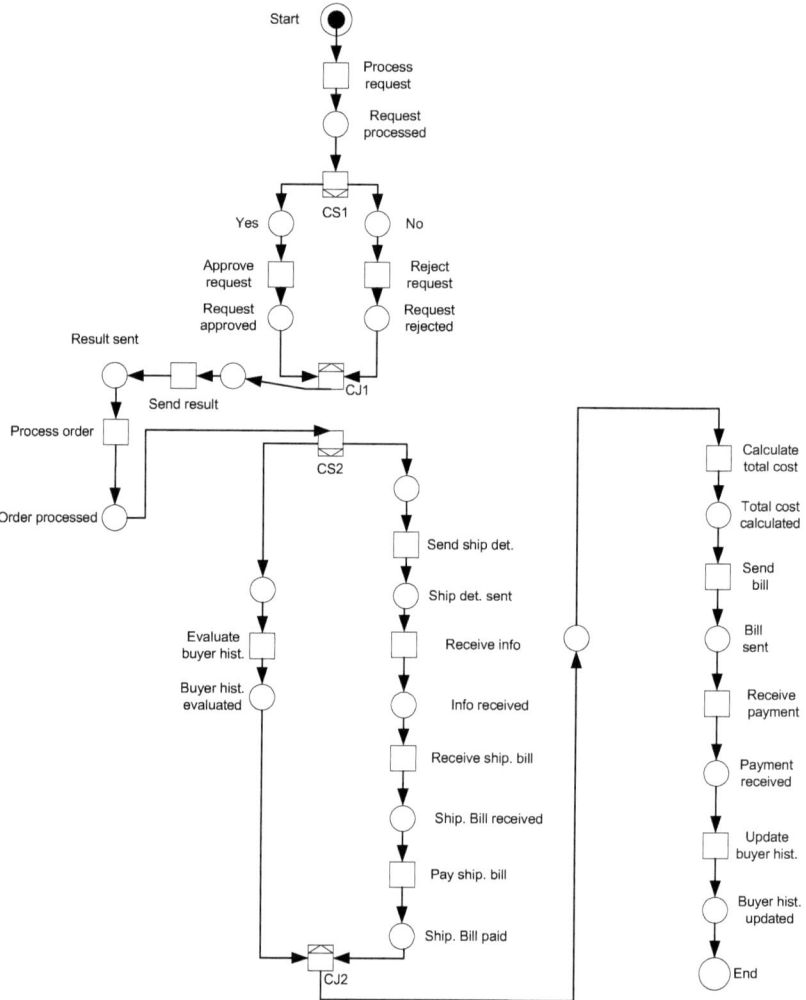

Figure 8.22.: By changing AND-split into XOR-split, the structural conformance is violated

8.3. Temporal Conformance

Temporal aspects are important quality criteria in business process execution. Temporal constraints, e.g. time between a request and a reply from a web service, are envisioned as part of the negotiations for setting up choreographies. It must be ensured that activities are performed in a timely manner and the right information is delivered to the right activity at the right time such that the overall temporal restrictions are satisfied. Choreographies and orchestrations may have deadlines which specify the latest point in time in which the last activity must finish execution. Temporal conformance checking assists organization to provide services with a higher quality of service (QoS) and hence be more competitive. Besides, it reduces the cost of the process as violation of temporal constraints leads to a kind of exception handling which is coupled with additional costs [212].

An algorithm for automated checking of the temporal constraints of the federated choreographies and generation of a valid temporal execution plan for choreographies and orchestrations is proposed. Based on this, it is possible to decide if the execution of the system leads to temporal exceptions and therefore modifications can be done if necessary. The proposed algorithm works in a distributed manner and there is no need for a central role or an organization for running the algorithm. Each participating partner possesses its local workflow model which interacts with other workflows. Because of the distributed functionality of the algorithm, one partner may need data from another partner to process locally. A partner can request and receive data which is only associated to accessible activities to this partner. Such activities are defined in a choreography and are anyway public to all participants of the choreography. In other words, data provider has not to reveal its private data to others and solely provide required data for interaction with other partners. This enables partners to hide their internal process logic whilst allow for interaction with other partners. Temporal conformance checking has a build-time and a run-time aspect. At build-time it is checked whether all orchestrations meet the temporal restrictions given by the choreographies they realize. At run-time the progress of execution has to be monitored to allow for diagnosis of potential violations of temporal constraints early enough such that counter-measures still can be taken in order to guarantee the correct functionality of the choreographies and orchestrations. Time management of the federated choreographies can be applied for three purposes:

Predictive time management: to predict the possible temporal behavior of the system and pre-calculate future possible violations of temporal constraints

Pro-active time management: to detect potential future violations and raise alarm in such a case such that counter-measure mechanisms can be triggered early enough. E.g. executing the shortest path if the deadline is about to pass

Reactive time management: to react and trigger exception handling mechanism if a temporal failure has already occurred

It should be ensured that the flow of information and tasks is done in a timely manner with consideration of the dependencies between activities which can reside in different choreographies and orchestrations of separate layers. For example if an activity a provides the input for another activity b, activity b must execute in a valid interval after activity a. In addition it must be checked that no explicitly assigned deadline is violated. Satisfaction of temporal restrictions of activities and assigned deadlines is necessary as organizations in the competitive world of business compete for highest possible efficiency. Besides, violation of constraints increases the cost of a process as each time an exception must be raised and exception handling mechanisms have to be triggered [212].

8.3.1. Related Works

The time management concepts come from a related field, namely workflow management research.

Maintaining Knowledge about Temporal Intervals

One of the earliest works on time properties is [29]. Allen describes a temporal representation using the concept of temporal intervals and introduces a hierarchical representation of relationships between temporal intervals applying constraints propagation techniques. This work describes thirteen ways in which an ordered pair of intervals can be related.

Time Constraints in Workflow Systems

Eder et al. in [110] present a model for calculation of temporal plans and propose some algorithms for calculation and incorporation of time constraints.

Managing Time in Workflow Systems

[109] provides a methodology for calculating temporal plans of workflows at design-time, instantiation-time and run-time. It considers several temporal constraints like lower-bound, upper-bound and fixed-date constraints and explains how these constraints can be incorporated. Moreover, a model for monitoring the satisfaction of temporal constraints at run-time is provided.

Temporal Modeling of Workflows with Conditional Execution Paths

[105] provides a technique for modeling and checking time constraints whilst conditional and parallel branches are discriminated. In addition, an unfolding-method for detection of scheduling conflicts is provided.

Dynamic Verification of Temporal Constraints in Production Workflows

Marjanovic in [187] represents the notions of duration space and instantiation space and describes a technique for verification of temporal constraints in production workflows.

8.3. Temporal Conformance

The approach presented in this book is complementary to that introduced in [187] in the way that a temporal plan for execution of all activities is calculated.

Temporal aspects of web services have been studied in [48, 161, 160].

On Temporal Abstractions of Web Service Protocols
[48] uses temporal abstractions of business protocols for their compatibility and replaceability analysis based on a finite state machine formalism.

Timed Modelling and Analysis in Web Service Compositions
Kazhamiakin, Pandya and Pistore in [161], as well as in *Representation, Verification, and Computation of Timed Properties in Web Service Compositions* [160], exploit an extension of timed automata formalism called web service time transition system (WSTTS) for modeling time properties of web services.

The approach presented in this work can cover cases which can be modeled in these works and additionally allows for definition of explicit deadlines. This work extends previous works by addressing the conformance and verification problem and provides an a priori execution plan at build-time (both best and worst case calculations) consisting of valid execution intervals for all activities of participating choreographies and orchestrations with consideration of the overall structure and temporal restrictions. The calculated execution plans can be monitored at run-time.

Summary and comparison of related works
Table 8.1 compares the related works on temporal issues. It summarizes the discussed papers, if the approach calculates temporal plans, if it is suitable for interacting workflows, i.e. in situations like interorganizational workflows or web service composition and if other consistency issues such as structural conformance are considered.

paper	calculation of temporal plans	Interacting entities	Other consistency issues
[29]	No	No	No
[110]	Yes	No	No
[109]	Yes	No	Yes
[105]	Yes	No	Yes
[187]	No	No	Yes
[48]	No	Yes	Yes
[161]	No	Yes	No
[160]	No	Yes	No
This book	Yes	Yes	Yes

Table 8.1.: Summary of related work on temporal aspects

8.3.2. Best Case, Worst Case Time Management of the Federated Choreographies

This approach calculates the best case and worst case temporal values for the federated choreographies. Best case is the case of execution of the shortest path in a flow. Worst case identifies the case when the longest path of a flow is taken and executed. The assumption is that activities have a fixed duration and each workflow has an assigned deadline. These assumptions are relaxed in other approaches presented for temporal conformance of the federated choreographies.

8.3.2.1. Prerequisites

Time is considered as discrete values expressed in some basic chronons like Minutes (M), Seconds (S) etc. The basic concepts used for calculation of temporal plans come originally from the field of project management and operations research [219] such as critical path method (CPM) [246] and program evaluation and review technique (PERT) [86] and its extended version (ePERT) [113]. There are two kinds of temporal constraints considered for this approach:

- **Implicit constraints** are derived implicitly from the structure of the process, e.g. an activity can start execution if and only if all of its predecessors have finished execution. This kind of constraints also can be referred to as *structural constraints*.

- **Explicit Constraints**, e.g. assigned deadlines, can be set explicitly by the process designer or enforced by law, regulations or business rules.

[109] identifies another temporal constraint called "fixed-date constraint" which is not used in this work. A fixed-date constraint is a time constraint that binds an event to some fixed date e.g. information updates are sent 15th of every month.

As the basic modeling language timed activity graphs or timed graphs [212] are used. They are familiar workflow graphs where nodes correspond to activities and edges the dependencies between activities, enriched with temporal information. Figure 8.23 shows an example of a timed workflow graph.

All activities have a unique name and two corresponding events. An event is either start of an activity (denoted a_s for an activity a) or its end (denoted a_e for an activity a). The relationship between a supporting and a supported choreography is modeled simply by event correspondence. $e_1 \equiv e_2$ denotes that event e_1 corresponds to event e_2. Note that e_1 and e_2 may belong to different choreographies and/or orchestrations. See figure 8.24 for an example of event correspondence. The notations used in figure 8.24 are explained in the following subsections. In the top part of the figure (case a), event correspondence is used for propagation of the temporal values of a complex activity a which is decomposed beneath. Start of the complex activity a corresponds to the start of the first activity (activity i) and the end of the complex activity a corresponds to the end of the last activity contained in the complex activity (activity j). Case b shows how event correspondence is used for

8.3. Temporal Conformance

propagation and copy of the temporal values of the same activity which is present in different choreographies and orchestrations. In this case as well, event correspondence is used to determine the corresponding events, i.e. to identify the start and the end of the corresponding activities. The propagation of temporal values is described in details in the subsection 8.3.2.3.

Activity Name	Activity Duration
Best Case Earlies Possible Start	Best Case Latest Allowed End
Worst Case Earlies Possible Start	Worst Case Latest Allowed End

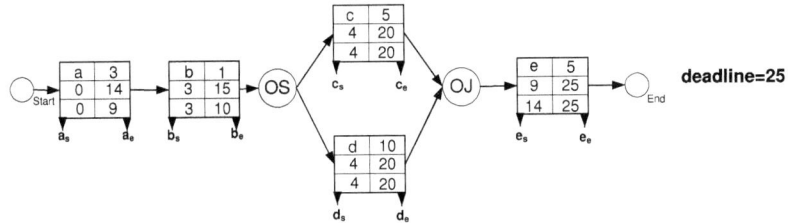

Figure 8.23.: An example of a timed graph with deadline= 25

All activities have durations. $a.d$ denotes the duration of an activity a. At the first use of a model an estimation of the activity durations, e.g. expert opinion, may be used. Later, workflow logs can be mined for actual activity durations. In the approach presented for best case and worst case calculations, deterministic values for activity durations are used. Then the proposed approach is adapted for interval-based (subsection 8.3.3) and stochastic temporal values (subsection 8.3.5). An interval in which an activity may execute is calculated. This interval is delimited by *earliest possible start* (eps-value) and *latest allowed end* (lae-value). $a.eps$ denotes the *eps*-value of an activity a and is the earliest point in time in which an activity a can start execution. $a.lae$ represents the latest point in time in which an activity a can finish execution in order to hold the assigned deadline. Both *eps* and *lae* values are calculated for *best case* and *worst case*. If there is a XOR-split in the workflow, there are multiple paths to be chosen and based on some evaluated conditions at runtime one of the available paths is executed. The best case is given, if the shortest path is executed and we have the worst case when the longest path is executed. It is possible that a XOR-split has other branches whose lengths lie between best and worst cases. In this work only best and worst cases are considered. If all branches of a XOR-split have the same length, both cases have the same *eps* and *lae*-values.

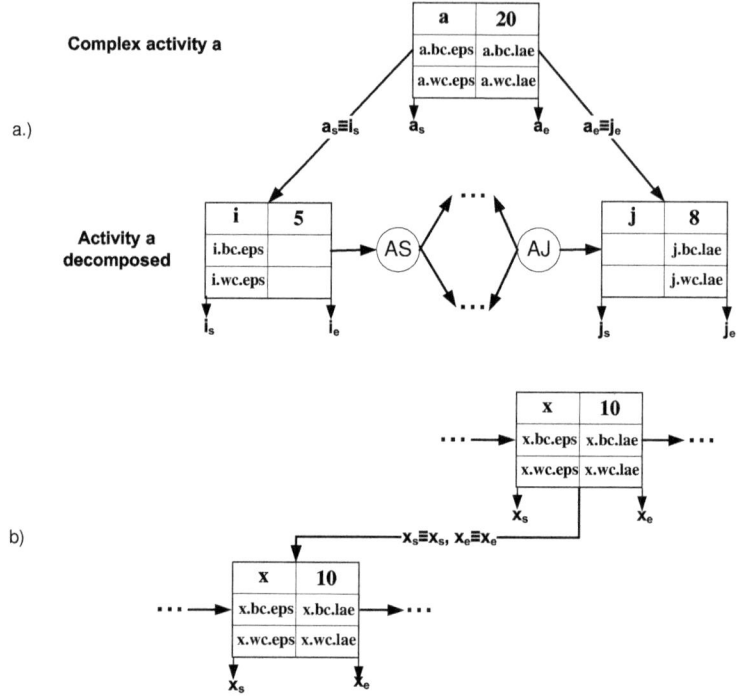

Figure 8.24.: a.) Propagation of the *eps* and *lae*-values of a complex activity. b) Propagation of values for the same activity in different graphs

eps-values are calculated in a forward pass by adding the *eps*-value of the predecessor to its duration. For example $b.eps = a.eps + a.d$ if an activity a is a predecessor of an activity b. If an activity a has multiple predecessors, e.g. if activity a is an immediate successor of an AND-join, the maximum of *eps*-values of predecessors of a is taken into account. The *eps*-value of the first activity or the set of first activities are set to 0.

In contrast to the *eps*-values, *lae*-values are calculated in a backward pass by subtracting the *lae*-value of the successor from its duration, e.g. $a.lae = b.lae - b.d$, if an activity b is a successor of an activity a. If an activity a has multiple successors, e.g. if activity a is an immediate successor of an AND-split, the minimum of *eps*-values of predecessors of a is taken into account. The *lae*-values of the last activity or the set of last activities are set to the assigned deadline. If no deadline is assigned, length of the longest path can be used instead of deadline. In this case the critical path has no buffer time. When parallel structures are present in the model, always the longest path (worst case calculation)

8.3. Temporal Conformance

between a split and its counterpart join nodes is considered. Hence, best case has the same temporal values as the worst case. The reason is that parallel-join must wait in any case for the longest branch of the parallel structure to commit. Figure 8.25 shows calculation of temporal values when AND-split and XOR-split are present in the model.

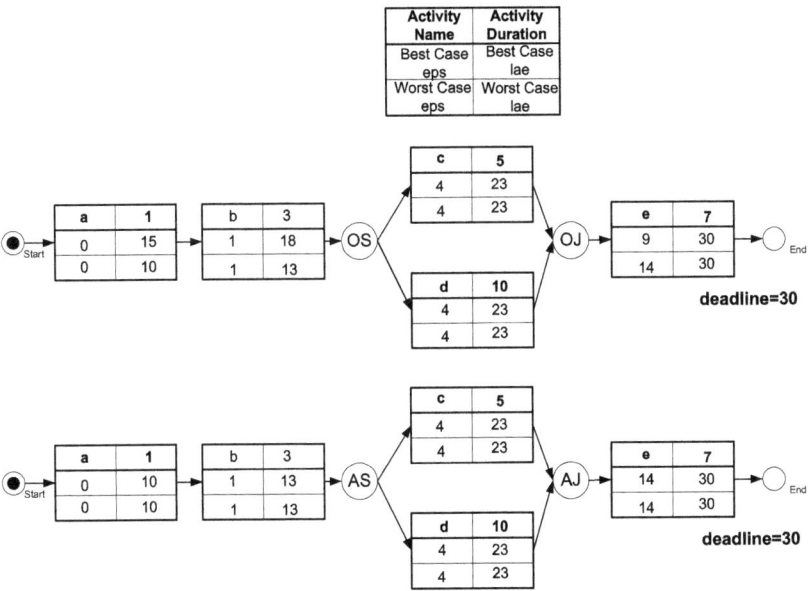

Figure 8.25.: Calculation of temporal values for AND-split and XOR-split

In addition to *eps* and *lae*-values, *earliest possible end* (*epe*-value) and *latest allowed start* (*las*-value) for the activities can be defined. However, given activity durations they may be calculated interchangeably applying the following formulas: $a.epe = a.eps + a.d$ and $a.lae = a.las + a.d$. For a more detailed discussion refer to [105]. Table 8.2 summarizes the calculation of temporal values.

8.3.2.2. The Proposed Approach

Figure 8.26 exemplary illustrates the starting point of the algorithm. The assumption is that there is only one global choreography present in the model. For the sake of readability, in figure 8.26 the views between choreographies and orchestrations are not depicted. As a mater of fact, because choreographies are composed of views, there is no need to calculate the temporal execution plans of the views separately, rather it suffices to calculate the temporal execution plans of the choreographies and check their temporal conformance. In this

Calculation of Temporal Values		
Forward Calculation	Best Case	Worst Case
Sequence	$a.eps.bc = b.eps.bc + a.d$	$a.eps.wc = b.eps.wc + a.d$
AND-join	$a.eps.bc = max(\{b.eps.bc + a.d\})$	$a.eps.wc = max(\{b.eps.wc + a.d\})$
XOR-join	$a.eps.bc = min(\{b.eps.bc + a.d\})$	$a.eps.wc = max(\{b.eps.wc + a.d\})$
$\forall$ immediate predecessors b of a		
Backward Calculation	Best Case	Worst Case
Sequence	$a.lae.bc = b.lae.bc - b.d$	$a.lae.wc = b.lae.wc - b.d$
AND-split	$a.lae.bc = min(\{b.lae.bc - b.d\})$	$a.lae.wc = min(\{b.lae.wc - b.d\})$
XOR-split	$a.lae.bc = max(\{b.lae.bc - b.d\})$	$a.lae.wc = min(\{b.lae.wc - b.d\})$
$\forall$ immediate successors b of a		

Table 8.2.: Calculation of temporal values

sense views are auxiliary constructs that do not contribute to the temporal conformance of the federated choreographies. How temporal execution plans of views can be basically calculated is explained in subsection 8.3.4.

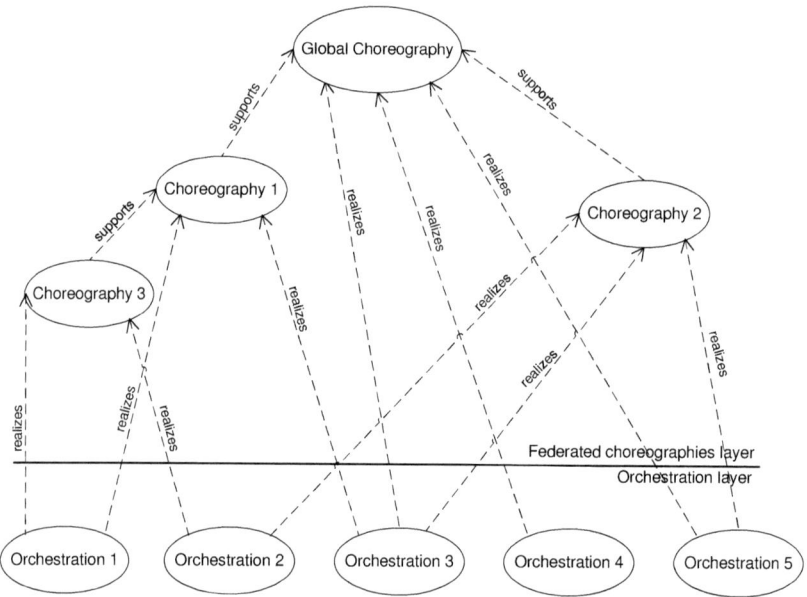

Figure 8.26.: Starting point of the algorithm

8.3. Temporal Conformance

The calculation of the timed graphs of participating choreographies and orchestrations is based on iteratively delimiting the initial intervals of activities because of implicit and explicit constraints. In addition, other choreographies and orchestration with a link may also impose a restriction on the calculated timed graph because of additional activities present in them. The imposed restriction further tightens the calculated interval. Note that a link identifies a dependency between choreographies and orchestration and is either a support relationship between two choreographies or a realization between a choreography and an orchestration. A valid execution interval is calculated when all factors affecting this interval are taken into account, which are:

1. Implicit constraints
2. Explicit constraints
3. Dependencies with other choreographies and orchestrations

Remember that the conformance condition must consistently be satisfied i.e. The sum of *eps*-value of an activity and its duration must be less or equal to its *lae*-value in both best and worst cases, i.e.

$\forall$ activities a: $a.bc.eps + a.d \leq a.bc.lae \wedge a.wc.eps + a.d \leq a.wc.eps$.

One important issue to be addressed is the case when one choreography has multiple supporting choreographies and/or realizing orchestrations as depicted in figure 8.27. The numbers beside the arrows show their order of execution. The method *"propagate"* is described in subsection 8.3.2.3.

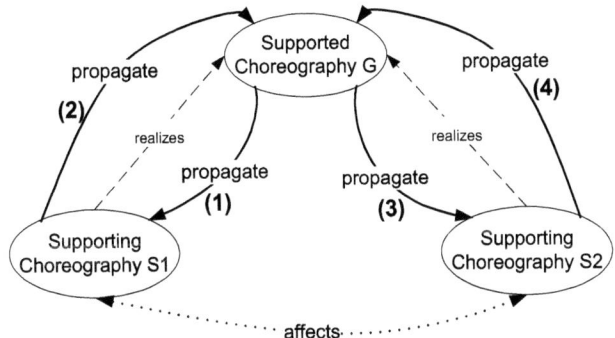

Figure 8.27.: Supported choreography with multiple incoming links

First, after initial calculation at G, temporal values are propagated from G to $S1$ (1), after recalculations at $S1$, they are again propagated upward to G (2). Note that a propagation from a source node to a target node may change the temporal values of the target node. This cycle is again repeated for *S2* (3,4). If *S2* again modifies the values of *G*, the most recently modified values may again impose a restriction on the values of the supporting choreography *S1*. In other words, two or more supporting choreographies and/or realizing orchestrations with the same supported choreography may affect each other indirectly even if they have no direct link to each other. This downward, upward cycle of propagation-recalculation, e.g. propagation from *G* to *S1*, recalculation at *S1*, propagation from *S1* to *G* and recalculation at *G*, must be iterated for all supporting choreographies and realizing orchestrations of a supported choreography as long as a stable state is reached. A stable state is reached if for all links, after propagation of temporal values from a source node to a target node, no modification of temporal values at the target node is necessary. In other words, no source node imposes a restriction on its target node(s) and no interval is further tightened after a propagation. The figures in appendix A show by a numeric example how this procedure and cycle of calculation-propagation-calculation works. The dependency between nodes of this example is illustrated in figure 8.27. If the values of a choreography or an orchestration are changed, this change can be propagated in both directions, i.e. to the choreography that it supports or realizes and/or to the choreographies or orchestrations by which it is supported or realized. After change of the values of a choreography or an orchestration *G*, all of its incoming and outgoing links are marked and the recalculated values are propagated for all links whose source or target node is *G*.

8.3.2.3. Methods

Following notations are used in the described methods: *a.bc.eps* and *a.bc.lae* denote the best case *eps* and *lae*-values respectively. *a.wc.eps* and *a.wc.lae* represent these values for the worst case. *a.d* identifies the duration of an activity *a*. *a.pred* and *a.succ* are the set of predecessors and successors of an activity *a* respectively. *a.pos* identifies the position of an activity *a* in a timed graph. a_s denotes the start-event of an activity *a* and a_e its end-event. *G.deadline* denotes the deadline of a timed graph *G*. *d.max* denotes the maximum allowed duration of a choreography or an orchestration. Upper case letters represent the graphs (choreographies or orchestrations) and lower case letters the activities.

The method *initialize(G* sets the *eps* and *lae*-values of activities a choreography or an orchestration to 0 and ∞ respectively. The reason is that in this approach the eps-values can always become greater and the lae-value can only become smaller when calculating timed graphs and delimiting the initial interval.

8.3. Temporal Conformance

The Method initialize(G)

---

1 **for** *all activities* $a \in G$ **do**
2     $a.wc.eps := 0$;
3     $a.bc.eps := 0$;
4     $a.wc.lae := \infty$;
5     $a.bc.lae = \infty$;
6 **endfor**

The Method calculate(G, G.deadline)

// -Forward Calculation-

1 **for** *all activities* $a \in G$ *in a topological order* **do**
    // -Worst Case-
2     $a.wc.eps = Max(Max\{b.wc.eps + b.d \mid b \in a.pred\}, a.wc.eps)$;
    // -Best Case-
3   **if** *a is an immediate successor of a XOR-Join* **then**
4        $a.bc.eps = Max(Min\{b.bc.eps + b.d \mid b \in a.pred\}, a.bc.eps)$;
5   **else**
6        $a.bc.eps = Max(Max\{b.bc.eps + b.d \mid b \in a.pred\}, a.bc.eps)$;
7   **endif**
8 **endfor**

// -Backward Calculation-

9 **for** *all activities* $a \in G$ *with a.pos = end* **do**
    // -Worst Case-
10     $a.wc.lae := G.deadline$;
    // -Best Case-
11     $a.bc.lae := G.deadline$;
12 **endfor**

13 **for** *all activities* $a \in G$ *with a.pos $\neq$ end in a reverse topological order* **do**
    // -Worst Case-
14     $a.wc.lae := Min(Min\{c.wc.lae - c.d \mid c \in a.succ\}, a.wc.lae)$;
    // -Best Case-
15   **if** *a is an immediate predecessor of a XOR-Split* **then**
16        $a.bc.lae := Min(Max\{c.bc.lae - c.d \mid c \in a.succ\}, a.bc.lae)$;
17   **else**
18        $a.bc.lae := Min(Min\{c.bc.lae - c.d \mid c \in a.succ\}, a.bc.lae)$;
19   **endif**
20 **endfor**

The calculate($G, G.deadline$) method takes as input a choreography or an orchestration in graph representation and the output is the calculated timed graph for both best and worst cases.

This method consists of two parts. In the first part in a forward pass from the start node to the end node the eps-values are calculated. The existing *eps*-values are replaced by the calculated *eps* only if the calculated *eps* is greater. Again, *eps*-values can only become greater. The *Backward Calculation* part calculates the *lae*-values in a backward pass and replaces the existing *lae*-value by calculated values only if the calculated *lae*-values are smaller. This method is used for pre-calculation of timed graphs as well as for recalculation of a timed graph after propagation of *eps* and *lae*-values from another choreography or orchestration.

The Method **propagate**(G, H)

1 change := false;
  // -Propagation of *eps*-
2 **for** *all activities* $\{x \in H \mid \exists a \in G : x_s \equiv a_s\}$ *in a topological order* **do**
3 **endfor**
4 **if** $x.eps < a.eps$ **then**
5 **endif**
6 $x.bc.eps := a.bc.eps$;
7 $x.wc.eps := a.wc.eps$;
8 change := true;

  // -Propagation of *lae*-
9 **for** *all activities* $\{x \in H \mid \exists a \in G : x_e \equiv a_e\}$ *in a topological order* **do**
10   **if** $x.lae > a.lae$ **then**
11         $x.bc.lae := a.bc.lae$;
12         $x.wc.lae := a.wc.lae$;
13   change := true;
14   **endif**
15 **endfor**
16 **return** change;

8.3. Temporal Conformance

This method propagates the *eps* and *lae*-values from one choreography or orchestration to another. It uses event correspondence for propagation of the *eps* and *lae*-values from a source activity to a target activity. The correspondence of the start events are used for propagation of the *eps*-values and the correspondence of end events for the propagation of *lae*-values.

When a complex activity is decomposed, the *eps*-value is propagated to its first activity and the *lae*-value to its last activity respectively. The temporal values of other activities of the complex activity as well as the lae-value of the first activity and the eps-value of the last activity can be calculated using the *calculate(G, G.deadline)* method as described. Figure 8.24 illustrates two cases.

The Method **checkConformance(G)**

---

1 **for** *all activities $a \in G$ in a reverse topological order* **do**
2   **if** $a.wc.eps + a.d > a.wc.lae$ **then**
3   conf := false;
4   **else if** $a.bc.eps + a.d > a.bc.lae$ **then**
5   conf := false;
6   **endif**
7 **endfor**
8 return conf;

The above method checks if the conformance condition is fulfilled. It checks if the sum of *eps* and duration of an activity is less than or equal to *lae*. Otherwise the boolean variable *conf* is set to false. This condition must always be met for all activities of all choreographies and orchestrations.

8.3.2.4. Temporal Conformance Checking Algorithm

The algorithm consists of two parts:

1. The initialization and precalculation phase

2. The recalculation and conformance checking phase

The Algorithm **temporalConformanceFederation()**

// -initialization and precalculation-

1 conf := true;
2 initialize(C_g);
3 calculate(C_g);
4 conf := checkConformance (C_g);
5 **for** all directly and indirectly supporting choreographies and realizing orchestrations G of C_g in a topological order **do**
6   initialize(G);
7   change := propagate(C_g, G);
8   **if** change = true **then**
9   G.deadline := G.first.eps + G.d.max;
10   calculate (G);
11   **endif**
12   change: = propagate(G, C_g);
13   **if** change = true **then**
14   calculate(C_g);
15   conf := checkConformance(C_g);
16   mark all incoming and outgoing edges of C_g;
17   **endif**
18 **endfor**

// -recalculation and conformance checking-

19 **repeat**
20   select randomly a marked edge e such that G is the supported choreography and H the supporting choreography or realizing orchestration;
21   change: = propagate(G, H);
22   **if** change = true **then**
23   calculate H;
24   conf := checkConformance (H);
25   mark all incoming and outgoing edges $\in H$;
26   **endif**
27   unmark e;
28   change: = propagate(H, G);
29   **if** change = true **then**
30   calculate G;
31   conf := checkConformance (G);
32   mark all incoming and outgoing edges $\in G$;
33   **endif**
34 **until** all edges are unmarked $\lor$ conf = false ;

8.3. Temporal Conformance

In the first phase after initialization of the global choreography its *eps* and *lae*-values are calculated without consideration of other supporting choreographies and realizing orchestrations . That means only implicit and explicit constraints are taken into account. Note that maximum allowed duration is considered for calculating the deadline of supporting choreographies and realizing orchestrations. *d.max* is the maximum duration during which a workflow can execute whereas a deadline denotes a point in time. Like deadlines, *d.max* is given a priori. It suffices in this phase to propagate the values to each node only once. These values only serve as initial values for further calculations. Hence each node, except the global choreography, is visited only once. A boolean variable *change* serves as an indicator if temporal values of a node are changed. If this variable becomes true all incoming and outgoing links of the corresponding choreography or orchestration are marked. Start and target node of each marked link must be revisited and recalculated if any value is changed. Note that multiple marks on an edge have no additional effect.

The second phase, the recalculation and conformance checking phase, consists of recalculation of the precalculated values in the first phase. For all marked edges, the cycle of propagation-recalculation is repeated until a stable state is reached or the conformance condition is violated. A stable state is reached if all marked edges are unmarked.

Figure 8.28 shows the end results of the graphs in figure 8.27. For a detailed calculation refer to figures A.1- A.15 in appendix A.

At this stage the system has reached a stable state and the final temporal plans of the supported choreography G and its two supporting choreographies $S1$ and $S2$ are calculated. It can be seen that same activities, no matter in which choreography, have the same temporal values. At the first glance, the lae-values of the activity e in the supported choreography G and the supporting choreography $S1$ are different, namely 50 and 52. Note that this is because of the absolute deadline of 50 for the supported choreography G and the maximum duration of 50 for the supporting choreography $S1$. A deadline is a time point whilst maximum duration identifies a period of time. When considering the difference between absolute deadline and maximum duration, the activity e has as well the same temporal value.

8.3.2.5. Implementation and Proof of Concept

A prototype of the proposed approach as proof of concept has been implemented. The workflow specifications of choreographies and orchestrations together with assigned deadlines, maximum durations and their dependencies are read as input. For each choreography or orchestration two inputs are required: An XML-file containing the structure of the workflow and a second XML-file containing the temporal information. The first file includes the activities and the dependencies between activities. The second file contains duration of the activities, assigned deadline and granularity of time. In addition to temporal information, it is possible to assign costs to activities and the total process execution cost can be calculated. The required XML-files for the graph depicted in figure 8.29 are presented in the following listings:

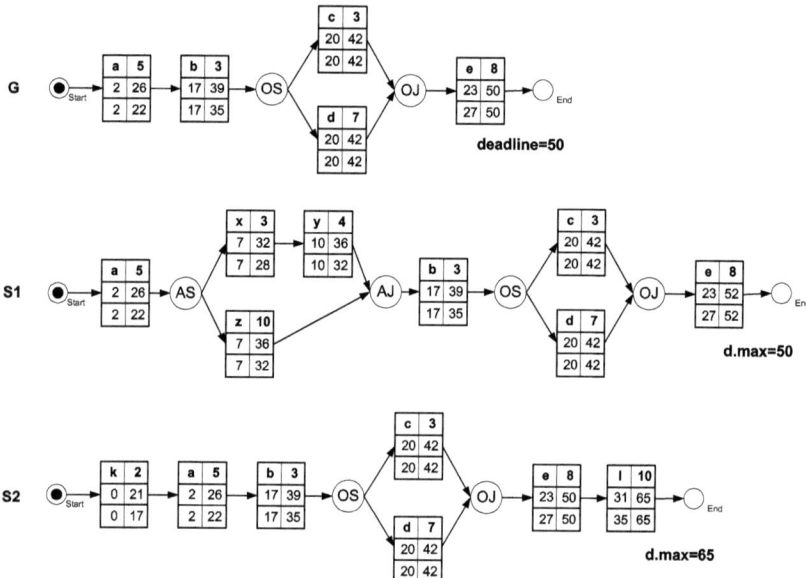

Figure 8.28.: After recalculation of S2

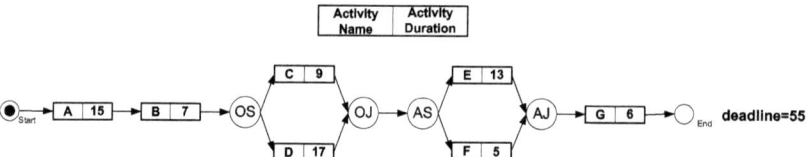

Figure 8.29.: A sample graph as input

8.3. Temporal Conformance

Listing 8.1: Structure of the graph in figure 8.29

```xml
<graph name="Global Choreography" description="Simple Workflow">

    <!--
        * structure: FIRST..A..B..Or[C,D]..And[E,F]..G..LAST
        * only joins may have multiple predecessors
        * only splits may have multiple successors
        * there must be exactly one node of type BEGIN
        * there must be exactly one node of type END
        * the graph must be acyclic
    -->

    <node name="FIRST" type="BEGIN" description="Start of the workflow" />
    <node name="A" type="ACTIVITY" description="The activity A" />
    <node name="B" type="ACTIVITY" description="The activity B" />
    <node name="C" type="ACTIVITY" description="The activity C" />
    <node name="D" type="ACTIVITY" description="The activity D" />
    <node name="E" type="ACTIVITY" description="The activity E" />
    <node name="F" type="ACTIVITY" description="The activity F" />
    <node name="G" type="ACTIVITY" description="The activity G" />
    <node name="OS1" type="ORSPLIT" description="The or-split OS1" />
    <node name="OJ1" type="ORJOIN" description="The or-join OJ1" />
    <node name="AS1" type="ANDSPLIT" description="The and-split AS1" />
    <node name="AJ1" type="ANDJOIN" description="The and-join AJ1" />
    <node name="LAST" type="END" description="End of the workflow" />

    <edge predecessor="FIRST" successor="A" description=" " />
    <edge predecessor="A" successor="B" description=" " />
    <edge predecessor="B" successor="OS1" description=" " />
    <!-- start or -->
    <edge predecessor="OS1" successor="C" description=" " />
    <edge predecessor="OS1" successor="D" description=" " />
    <edge predecessor="C" successor="OJ1" description=" " />
    <edge predecessor="D" successor="OJ1" description=" " />
    <!-- end or -->
    <edge predecessor="OJ1" successor="AS1" description=" " />
    <!-- start and -->
    <edge predecessor="AS1" successor="E" description=" " />
    <edge predecessor="AS1" successor="F" description=" " />
    <edge predecessor="E" successor="AJ1" description=" " />
    <edge predecessor="F" successor="AJ1" description=" " />
    <!-- end and -->
    <edge predecessor="AJ1" successor="G" description=" " />
    <edge predecessor="G" successor="LAST" description=" " />

</graph>
```

Listing 8.2: Temporal data of the graph in figure 8.29

```
<dataset
    refersTo="Global Choreography"
    dataSetDescription="Empirical Data">
    <!-- The overall process DEADLINE; defined as deadline for last node. -->
    <time refersToNode="LAST" type="DEADLINE" value="55" granularity="MINUTES" />

    <!-- Durations: activities not listed are assumed to have duration 0 -->
    <time refersToNode="A" type="DURATION" value="15" />
    <time refersToNode="B" type="DURATION" value="7" />
    <time refersToNode="C" type="DURATION" value="9" />
    <time refersToNode="D" type="DURATION" value="17" />
    <time refersToNode="E" type="DURATION" value="13" />
    <time refersToNode="F" type="DURATION" value="5" />
    <time refersToNode="G" type="DURATION" value="6" />

    <!-- Costs: activities not listed are assumed to have cost 0 -->

</dataset>
```

The prototype reads the XML-Files as input and convert the XML-description of the choreographies and orchestrations into directed acyclic graphs. After that, the prototype calculates the execution plan for all participating choreographies and orchestrations and checks if the conformance condition is met for all involved nodes. The prototype has been implemented under JAVA and has been validated in the framework of the European project WS-Diamond [11]. Table 8.3 at the end of this subsection shows the experimental results, applied on data sets consisting of different number of choreographies and/or orchestrations and different number of activities.

The above presented approach considers implicit and explicit constraints when calculating time graphs. However, in a straightforward manner upper-bound and lower-bound constraints can also be considered. Lower-bound and upper-bound constraints can be used for modeling interval-based duration of activities rather than deterministic values. See subsection 8.3.3 for a modified version of the algorithm that considers lower-bound and upper-bound constraints.

The approach for checking the temporal conformance of the federated choreographies with deterministic fixed-values are also separately presented in [114].

8.3.2.6. Proof of Termination and Complexity Analysis

There are two possibilities: either there is a stable state or there is no such a stable state. A stable state is a state in which the same activities in all choreographies or orchestrations have the same temporal values and after a propagation from a source choreography or orchestration to a target choreography or orchestrationn, no changes are made to the

8.3. Temporal Conformance

temporal values of the target choreography or orchestration. The algorithm terminates in both cases.

Case 1: There is a stable state. Let $\mid e \mid$ denote the cardinality of edges and $\mid me \mid$ the cardinality of marked edges. It is obvious that always $\mid me \mid \leq \mid e \mid$ is valid. Because the number of choreographies and orchestrations are finite, it follows that the number of edges is also finite, i.e. $\mid me \mid \leq \mid e \mid < \infty$. In this case after a finite number of steps (propagation and recalculation) all the same activities that reside in different choreographies and orchestrations have the same temporal values and the stable state is reached. That means $\mid me \mid = \varnothing$ and the algorithm terminates.

Case 2: There is no stable state. The absence of the stable state means that number of marked edges can never be empty, i.e. $\mid me \mid = \varnothing$ is never valid. It implies that there is at least one propagation that changes the temporal values of a target choreography or orchestration. In the algorithm, change of a temporal value means that the *lae*-value becomes smaller, the *eps*-value becomes greater or both. In any of these cases because there is a finite number of chronons between the time points, $eps + a.d > lae$ becomes true in a finite number of steps which violates the conformance condition and the algorithm terminates.

Complexity Analysis

The problem can be decided in polynomial time and the algorithm has a worst case time complexity of $O(\delta \times m \times n^3)$, where δ denotes the maximum value of assigned deadlines and maximum durations of all choreographies and orchestrations, m the total number of choreographies and orchestrations in the model and n the maximum number of activities contained in the graph of a participating choreography or orchestration.

The method *initialize(G)* has a worst case complexity of $O(n)$. The method *calculate(G, G.deadline)* has a worst case complexity of $O(n^2)$. The method *propagate(G, H)* has a worst case complexity of $O(n)$. The method *checkConformance(G)* has a worst case complexity of $O(n)$.

The first part of the algorithm *temporalConformanceFederation()*, the initialization and precalculation phase, has a complexity of $O(m \times n^2)$, n and m as defined before. In this phase, the propagations and calculations are performed only once from the global choreography to all of its directly and indirectly choreographies and orchestrations for precalculation purposes. Hence the first part of the algorithm has a complexity of $O(m \times n^2)$.

In the second part of the algorithm, the recalculation and conformance checking phase, the cycle of calculation-propagation-calculation is repeated as long as a stable state is reached or the conformance condition is violated. The worst case is given if in one cycle of iterations, the number of chronons between eps-value of an activity and its lae-value becomes only one unit smaller, i.e. if eps-value becomes only one unit greater or lae-value becomes only one unit smaller. The total number of chronons in the model equals $n \times m \times \delta$, where n, m and δ as defined before. Note that if a choreography or an orchestration starts at time point 0 its maximum duration can be treated the same as assigned deadline. The worst case complexity of the second part of the algorithm is therefore $O(\delta \times m \times n^3)$. Consequently, the worst case complexity of the overall algorithm is $O(\delta \times m \times n^3)$.

Nr.	Number of workflows	Number of activities	Deadline	Execution time (MS)
1	3	39	50	161
2	3	78	100	187
3	3	117	150	244
4	3	156	200	294
5	3	195	250	306
6	5	81	50	200
7	5	160	100	250
8	5	239	150	284
9	5	318	200	317
10	5	397	250	356
11	6	498	250	391
12	7	599	250	422
13	8	700	250	469
14	9	801	250	515
15	10	902	250	563
16	11	1003	250	609
17	12	1104	250	656
18	13	1205	250	703
19	14	1306	250	734
20	15	1407	250	766
21	16	1508	250	828
22	17	1609	250	875
23	18	1710	250	907
24	19	1811	250	922
25	20	1912	250	969

Table 8.3.: Data sets with different numbers of flows and activities

8.3.3. Interval-Based Calculations of Temporal Conformance

The approach presented in subsection 8.3.2.2 considers only implicit constraints (structure of the process) and explicit constraints (assigned temporal restriction). Here a modified

8.3. Temporal Conformance

version of the algorithm is represented that caters for representation of upper-bound and lower-bound constraints [109].

Lower-bound constraint identifies the minimum temporal distance between two events. Let a be the source event and b the destination event. $lbc(a, b, \delta)$ denotes that between the event a and the event b at least δ time points must pass.

Upper-bound constraint identifies the maximum temporal distance between two events. Let a be the source event and b the destination event. $ubc(a, b, \delta)$ denotes that between the event a and the event b at most δ time points can pass.

Such constraints can be used for modeling interval-based, variable duration of activities by insertion of upper-bound and lower-bound constraints between start event and end event of each activity as depicted in figure 8.30. In this figure $a.d \in [0, 10]$ and $b.d \in [0, 15]$.

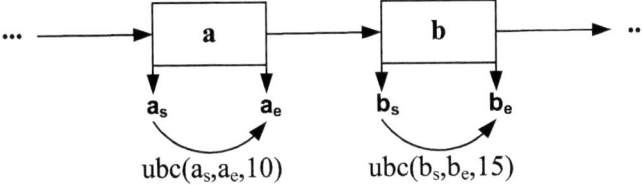

Figure 8.30.: Modeling variable duration of activities with upper-bound and lower-bound constraints

The temporal conformance algorithm for lower-bound and upper-bound constraints uses following methods:

- initialize(G)
- calculate($G, G.deadline$)
- incorporateUbc($G, \{ubc(s, d, \delta)\}$)
- propagate(G, H)
- checkConformance(G)

The methods initialize(G), propagate(G, H) and checkConformance(G) are the same as those described in subsection 8.3.2.3 and therefor are not again described here. The adapted versions of the method calculate($G, G.deadline$) and the method incorporateUbc($G, \{ubc(s, d, \delta)\}$) which is used for incorporation of upper-bound constraints into a timed graph are described at the end of this subsection. Finally, the overall algorithm for checking the interval-based temporal conformance is presented.

The method *calculate(G, G.deadline* takes as input a choreography or an orchestration in graph representation and as output it calculates the timed graph for both best case and worst case.

This method consists of two parts. In the first part in a forward pass from the start node to the end node the eps-values are calculated. Three values are considered: the existing eps-values, the newly calculated eps-values and possible lower-bound constraints. Depending on the position of the activity in the flow (e.g. immediate successor of a XOR-join or source of a lower-bound constraint) the valid eps value is calculated. The *Backward Calculation* part calculates the *lae*-values in a backward pass by again considering three values i.e. existing lae-values, newly calculated lae-values and possible lower-bound constraints. This method is used for precalculation of timed graphs as well as for recalculation of the timed graph after propagation of *eps* and *lae*-values from another choreography or orchestration.

The method incorporateUbc($G, \{ubc(s,d,\delta)\}$) incorporates the upper-bound constraints into a choreography or an orchestration. It first checks if the consistency condition of the upper-bound constrains are violated, i.e. if $s.eps + \delta < d.eps$ and $s.lae + \delta < d.lae$. Where δ denotes the value of the upper-bound constraint, *s.eps* and *s.lae* denote the eps and lae-value of the source activity and *d.eps* and *d.lae* identify the eps and lae-value of the destination activity respectively.

These conditions must be valid for both best case and worst case. If this condition is violated, it is tried to incorporate the *ubc* by shifting the temporal values of the source activity of the *ubc*. The eps-value of the source activity is set to : $s.wc.eps := d.wc.eps - \delta$. First, it is checked if the conformance condition is still fulfilled. In other words, it is checked if $a.eps + a.d \leq a.lae$ for both worst and base cases (method *checkConformance(G)*). After this, the temporal value of the graph is again calculated (method *calculate (G,G.deadline)*). If the temporal value of the source activity of the *ubc* is not changed, the *ubc* is incorporated. Otherwise a violation is occurred. In a backward calculation the lae-values are calculated and incorporated. Temporal values are calculated for both best and worst cases.

8.3.3.1. Calculation of Timed Graphs and Temporal Conformance Checking

The algorithm *temporalConformanceFederationUbcLbc()* except for the additional method incorporateUbc($G, \{ubc(s,d,\delta)\}$), works in a similar manner as in subsection 8.3.2.3

8.3. Temporal Conformance   151

8.3.4. Calculation of Temporal Execution Plans of Views

In this subsection calculation of temporal execution plans of views is presented. Views and construction of views are presented in chapter5. However because views are rather supporting and auxiliary constructs, the temporal conformance of views are not necessarily important for the temporal conformance of an interorganizational workflow. On the other hand, there are situations in which one needs to calculate the temporal execution plans of the views. For example in business-to-costumer situations where a human actor interacts with a view of a flow, it is necessary to calculate the temporal execution plan of the view such that the customer knows in which interval he can send messages and in which interval he can expect messages from a service provider. It is assumed that each workflow has a deadline and based on the calculation of the temporal plans of a private workflow, the temporal plans of its views are calculated. In other words a valid interval in which an activity, executable or aggregated, can execute is calculated. How temporal execution plans of workflows are calculated is described in subsection 8.3.2.1.

8.3.4.1. Calculation of Timed Graphs of Views

As explained, two ways for constructing views are considered: application of the abstraction operator and aggregation. If the abstraction operator is applied on an executable private workflow process, there is no need to recalculate the temporal execution plan of the view. In this case, after calculation of the temporal plan of a private process, the calculated values can be directly taken over for the activities contained in the view. See figure 8.31 for an example.

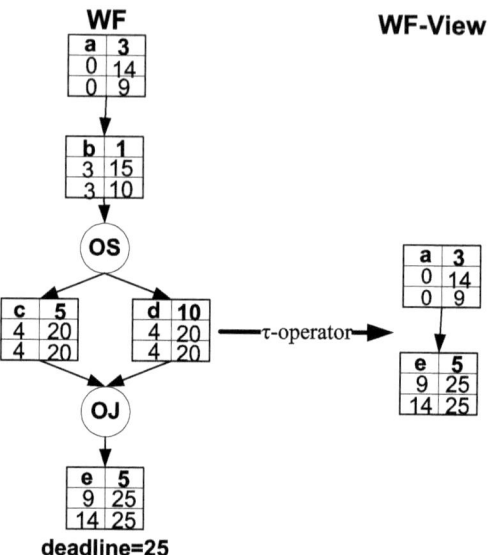

Figure 8.31.: Temporal plan of a WF and its view by application of τ-operator

If aggregation is applied, the temporal values of the aggregated activities in views can be calculated in a straightforward manner. The duration of the aggregated activity is sum of the durations of the executable activities contained in it. Note that the parallel or join structure can be considered as one activity because the length of its longest path is taken as its duration. This yields to a worst case estimation of the duration of an aggregated activity. For the interacting partner it is important to know in which time interval they can interact with the workflow. Hence, worst case duration for the aggregated activities is a reasonable estimation. This yields always to a temporally valid interaction with the view and therefore guarantees the correct temporal behavior of the flow. The eps-value of an aggregated activity is the eps-value of its first executable activity or the maximum value of the set of its first executable activities. The lae-value of an aggregated activity is the lae-value of its last executable activity or the minimum value of the set of its last executable activities. The temporal values of other activities that are not contained in another aggregated activity can be taken over directly from temporal plan of the private workflow.

8.3. Temporal Conformance

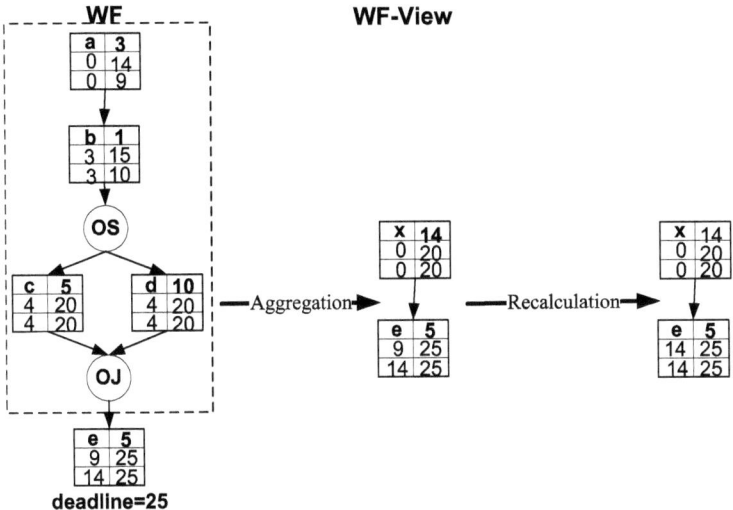

Figure 8.32.: Temporal plan of a view by application of aggregation

Figure 8.32 shows an example for this case. As can be seen in figure 8.32, the aggregated activity x has a duration of 14 time units, whereas the activity e in the view has a best case eps-value of 9 time units. It implies that the aggregated activity e in the view of figure 8.32 can start execution before the aggregated activity x (its direct predecessor) has finished execution, which is a violation of the structural constraints. The reason is that the aggregated activity x reflects its worst case value whilst 9 is the eps-value of activity e if the aggregated activity x execute its shortest path and terminates at best case. To resolve this issue, it is necessary to recalculate the *eps*-values of the view. Note that the *lae*-values remain unaffected. This can be done in the same way as explained before (the forward pass calculation). The end results are depicted in the right most part of the figure 8.32.

The approach for calculating the temporal execution plans of the views are also separately presented in [115]. This work proposes another form for checking the temporal conformance of the flows of the interacting partners.

8.3.5. Probabilistic Time Management of the Federated Choreographies

In this subsection another approach for time management of the federated choreographies is presented that caters for a new set of questions regarding time management and temporal conformance of the federated choreographies. In real life applications, it is almost impossible to give exact statements about temporal constraints such as how long the execution of a business process takes. This is mainly because of two issues:

- Variable duration of activities

- (Unknown) branching probabilities at conditional nodes

By application of the probabilistic approach one can answer questions such as with which probability a choreography or an orchestration will finish execution such that the assigned deadline is not violated or with which probability the remaining execution time is equal or less than t time points. The uncertainty associated with such statements arises from two factors mentioned above. Contrary to the previous approach, the probabilistic approach does not consider best case (when the shortest path of a graph is executed) and worst case (when the longest path of a graph is executed) when calculating timed graphs. Figure 8.33 shows an example of a graph with branching probabilities. The branching probability of each path is shown on the arc. For example, in 40% of cases the activity c is executed and in 60% the activity d. After activity c, in 10% of cases the activity e is executed whilst in 90% of cases the activity f. Given the paths are independent from each other, the path containing both activities c and e is executed with the probability of $p = 0.4 \times 0.1 = 0.04$. Table 8.4 shows the execution probability of each path of the probabilistic timed graph in figure 8.33. Note that the sum of the probabilities of execution paths must be always 1, i.e. let G be a probabilistic timed graph with $n \in \mathbb{N}$ distinct paths, where p_i identifies the execution probability of the i-th path: $\Sigma_{i=1}^{i=n}(p_i) = 1$.

8.3. Temporal Conformance

The Method **calculate**(G, G.deadline)

```
    // -Forward Calculation-
 1  for all activities a ∈ G in a topological order do
        // -Worst Case-
 2      if a is the destination of a lbc(s, a, δ) then
 3          a.wc.eps = Max({b.wc.eps + b.d | b ∈ a.pred}, a.wc.eps, s.wc.eps + δ)
 4      else
 5          a.wc.eps = Max({b.wc.eps + b.d | b ∈ a.pred}, a.wc.eps)
        // -Best Case-
 6      if a is the immediate successor of a XOR-Join then
 7          if a is destination of a lbc(s, a, δ) then
 8              a.bc.eps = Max(Min{b.bc.eps + b.d | b ∈ a.pred}, a.bc.eps, s.bc.eps + δ)
 9          else
10              a.bc.eps = Max(Min{b.bc.eps + b.d | b ∈ a.pred}, a.bc.eps)
11      else
12          if a is the destination of a lbc(s, a, δ) then
13              a.bc.eps = Max({b.bc.eps + b.d | b ∈ a.pred}, a.bc.eps, s.bc.eps + δ)
14          else
15              a.bc.eps = Max({b.bc.eps + b.d | b ∈ a.pred}, a.bc.eps)

    // -Backward Calculation-
16  for all activities a ∈ G with a.pos = end do
        // -Worst Case-
17      a.wc.lae := G.deadline;
        // -Best Case-
18      a.bc.lae := G.deadline;
19  for all activities a ∈ G with a.pos ≠ end in a reverse topological order do
        // -Worst Case-
20      if a is the source of a lbc(a, d, δ) then
21          a.wc.lae := Min({c.wc.lae − c.d | c ∈ a.succ}, a.wc.lae, d.wc.lae − δ)
22      else
23          a.wc.lae := Min({c.wc.lae − c.d | c ∈ a.succ}, a.wc.lae)
        // -Best Case-
24      if a is the immediate predecessor of a XOR-Split then
25          if a is the source of a lbc(a, d, δ) then
26              a.bc.lae := Min(Max{c.bc.lae − c.d | c ∈ a.succ}, a.bc.lae, d.bc.lae − δ)
27          else
28              a.bc.lae := Min(Max{c.bc.lae − c.d | c ∈ a.succ}, a.bc.lae)
29      else
30          if a is the source of a lbc(a, d, δ) then
31              a.bc.lae := Min({c.bc.lae − c.d | c ∈ a.succ}, a.bc.lae, d.bc.lae − δ)
32          else
33              a.bc.lae := Min({c.bc.lae − c.d | c ∈ a.succ}, a.bc.lae)
```

The Method **incorporateUbc**($G, \{ubc(s,d,\delta)\}$)

1 violation := false;
2 oldValue := 0;
3 **repeat**
4   **for** *all $ubc(s,d,\delta)$ in G* **do**
        // -Worst Case-
5   **if** $s.wc.eps + \delta < d.wc.eps$ **then**
6              $s.wc.eps := d.wc.eps - \delta$;
7              $oldValue := d.wc.eps$;
8   calculate($G, G.deadline$);
9   conf := checkConformance(G);
10   **if** $d.wc.eps \neq oldValue$ **then**
11   violation := true;

12   **if** $s.wc.lae + \delta < d.wc.lae$ **then**
13             $d.wc.lae := s.wc.lae + \delta$;
14             $oldValue := s.wc.lae$;
15   calculate($G, G.deadline$);
16   conf := checkConformance(G);
17   **if** $s.wc.lae \neq oldValue$ **then**
18   violation :=true;

        // -Best Case-
19   **if** $s.bc.eps + \delta < d.bc.eps$ **then**
20             $s.bc.eps := d.bc.eps - \delta$;
21             $oldValue := d.bc.eps$;
22   calculate($G, G.deadline$);
23   conf := checkConformance(G);
24   **if** $d.bc.eps \neq oldValue$ **then**
25   violation := true;

26   **if** $s.bc.lae + \delta < d.bc.lae$ **then**
27             $d.bc.lae := s.bc.lae + \delta$;
28             $oldValue := s.bc.lae$;
29   calculate($G, G.deadline$);
30   conf := checkConformance(G);
31   **if** $s.bc.lae \neq oldValue$ **then**
32   violation :=true;

33 **until** *violation = true $\vee$ conf = false $\vee$ all $Ubc(s,d,\delta)$ are incorporated* ;

8.3. Temporal Conformance

The Algorithm temporalConformanceFederationUbcLbc()

// -initialization and precalculation-

1. conf := true;
2. initialize(C_g);
3. calculate(C_g);
4. incorportaeUbc(G, \{s, d, δ\})
5. conf := checkConformance; (C_g);
6. **for** *all directly and indirectly supporting choreographies and realizing orchestrations G of C_g in a topological order* **do**
7.   initialize(G);
8.   change := propagate(C_g, G);
9.   **if** *change = true* **then**
10.   G.deadline := G.first.eps + G.d.max;
11.   calculate (G);
12.   **endif**
13.   change: = propagate(G, C_g);
14.   **if** *change = true* **then**
15.   calculate(C_g);
16.   conf := checkConformance(C_g);
17.   mark all incoming and outgoing edges of C_g;
18.   **endif**
19. **endfor**

// -recalculation and conformance checking-

20. **repeat**
21.   select randomly a marked edge *e* such that G is the supported choreography and H the supporting choreography or realizing orchestration;
22.   change: = propagate(G, H);
23.   **if** *change = true* **then**
24.   calculate H;
25.   conf := checkConformance (H);
26.   mark all incoming and outgoing edges $\in H$;
27.   **endif**
28.   unmark *e*;
29.   change: = propagate(H, G);
30.   **if** *change = true* **then**
31.   calculate G;
32.   conf := checkConformance (G);
33.   mark all incoming and outgoing edges $\in G$;
34.   **endif**
35. **until** *all edges are unmarked $\lor$ conf = false* ;

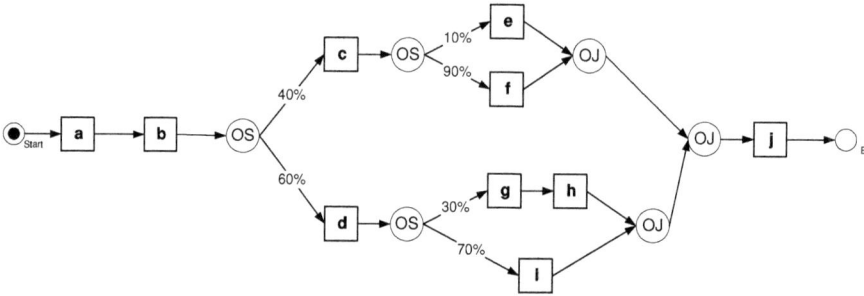

Figure 8.33.: A sample timed graph with branching probabilities

Number	Path	Probability
1	abcej	$0.4 \times 0.1 = 0.04$
2	abcfj	$0.4 \times 0.9 = 0.36$
3	abdghj	$0.6 \times 0.3 = 0.18$
4	abdij	$0.6 \times 0.7 = 0.42$

Table 8.4.: Execution probability of each path of the graph in figure 8.33

8.3.5.1. Probabilistic Model Description

In order to express the variable duration of activities, the notion of time histograms [221, 106] has been used. A duration histogram, basically, is a data structure for representation of the (probabilistic and variable) duration of basic activities, complex activities, subworkflows and workflow itself. A duration histogram is a tuple (p, d), where p is a probability and d a duration. For example the probabilistic duration of an activity can be represented as $\{(0.1, 10), (0.25, 12), (0.32, 15), (0.33, 20)\}$ which can be interpreted as follows: the duration of this activity is with the probability 10%, 10 time points, with the probability 25%, 12 time points, with the probability 32%, 15 time points and with the probability 33%, 20 time points. Note that the values for activity or workflow durations can be extracted from empirical data e.g. workflow logs and by lack of such data other sources or estimations such as expert opinion may be used. If in a duration histogram there is any tuples whose time values are the same, these tuples must be merged by adding the probabilities of tuples with the same duration. A workflow graph augmented with stochastic temporal information for activities and nodes is referred to as probabilistic timed graph. Figure 8.34 illustrates an example of such a probabilistic timed graph. The duration of activities are given in the table above the graph.

8.3. Temporal Conformance

All control nodes, i.e. start node, end node, XOR-split, XOR-join, AND-split and AND-join, have the duration 0. The deadline of the workflow is also given in form of a (probability, duration) tuple. Further, it is assumed that there is no delay between end of an activity and start of its successor or the set of its successors.

Analogous to duration Histograms (d-histograms), [221] defines e-histograms for presentation of e-values and l-histograms for presentation of l-values. e-values are earliest possible start values (eps-values) and/or earliest possible end values (epe-values). l-values are latest allowed start values (las-values) and/or latest allowed end values (lae-values). Note that e-histograms and l-histograms must be interpreted in a different way different than d-histograms.

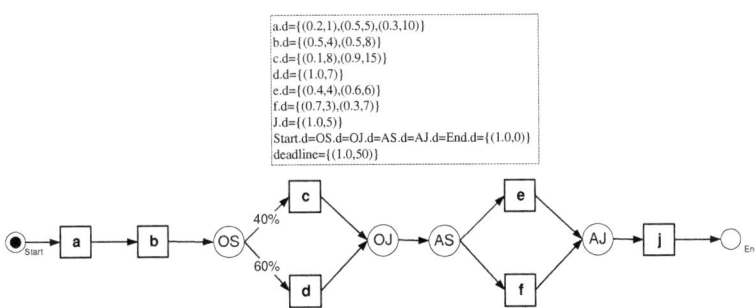

Figure 8.34.: A sample probabilistic timed graph (PTG)

8.3.5.2. Histogram Operations

In order to calculate the execution plan and temporal values (eps-values, epe-values, las-values and lae-values) of a probabilistic timed graph, operations on histograms are necessary. Theses histograms operations are briefly introduced in this subsection.

The *histogram addition* generates the cartesian product of the tuples of two histograms, where probabilities are multiplied and time values are added: $\{(0.25, 3), (0.75, 5)\} + \{(0.5, 3), (0.5, 5)\} = \{(0.125, 6), (0.125, 8), (0.375, 8), (0.375, 10)\}$. Resulting tuples with equal time values are *aggregated*, which means they are merged by summing up their probabilities: $\{(0.125, 6), (0.5, 8), (0.375, 10)\}$.

The *histogram subtraction* $h_1 - h2$ is a variation of the addition, with the only difference that time values for the resulting tuples are subtracted. For example Let $h_1 = \{(0.5, 10), (0.5, 15)\}$ and $h_2 = \{(0.3, 3), (0.7, 7)\}$, then $h_1 - h2 = \{(0.15, 7), (0.35, 3), (0.15, 12), (0.35, 8)\}$. In this example there is no need for aggregation as all durations have unique values.

The *histogram conjunction* also generates a cartesian product. Again probabilities are multiplied, but this time the maximum time value of each tuple-combination determines the time value of the resulting tuple. Therefore it is also called the *max-conjunction*: $\{(0.25, 3), (0.75, 5)\} \wedge_{max} \{(0.5, 3), (0.5, 5)\} = \{(0.125, 3),$
$(0.125, 5), (0.375, 5), (0.375, 5)\}$. Again the final resulting histogram has to be aggregated, which results in $\{(0.125, 3), (0.875, 5)\}$. A variation of this operation is the *min-conjunction* which determines the time value of the resulting tuple by applying a minimum-operation. $\{(0.25, 3), (0.75, 5)\} \wedge_{min} \{(0.5, 3), (0.5, 5)\} = \{(0.125, 3), (0.125, 3), (0.375, 3), (0.375, 5)\}$ which yields to $\{(0.625, 3), (0.375, 5)\}$.

The *weight*-operation multiplies all probabilities in a histogram with a given probability: $\{(0.25, 3), (0.75, 5)\} * 0.25 = \{(0.0625, 3), (0.1875, 5)\}$ and $\{(0.5, 3), (0.5, 5)\}$ $*0.75 = \{(0.375, 3), (0.375, 5)\}$. Please note that the weight operation produces an *invalid* histogram, as the sum of probabilities is less than 1.0. Therefore it always appears in combination with the *histogram disjunction*, which merges two weighted histograms: $\{(0.0625, 3), (0.1875, 5)\} \vee \{(0.375, 3), (0.375, 5)\} = \{(0.0.625, 3),$
$(0.1875, 5), (0.375, 3), (0.375, 5)\}$; and the aggregation which yields to $\{(0.4375, 3), (0.5625, 5)\}$.

Both, conjunction and disjunction, are commutative and associative, therefore they can be extended to k histograms, e.g.: $h = h_1 \vee \ldots \vee h_k = \bigvee h_i$, where $1 \leq i \leq k$.

The *histogram comparison* is applied for comparing two histograms with each other. Unlike discrete values, two histograms h_1 and h_2 may partially overlap. Thus an expression like $h_1 < h_2$ can be true and false at the same time, each at least up to a certain degree. Therefore, the comparison of two histograms h_1 and h_2 with the comparison-operator $\bowtie \in \{\leq, <, =, >, \geq\}$ for a given degree $0 \leq deg \leq 1$ is defined as follows:

$$h_1 \bowtie_{deg} h_2 = \begin{cases} true & : \quad \Sigma p_1 * p_2 \geq deg \wedge t_1 \bowtie t_2, \forall (p_1, t_1) \in h_1, \forall (p_2, t_2) \in h_2 \\ false & : \quad otherwise \end{cases}$$

8.3. Temporal Conformance

Based on the histograms h_1 and h_2, depicted in Figure 8.35, we can make the following statements: up to a degree of 0.545, h_1 is greater than h_2 and up to a degree of 0.35, h_1 is equal to h_2. Thus, for instance, the following expressions are true: $h_1 <_{0.05} h_2$, $h_1 >_{0.25} h_2$, $h_1 >_{0.545} h_2$, and the following are false: $h_1 >_{0.7} h_2$, $h_1 \geq_{0.9} h_2$. In order to check the total histogram equality the certainty degree must be set to 1.0: $h_1 =_{1.0} h_2$ and to ensure that two histograms have no overlapping regions at all, they must be compared with the certainty degree of 1.0: $h_1 <_{1.0} h_2$ or $h_1 >_{1.0} h_2$.

t_1	p_1
0.15	10
0.50	15
0.35	20

Histogram h_1

t_2	p_2
0.30	9
0.70	15

Histogram h_2

$p_1 * p_2$	t_1		t_2
0.045	10	>	9
0.150	15	>	9
0.105	20	>	9
0.105	10	<	15
0.350	15	=	15
0.245	20	>	15

$t_1 > t_2$: 54.5 %
$t_1 = t_2$: 35.0 %
$t_1 < t_2$: 10.5 %
$t_1 <= t_2$: 45.5 %
$t_1 => t_2$: 89.5 %

Figure 8.35.: Calculating the values for histogram comparison

A relaxed certainty allows for overlapping regions, which might prove useful especially if there are (extreme) outliers in histograms. For example imagine that the mean of a histogram h_3 is 5 and it contains one extreme outlier, the tuple (0.005,1000). Even with a histograms h_4 that contains much higher time values, a <-comparison with 100%-certainty always yields *false*. Therefore, relaxing the certainty-value just by 0.01% will avoid most conformance-conflicts (still, one day this highly improbable case might occur).

8.3.5.3. Calculation of Probabilistic Timed Graphs

e-histograms (eps-histograms, epe-histograms) of nodes of a workflow can be calculated by applying the forward calculation rules in a topological order. These rules are specified in table 8.5 according to the node types. In table 8.5, *node.eps* denotes the eps-histogram of the current node, *node.epe* its epe-histogram, *node.d* the duration histogram of the current node, *pred.epe* identifies the epe-histogram of the predecessor node, *node.Pred* the set of predecessor nodes of the current node and $p_{pred \Rightarrow node}$ identifies the execution probability of the edge connecting the predecessor node to the current node.

Except for nodes with multiple incoming paths, i.e. AND-join, XOR-join, the duration-histograms are summed up to calculate the according e-histograms. For AND-joins the max-conjunction is applied because the longest path (or histogram-tuple) determines the resulting tuple. For XOR-joins, the histograms of predecessors are weighted with the according branching probability and subsequently they are merged applying the conjunction.

Analogously, for calculation of l-histograms (las-histograms and lae-histograms) the backward calculation rules, as specified in table 8.6, have to be applied in a backward

type of node	node.eps =	node.epe =
Start	$\{(1.0, 0)\}$	$node.eps + node.d$
End	$pred.epe$	$node.eps + node.d$
Activity	$pred.epe$	$node.eps + node.d$
AND-split	$pred.epe$	$node.eps + node.d$
XOR-split	$pred.epe$	$node.eps + node.d$
AND-join	$\forall pred \in node.Pred : \bigwedge_{max}(pred.epe)$	$node.eps + node.d$
XOR-join	$\forall pred \in node.Pred : \bigvee(pred.epe * p_{pred \Rightarrow node})$	$node.eps + node.d$

Table 8.5.: Calculation of e-histograms

topological order. In table 8.6 *node.lae* refers to the lae-histogram of the current node, *node.las* the las-histogram of the current node, $\{(1.0, \delta)\}$ denotes the assigned deadline, *node.d* the duration histogram of the current node, *succ.las* identifies the las-histogram of the successor node, *node.Succ* the set of successor nodes of the current node and $p_{node \Leftarrow succ}$ the execution probability of the edge connecting the current node with the successor node.

When reversing the direction of calculation, beginning from the end-node to the start-node, histogram subtraction is applied instead of histogram addition. lae-histogram of the end-node is initialized with the assigned deadline. Special rules must be applied when calculating the l-histograms of the nodes with multiple outgoing paths, AND-split and XOR-split. lae-histogram of an AND-split is calculated by a min-conjunction over its outgoing paths. XOR-splits are calculated by a weighted disjunction of the outgoing paths.

type of node	node.lae =	node.las =
End	$\{(1.0, \delta)\}$	$node.lae - node.d$
Start	$succ.las$	$node.lae - node.d$
Activity	$succ.las$	$node.lae - node.d$
AND-join	$succ.las$	$node.lae - node.d$
XOR-join	$succ.las$	$node.lae - node.d$
AND-split	$\forall succ \in node.Succ : \bigwedge_{min}(succ.las)$	$node.lae - node.d$
XOR-split	$\forall succ \in node.Succ : \bigvee(succ.las * p_{node \Leftarrow succ})$	$node.lae - node.d$

Table 8.6.: Calculation of l-histograms

As a numeric example, using the forward and backward calculation rules for e-histograms and l-Histograms in table 8.5 and table 8.6, the temporal values of the graph depicted in figure 8.34 are calculated. In the tables 8.7, 8.8 and 8.9 at the end of this chapter only the final results are represented. For a detailed calculation of the temporal value please refer to appendix B.

8.3. Temporal Conformance

8.3.5.4. The Proposed Approach

In the previous subsection the best case, worst case approach for temporal conformance of federated choreographis has been presented. In this subsection, the probabilistic approach is discussed, i.e. how it can be checked that federated choreographies are temporally conformant, given the stochastic information for activity durations and branching probabilities. The proposed approach for probabilistic management of the federated choreographies uses basically the same principle as presented for the best case, worst case calculations (see subsection 8.3.2.2). As already mentioned, the difference between two approaches is that probabilities for possible durations of activities and branches of decision nodes have been considered. In this approach there is no need to calculate the best case and worst cases. Hence, In the following subsections a modification of methods for the probabilistic approach have been presented.

8.3.5.5. Methods

Method *initialize* This method initializes all e-histograms and l-histograms in a given graph. The variable $a.eps'$ and $a.lae'$ are used for the propagation of interval restrictions. Histograms are initialized at the first step of the algorithm.

The Method **initialize(G)**
1 **for** *all activities* $a \in G$ **do**
2 $\quad$ $a.eps := \{(1.0, 0)\};$
3 $\quad$ $a.lae := \{(1.0, \infty)\};$
4 $\quad$ $a.eps' := \varnothing;$
5 $\quad$ $a.lae' := \varnothing;$
6 **endfor**

Method *propagate* This method propagates time-interval restrictions on activities from a source chorecography or orchestration G to a target choreography or orchestration H. The propagation is performed only if the propagated values further constrain the existing values of the target choreography or orchestration, i.e. interval [eps,lae] of the target choreography or orchestration becomes tighter. This means that propagation will only occur if eps increases or lae decreases. The parameter*certainty* defines the probability (degree) applied for histogram comparison operations (see also subsection 8.3.5.2). A 100%-certainty ensures that the compared histograms have no overlapping regions at all, but a very high certainty will be more vulnerable to non-conformance conflicts than lower ones (see method *checkConformance* for further details). The propagated histograms will be stored in $x.eps'$ and $x.lae'$ of an activity x for further usage in the subsequent calculation of probabilistic timed graphs. The method uses event correspondence for propagation of *eps*- and *lae*-histograms from a source activity to a target activity. The correspondence of start events are used for propagation of *eps*-histograms and the correspondence of end events for propagation of *lae*-histograms.

The Method **propagate(*G*, *H*, certainty)**

---

1 change := false;
2 **for** *all activities* $\{x \in H \mid \exists a \in G : x_s \equiv a_s\}$ *in a topological order* **do**
      // -propagation of *eps*-
3   **if** *x.eps* $<_{certainty}$ *a.eps* **then**
4   *x.eps'* := *a.eps*;
5   change := true;
6   **endif**
      // -propagation of *lae*-
7   **if** *x.lae* $>_{certainty}$ *a.lae* **then**
8   *x.lae'* := *a.lae*;
9   change := true;
10   **endif**
11 **endfor**

Method *calculate* Input parameter is a choreography or an orchestration. This method is used for pre-calculation of probabilistic timed graphs as well as for recalculations after interval propagations. Basically this method uses the same technique for calculation of probabilistic timed graphs as described in subsection 8.3.5.3 for forward and backward-calculation of eps-histograms and lae-histograms. It must be considered that the execution interval of an activity *a* (eps and lae-histogram) may already be restricted due to a prior propagation from another orchestration and/or choreography (stored in *a.eps'* and *a.lae'*). If this is the case the calculated histogram is merged with the propagated histogram. As this merge has exactly the same semantics as an ordinary AND-structure, the histogram conjunction operations (max for eps, min for lae) can be used. This ensures that the eps-histogram only increases and the lae-histogram only decreases, hence further restricting the valid interval.

8.3. Temporal Conformance

The Method calculate(G)

1 **for** all nodes $n \in N, G = (N, E)$ in forward topological order **do**
2   calculate $n.eps$ according to Table 8.5;
3   **if** $n.type = activity \wedge n.eps' \neq \varnothing$ **then**
4          $n.eps := n.eps \wedge_{max} n.eps'$;
5          $n.eps' = \varnothing$;
6   **endif**
7   calculate $n.epe$ according to Table 8.5;
8 **endfor**

9 **for** all nodes $n \in N, G = (N, E)$ in backward topological order **do**
10   calculate $n.lae$ according to Table 8.6;
11   **if** $n.type = activity \wedge n.lae' \neq \varnothing$ **then**
12          $n.lae := n.eps \wedge_{min} n.eps'$;
13          $n.eps' = \varnothing$;
14   **endif**
15   calculate $n.las$ according to Table 8.6;
16 **endfor**

Method checkConformance This method checks if the basic conformance conditions are satisfied:

1. The earliest possible start time of an activity must always be less than or equal to its latest allowed start time, i.e. $\forall$ activities a: $a.eps \leq a.las$

2. The earliest possible start time of an activity must not exceed its earliest possible end time, i.e. $\forall$ activities a: $a.eps \leq a.epe$

Otherwise the boolean variable *conf* is set to false, which stops the algorithm. This condition must always be met for all activities of all choreographies and orchestrations. For the same reason as before, the variable *certainty* is used for histogram comparison operations. A 100%-certainty ensures that the compared histograms have no overlapping regions at all, but a very high certainty is more vulnerable to non-conformance conflicts than lower ones. A relaxed certainty allows for overlapping regions, which might prove useful when dealing with outliers. Furthermore it is possible to use the certainty as an adjusting bolt, to select a strategy from very conservative (strict) to risky which allows more possible violations during run-time.

The Method **checkConformance(G,certainty)**

1 **for** *all activities $a \in G$ in a reverse topological order* **do**
2   **if** *a.eps* $>_{certainty}$ *a.las* **then**
3   conf := false;
4   **else if** *a.eps* $>_{certainty}$ *a.epe* **then**
5   conf := false;
6   **endif**
7 **endfor**
8 return conf;

8.3.5.6. Temporal Conformance Checking Algorithm

The algorithm consists of two parts:

1. The initialization and precalculation phase

2. The recalculation and conformance checking phase

Note that the algorithm needs a *certainty*-value as input-parameter. The higher this value, the stricter the conformance check.

In the first phase the global choreography is initialized and then its histograms are calculated. After checking the conformance condition of the global choreography, all of its supporting choreographies and realizing orchestrations O are initialized, followed by the propagation from the global choreography and calculation of their timed graphs (e and l-histograms). Note that the value *d.max* denotes the explicitly defined maximum durations for graphs (orchestration or choreography), which is needed to initialize the according deadline δ necessary for the backward calculation of a timed graph. In this phase propagation only occurs between all directly or indirectly supporting choreographies and realizing orchestrations of the global choreography and vice versa. The resulting e and l-histograms serve as initial values for further calculations.

Each calculation is followed by an initial basic conformance check. The value of the flag *conf* signals if temporal conformance can be guaranteed at least up to the given certainty-value. The only reason why the check may fail at this stage is a too tight deadline caused by a too low maximum duration. A boolean variable *change* serves as an indicator if temporal values of a node are changed. If this variable becomes true all incoming and outgoing links of the corresponding choreography or orchestration are marked. Source and target node of each marked link will be revisited and eventually recalculated in the next phase. Multiple marks on an edge have no additional effect. If the temporal conformance condition is not violated, the second phase of the algorithm starts: recalculation and conformance checking. For all marked edges, the cycle of propagation, recalculation, and conformance-check is repeated until a stable state is reached or the conformance condition is violated. A stable state is reached if no edge has a mark on it.

The Algorithm **temporalConformanceFederation(certainty)**

```
   // -initialization and precalculation-
1  conf := true;
2  initialize(C_g);
3  calculate(C_g);
4  conf := checkConformance (C_g, certainty);
5  for all directly and indirectly supporting choreographies and realizing orchestrations G of C_g
   in a topological order do
6      initialize(G);
7      change := propagate(C_g, G, certainty);
8      if change = true then
9          G.deadline := G.first.eps + G.d.max;
10         calculate (G);
11     endif
12     change: = propagate(G, C_g, certainty);
13     if change = true then
14         calculate(C_g);
15         conf := checkConformance(C_g, certainty);
16         mark all incoming and outgoing edges of C_g;
17     endif
18 endfor

   // -recalculation and conformance checking-
19 repeat
20     select randomly a marked edge e such that G is the supported choreography and
       H the supporting choreography or realizing orchestration;
21     change: = propagate(G, H, certainty);
22     if change = true then
23         calculate H;
24         conf := checkConformance(H, certainty);
25         mark all incoming and outgoing edges ∈ H;
26     endif
27     unmark e;
28     change: = propagate(H, G, certainty);
29     if change = true then
30         calculate G;
31         conf := checkConformance(G, certainty);
32         mark all incoming and outgoing edges ∈ G;
33     endif
34 until all edges are unmarked ∨ conf = false ;
```

8.3. Temporal Conformance

Let G, S1 and S2 be the choreographies depicted in figure 8.27. The graph of the *Supported Choreography G* is presented by the graph illustrated in figure 8.36. The graphs of the *supporting choreography S1* and the *supporting choreography S2* are illustrated in figure 8.37 and figure 8.38 respectively. The supported choreography is linked to the supporting choreographies as follows:

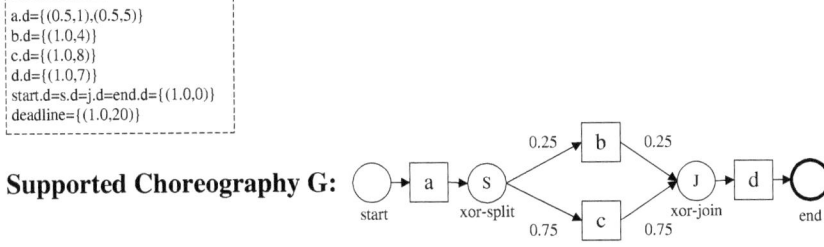

Figure 8.36.: Supported choreography G

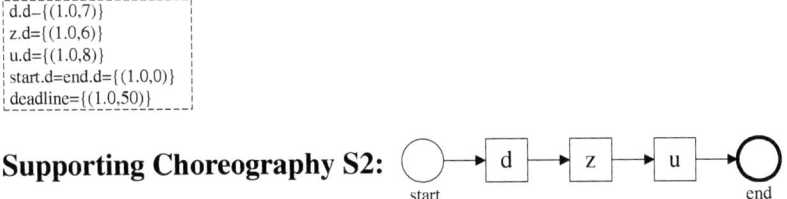

Figure 8.37.: Supporting choreography S1

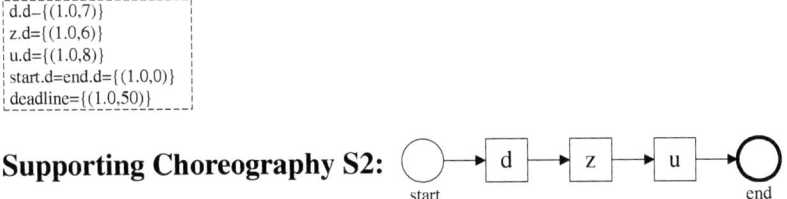

Figure 8.38.: Supporting choreography S2

- By the corresponding node b, which is one of the conditional nodes in G and the middle nodes in S1. Both nodes refer to the same activity, and therefor they have the same duration.

- By the corresponding node d, which is the last activity in G and the first activity in S2.

- Activities a and c in C correspond to further orchestrations or choreographies which are not consider here.

For the algorithm a very strict *certainty* = 99% is defined. The first phase starts with the initialization and calculation of G. The temporal values are represented in the following listing:

$$
\begin{array}{rl}
\multicolumn{2}{c}{\textit{Forward Calculation : starting with time point 0}} \\
a.eps &= start.epe = start.eps = \{(1.0, 0)\} \\
s.eps &= a.epe = a.d + a.eps = \{(0.5, 1), (0.5, 5)\} \\
b.eps &= c.eps = s.epe = s.eps \\
b.epe &= b.d + b.eps = \{(0.5, 5), (0.5, 9)\} \\
c.epe &= c.d + b.eps = \{(0.5, 9), (0.5, 13)\} \\
j.eps &= (b.epe * 0.25) \vee (c.epe * 0.75) = \{(0.125, 5), (0.5, 9), (0.375, 13)\} \\
d.eps &= j.epe = j.eps \\
end.epe &= end.eps = d.epe = d.d + d.eps = \{(0.125, 12), (0.5, 16), (0.375, 20)\} \\
\multicolumn{2}{c}{\textit{Backward Calculation : starting with deadline } \delta = 20} \\
d.lae &= end.las = end.lae = \{1.0, \delta)\} \\
b.lae &= c.lae = j.las = j.lae = d.las = d.lae - d.d = \{(1.0, 13)\} \\
b.las &= b.lae - b.d = \{(1.0, 9)\} \\
c.las &= c.lae - c.d = \{(1.0, 5)\} \\
s.lae &= (b.las * 0.25) \vee (c.las * 0.75) = \{(0.25, 9), (0.75, 5)\} \\
a.lae &= s.las = s.lae \\
start.las &= start.lae = a.las = a.lae - a.d = \{(0.125, 8), (0.75, 4), (0.125, 0)\}
\end{array}
$$

The initialization of the eps and lae-histograms of S1 (with 0 and ∞ values respectively) is followed by the propagation between corresponding nodes of G and S1 (activity b). Propagation only occurs if it further constrains the interval [eps,lae] of S1.b. The method *propagate* first checks if $S1.b.eps <_{0.99} G.b.eps$; this is the case, therefore $S1.b.eps' = \{(0.5, 1), (0.5, 5)\}$. Analogously the lae-histograms is checked: as $S1.b.lae >_{0.99} G.b.lae$, the method *propagate* sets the intermediate $S1.b.lae' = \{(1.0, 13)\}$. Now the calculation of S1

8.3. Temporal Conformance

starts as described in method *calculate(G)* (calculation-details only for max-conjunction at b.eps and min-conjunction at b.lae):

$$
\begin{aligned}
x.eps &= start.epe = start.eps = \{(1.0, 0)\} \\
b.eps &= x.epe = \{(1.0, 1)\} \\
b.eps &= b.eps \wedge_{max} b.eps' = \{(0.5, 1), (0.5, 5)\} \\
y.eps &= b.epe = \{(0.5, 1), (0.5, 5)\} \\
end.epe &= end.eps = y.epe = \{(0.5, 2), (0.5, 6)\}
\end{aligned}
$$

$$
\begin{aligned}
y.lae &= end.las = end.lae = \{1.0, 20)\} \\
b.lae &= y.las = \{(1.0, 19)\} \\
b.lae &= b.lae \wedge_{min} b.lae' = \{(1.0, 13)\} \\
x.lae &= b.las = \{(1.0, 9)\} \\
start.las &= start.lae = x.las = \{(0.5, 8), (0.5, 4)\}
\end{aligned}
$$

In the next step the calculated values must be propagated from S1 to G, if the according propagation conditions apply for *b.eps* and *b.lae*. This is not the case, therefore the timed graph of G does not change and the existing values remain the same. In this stage the initialization and precalculation starts for S2. After the initialization, the method *propagate* sets $S2.d.eps = \{(0.125, 5), (0.5, 9), (0.375, 13)\}$ and $S2.d.lae = \{(1.0, 20)\}$, and the subsequent calculation of the probabilistic timed graph continues:

$$
\begin{aligned}
d.eps &= start.epe = start.eps = \{(1.0, 0)\} \\
d.eps &= d.eps \wedge_{max} d.eps' = \{(0.125, 5), (0.5, 9), (0.375, 13)\} \\
z.eps &= d.epe = \{(0.125, 12), (0.5, 16), (0.375, 20)\} \\
u.eps &= z.epe = \{(0.125, 18), (0.5, 22), (0.375, 26)\} \\
end.epe &= end.eps = u.epe = \{(0.125, 26), (0.5, 30), (0.375, 34)\}
\end{aligned}
$$

$$
\begin{aligned}
u.lae &= end.las = end.lae = \{(1.0, 50)\} \\
z.lae &= u.las = \{(1.0, 42)\} \\
d.lae &= z.las = \{(1.0, 36)\} \\
d.lae &= d.lae \wedge_{min} d.lae' = \{(1.0, 20)\} \\
start.las &= start.lae = d.las = d.las = \{(1.0, 13)\}
\end{aligned}
$$

The reverse propagation – of d from $S1$ to G – does not change any value in the timed graph of G. As no further choreographies exist, and no marked edges are left, the algorithm terminates successfully. This specific composition temporally conforms, and no deadline is violated if the real durations of activities adhere to the estimated/mined durations. The build-time calculations are now complete.

The probabilistic approach for time management of choreographies is also separately presented in [111].

8.3.5.7. Proof of Termination and Complexity Analysis

Analogues to the argumentation in subsection 8.3.2.6 it can be proved that the proposed algorithm terminates. The algorithm terminates in two cases: (1) as the number of edges is finite, a stable state will be reached in a finite number of steps. Or (2), if such a stable state does not exist, after a finite number of steps the conformance condition will be violated, because with each iteration the *lae* becomes smaller and the *eps* value greater until $eps >_{certainty} lae$, since there is only a finite number of chronons between time points. The same argumentation for the complexity analysis also applies here.

8.3.5.8. Run-time Applications

During run-time the probabilistic timed graph of each choreography and orchestration can be used for several purposes, for instance (given that the time values specify *hours*):

- Pre-dispatching of time-frames for all activities of the choreography and all orchestrations, as soon as the first activity a of the orchestration starts; e.g. the owner of orchestration $O2$ can be notified, that d will be called in $\{(0.125,5),(0.5,9),(0.375,13)\}$ hours and should be finished in $\{(1.0,36)\}$ hours.

- If, for instance, b ends 20 hours after the start of the process (choreography), then a deadline violation will occur with a 'probability' of 100% (according to b.lae). With the availability of this information, the administrator is able to trigger counter-measure issues to avoid the upcoming temporal failure and deadline violation.

8.3.6. Temporal Aspects of BPEL Processes

The methods and techniques proposed here can be used for time management of processes in WS-BPEL. As noted before, in WS-BPEL orchestrations can be modeled as executable processes and choreographies as abstract processes. Figure 8.39 illustrates schematically the cycle form process design to temporal conformance checking.

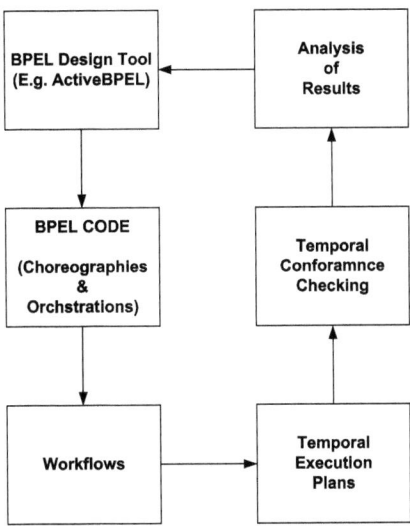

Figure 8.39.: From process design to temporal conformance checking

Processes can be designed using tools such as ActiveBPEL [10] or Oracle BPEL designer [13]. Using these tools choreographies and orchestrations can be defined and modeled. After definition of the choreographies and the orchestrations the underlying workflow of the modeled choreographies and orchestrations can be extracted. Based on the methods and techniques introduced in this book, temporal execution plans of the involved choreographies and orchestrations can be calculated and subsequently can be checked if the model is temporally conformant or are there any changes necessary. When there is some temporal inconsistencies, it may be possible to solve this issue with some modification such as extension of the deadline or defining alternatives for some activities with shorter execution durations. After checking the temporal conformance of the model, the results can be considered for possible redesigning of the process at process designer. Eder et. al in [112] propose a technique for time management of different communication patterns between processes such as request/reply or solicit response. Using the techniques presented in [112] different communication patterns in WS-BPEL can be modeled and handled.

8.4. Correctness of View-Based Interorganizational Workflows

The architecture of the view-based interorganizational workflows are illustrated in figure 5.1. The choreography is a workflow composed of views and it must be ensured that it conforms to correctness criteria. It must be checked that activities contained in the choreography are only those contained in the views. A choreography is order-preserving with respect to the views and the choreography itself is a valid full-blocked workflow definition.

Definition 8.39: **(Correctness of Interorganizational Workflows)**
Let $C = (N_C, E_C)$ be a choreography and $V_i = (N_{v_i}, E_{v_i}), 1 \leq i \leq n$ the workflow views. A choreography C is correct with respect to $V_i, 1 \leq i \leq n$ if and only if:

(a) C is a valid full-blocked workflow

(b) $\forall i : V_i$ is a correct view on C

(c) C is composed of the activities of V_i, i.e. $\forall$ activity $a : a \in N_C \Rightarrow \exists V_i : a \in N_{v_i}$

Note that only activities contained in the Choreography C must also be contained in a view and not the control nodes. The reason is that the structure of the activities in the choreography can be different than that in views. In other words, the choreography can present the activities of the views in a new ordering.

8.4. Correctness of View-Based Interorganizational Workflows 175

	Forward Calculation: starting with time point 0
start.eps=	{(1.0,0)}
start.epe =	{(1.0,0)}
a.eps =	{(1.0,0)}
a.epe =	{(0.2,1), (0.5,5), (0.3,10)}
b.eps =	{(0.2,1), (0.5,5), (0.3,10)}
b.epe =	{(0.1,5),(0.35,9), (0.25,13), (0.15,14),(0.15,18)}
OS.eps =	{(0.1,5), (0.35,9), (0.25,13), (0.15,14), (0.15,18)}
OS.epe =	{(0.1,5), (0.35,9), (0.25,13), (0.15,14), (0.15,18)}
c.eps =	{(0.1,5), (0.35,9), (0.25,13), (0.15,14), (0.15,18)}
c.epe =	{(0.01,13),(0.035,17), (0.09,20), (0.025,21), (0.015,22), (0.315,24), (0.015,26), (0.225,28), (0.135,29), (0.135,33)}
d.eps =	{(0.1,5), (0.35,9), (0.25,13), (0.15,14), (0.15,18)}
d.epe =	{(0.1,12), (0.35,16),(0.25,20), (0.15,21), (0.15,25)}
OJ.eps =	{(0.06,12), (0.004,13), (0.21,16), (0.014,17), (0.186,20), (0.1,21), (0.006,22), (0.126,24), (0.09,25), (0.006,26), (0.09,28), (0.054,29), (0.054,33)}
OJ.epe =	{(0.06,12), (0.004,13), (0.21,16), (0.014,17), (0.186,20), (0.1,21), (0.006,22), (0.126,24), (0.09,25), (0.006,26), (0.09,28), (0.054,29), (0.054,33)}
AS.eps =	{(0.06,12), (0.004,13), (0.21,16), (0.014,17), (0.186,20), (0.1,21), (0.006,22), (0.126,24), (0.09,25), (0.006,26), (0.09,28), (0.054,29), (0.054,33)}
AS.epe =	{(0.06,12), (0.004,13), (0.21,16), (0.014,17), (0.186,20), (0.1,21), (0.006,22), (0.126,24), (0.09,25), (0.006,26), (0.09,28), (0.054,29), (0.054,33)}
e.eps =	{(0.06,12), (0.004,13), (0.21,16), (0.014,17), (0.186,20), (0.1,21), (0.006,22), (0.126,24), (0.09,25), (0.006,26), (0.09,28), (0.054,29), (0.054,33)}
e.epe =	{(0.024,16), (0.0016,17), (0.036,18), (0.0024,19), (0.084,20), (0.0056,21), (0.126,22), (0.0084,23), (0.0744,24), (0.04,25), (0.114,26), (0.06,27), (0.054,28), (0.036,29), (0.078,30), (0.054,31), (0.0396,32), (0.0216,33), (0.054,34), (0.0324,35), (0.0216,37), (0.0324,39)}
f.eps =	{(0.06,12),(0.004,13), (0.21,16), (0.014,17), (0.186,20), (0.1,21), (0.006,22), (0.126,24), (0.09,25), (0.006,26), (0.09,28), (0.054,29), (0.054,33)}
f.epe =	{(0.042,15), (0.0028,16), (0.165,19), (0.011,20), (0.1932,23), (0.0742,24), (0.0042,25), (0.144,27), (0.093,28), (0.006,29), (0.1008,31), (0.0648,32), (0.0018,33), (0.027,35), (0.054,36), (0.0162,40)}
AJ.eps =	{(0,0010752,16), (0,00007168,17), (0,0016128,18), (0,01066752,19), (0,0192512,20), (0,00123648,21), (0,0278208,22), (0,05749632,23), (0,05769168,24), (0,02121808,25), (0,0561336,26), (0,1125456,27), (0,0929928,28), (0,0302568,29), (0,0573612,30), (0,12019032,31), (0,08088192,32), (0,02100888,33), (0,0487512,34), (0,05479272,35), (0,0553176,36), (0,02125008,37), (0,03187512,39), (0,0162,40)}
AJ.epe =	{(0,0010752,16), (0,00007168,17), (0,0016128,18), (0,01066752,19), (0,0192512,20), (0,00123648,21), (0,0278208,22), (0,05749632,23), (0,05769168,24), (0,02121808,25), (0,0561336,26), (0,1125456,27), (0,0929928,28), (0,0302568,29), (0,0573612,30), (0,12019032,31), (0,08088192,32), (0,02100888,33), (0,0487512,34), (0,05479272,35), (0,0553176,36), (0,02125008,37), (0,03187512,39), (0,0162,40)}

Table 8.7.: Forward Calculation: starting with time point 0

	Forward Calculation: starting with time point 0 (cntd.)			
j.eps =	{(0,0010752,16),	(0,00007168,17),	(0,0016128,18),	(0,01066752,19),
	(0,0192512,20),	(0,00123648,21),	(0,0278208,22),	(0,05749632,23),
	(0,05769168,24),	(0,02121808,25),	(0,0561336,26),	(0,1125456,27),
	(0,0929928,28),	(0,0302568,29),	(0,0573612,30),	(0,12019032,31),
	(0,08088192,32),	(0,02100888,33),	(0,0487512,34),	(0,05479272,35),
	(0,0553176,36), (0,02125008,37), (0,03187512,39), (0,0162,40)}			
j.epe =	{(0,0010752,21),	(0,00007168,22),	(0,0016128,23),	(0,01066752,24),
	(0,0192512,25),	(0,00123648,26),	(0,0278208,27),	(0,05749632,28),
	(0,05769168,29),	(0,02121808,30),	(0,0561336,31),	(0,1125456,32),
	(0,0929928,33),	(0,0302568,34),	(0,0573612,35),	(0,12019032,36),
	(0,08088192,37),	(0,02100888,38),	(0,0487512,39),	(0,05479272,40),
	(0,0553176,41), (0,02125008,42), (0,03187512,44), (0,0162,45)}			
End.eps =	{(0,0010752,21),	(0,00007168,22),	(0,0016128,23),	(0,01066752,24),
	(0,0192512,25),	(0,00123648,26),	(0,0278208,27),	(0,05749632,28),
	(0,05769168,29),	(0,02121808,30),	(0,0561336,31),	(0,1125456,32),
	(0,0929928,33),	(0,0302568,34),	(0,0573612,35),	(0,12019032,36),
	(0,08088192,37),	(0,02100888,38),	(0,0487512,39),	(0,05479272,40),
	(0,0553176,41), (0,02125008,42), (0,03187512,44), (0,0162,45)}			
End.epe =	{(0,0010752,21),	(0,00007168,22),	(0,0016128,23),	(0,01066752,24),
	(0,0192512,25),	(0,00123648,26),	(0,0278208,27),	(0,05749632,28),
	(0,05769168,29),	(0,02121808,30),	(0,0561336,31),	(0,1125456,32),
	(0,0929928,33),	(0,0302568,34),	(0,0573612,35),	(0,12019032,36),
	(0,08088192,37),	(0,02100888,38),	(0,0487512,39),	(0,05479272,40),
	(0,0553176,41), (0,02125008,42), (0,03187512,44), (0,0162,45)}			

Table 8.8.: Forward Calculation: starting with time point 0 (cntd.)

8.4. Correctness of View-Based Interorganizational Workflows

	Backward Calculation: starting with deadline= 50
End.lae =	{ 1.0, 50)}
End.las =	{ 1.0, 50)}
j.lae =	{ 1.0, 50)}
j.las =	{(1.0,45)}
AJ.lae =	{(1.0,45)}
AJ.las =	{(1.0,45)}
e.ale =	{(1.0,45)}
e.las =	{(0.4,41),(0.6,39)}
f.ale=	{(1.0,45)}
f.las=	{(0.7,42),(0.3,38)}
AS.lae=	{(0.3,38),(0.42,39),(0.28,41)}
AS.las=	{(0.3,38),(0.42,39),(0.28,41)}
OJ.lae =	{(0.3,38),(0.42,39),(0.28,41)}
OJ.las =	{(0.3,38),(0.42,39),(0.28,41)}
c.lae =	{(0.3,38),(0.42,39),(0.28,41)}
c.las =	{(0.27,23),(0.378,24),(0.252,26),(0.03,30),(0.042,31),(0.028,33)}
d.lae =	{(0.3,38),(0.42,39),(0.28,41)}
d.las =	{(0.3,31),(0.42,32),(0.28,34)}
OS.lae =	{(0.108,23), (0.1512,24), (0.1008,26), (0.012,30), (0.1968,31), (0.252,32), (0.0112,33), (0.168,34)}
OS.las =	{(0.108,23), (0.1512,24), (0.1008,26), (0.012,30), (0.1968,31), (0.252,32), (0.0112,33), (0.168,34)}
b.lae =	{(0.108,23), (0.1512,24), (0.1008,26), (0.012,30), (0.1968,31), (0.252,32), (0.0112,33), (0.168,34)}
b.las =	{(0,054,15), (0,0756,16), (0,0504,18), (0,054,19), (0,0756,20), (0,0564,22), (0,0984,23), (0,126,24), (0,0056,25), (0,09,26), (0,0984,27), (0,126,28), (0,0056,29), (0,084,30)}
a.lae =	{(0,054,15), (0,0756,16), (0,0504,18), (0,054,19), (0,0756,20), (0,0564,22), (0,0984,23), (0,126,24), (0,0056,25), (0,09,26), (0,0984,27), (0,126,28), (0,0056,29), (0,084,30)}
a.las =	{(0,0162,5), (0,02268,6), (0,01512,8), (0,0162,9), (0,04968,10), (0,0378,11), (0,01692,12), (0,05472,13), (0,0756,14), (0,0546,15), (0,027,16), (0,0678,17), (0,0978,18), (0,0798,19), (0,028,20), (0,05628,21), (0,06888,22), (0,0882,23), (0,00392,24), (0,06,25), (0,01968,26), (0,0252,27), (0,00112,28), (0,0168,29)}
Start.lae =	{(0,0162,5), (0,02268,6), (0,01512,8), (0,0162,9), (0,04968,10), (0,0378,11), (0,01692,12), (0,05472,13), (0,0756,14), (0,0546,15), (0,027,16), (0,0678,17), (0,0978,18), (0,0798,19), (0,028,20), (0,05628,21), (0,06888,22), (0,0882,23), (0,00392,24), (0,06,25), (0,01968,26), (0,0252,27), (0,00112,28), (0,0168,29)}
Start.las =	{(0,0162,5), (0,02268,6), (0,01512,8), (0,0162,9), (0,04968,10), (0,0378,11), (0,01692,12), (0,05472,13), (0,0756,14), (0,0546,15), (0,027,16), (0,0678,17), (0,0978,18), (0,0798,19), (0,028,20), (0,05628,21), (0,06888,22), (0,0882,23), (0,00392,24), (0,06,25), (0,01968,26), (0,0252,27), (0,00112,28), (0,0168,29)}

Table 8.9.: Backward Calculation: starting with deadline= 50

Chapter 9

A General Case of Interorganizational Workflows

In the previous chapter the concept of the federate choreographies (section 7.2) has been introduced and structural conformance (section 8.2) and temporal conformance (section 8.3) of the federated choreographies have been studied and algorithms for the conformance checking have been proposed.

In this chapter a more general case of interorganizational workflows is presented and adapted versions of the conformance checking algorithms for this case are proposed.

9.1. A More General Architecture for Interorganizational Workflows

For a more general scenario of interorganizational workflows it is assumed that an interorganizational workflow is composed of a set of choreographies and orchestrations. Choreographies, again, are abstract processes that define the message exchange protocols among involved partners and orchestrations are in charge of realizing the abstract activities defined in a choreography. Figure 9.1 illustrates this scenario. In contrast to the federated choreographies (compare figure 7.10) in this architecture the choreographies are independent from each other. i.e. there is no support-link between two choreographies. However, in this model, as well, partners can take part in several choreographies and their according parts must be realized in their orchestrations which is run and controlled only by its owner. For example *Partner* 4 takes part in *choreography* 1, *choreography* 2 and *choreography* 3 and hence parts of these three choreographies that belong to partner 4 must be realized in his orchestrations. In addition, there is no *global choreography* in the model rather a set of independent choreographies. Remember that the global choreography is a choreography that is only supported by other choreographies and in turn supports no choreography. The global choreography captures the core of business process. In contrast, in this model the business process is divided among a set of independent choreographies. If there is only one choreography present in the model, we have the typical scenario, i.e. one shared choreography and a set of orchestrations, one for each partner.

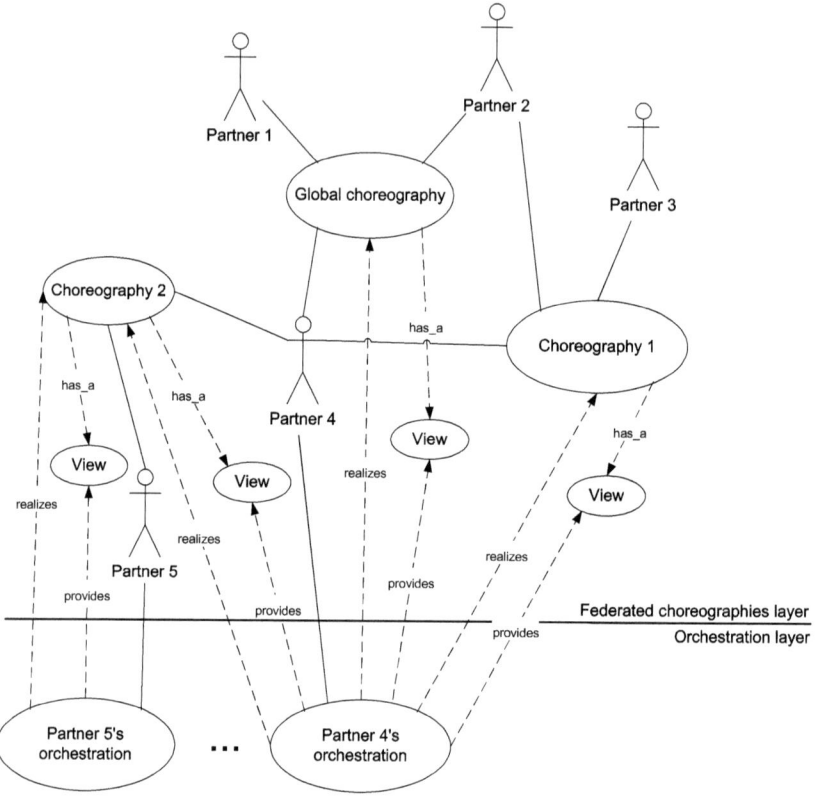

Figure 9.1.: A typical scenario: a set of choreographies and orchestrations

9.2. Conformance Issues

Indeed, it must be ensured that the underlying model of an interorganizational workflow is conflict-free and its execution leads to no failures. For this aim, in this section the modified version of the structural and temporal conformance are presented. Note that the proposed algorithms in this section uses the same underlying methods and concepts as used for the federated choreographies and therefore description of methods, mathematical background, concepts and calculations are omitted in this section and only the conformance checking algorithms are presented.

9.2.1. Structural Conformance

In this scenario, it must be checked that structural conformance conditions are satisfied, i.e. orchestrations do not violate the structural requirements imposed by the choreographies they realize.

For the structural conformance checking the algorithm presented in subsection 8.2.1 can be directly used. Note that in this architecture there is no support-link in the model and the algorithm checks only the realize links, i.e. the links between realized choreographies and realizing orchestrations.

9.2.2. Temporal Conformance

The aim of the temporal conformance checking is to ensure that execution of an interorganizational workflow leads to no temporal failures and enabling predictive and pro-active time management such that counter-measures can be taken early enough to guarantee the correct execution of the flow. In this case like the case of the federated choreographies by application of the same underlying methods a valid temporal execution plan for all activities are computed at design-time. The computed temporal plans at design-time can be monitored at run-time. The same both approaches of temporal conformance checking is also applied for this scenario i.e. the best case, worst case calculations and the probabilistic approach.

9.2.2.1. Best Case, Worst Case Calculations

In this case, there is no global choreography as well as no support-link in the model. Hence, in the initialization and precalculation phase instead of initializing and calculating the timed graph of the global choreography and subsequently all of its directly and indirectly supporting choreographies and realizing orchestrations, this cycle must be done along all of the realize-links in the model. That means from realized choreographies to their realizing orchestrations and vice versa. However it must be noted that also in this case choreographies may affect each other indirectly even when they are independent of each other.

If the model consists of a set of *clusters* of independent orchestrations and choreographies, as depicted in figure 9.2, temporal values can be calculated in a straightforward manner. Clusters here refer to one choreography together with its realizing orchestrations (cf. typical scenario in figure 7.2). Independent clusters means that there is no link from one cluster to another one, i.e. each cluster is temporally independent and imposes no temporal restriction on other clusters. As it can be seen, figure 9.2 is composed of two independent clusters. In such a case temporal calculations can be done in a straightforward manner and each cluster is handled separately. Initialization and synchronization of each cluster must be done, as well, independently. Note that in figures 9.2 and 9.2 views are not depicted as they do not contribute to the temporal conformance of the whole model.

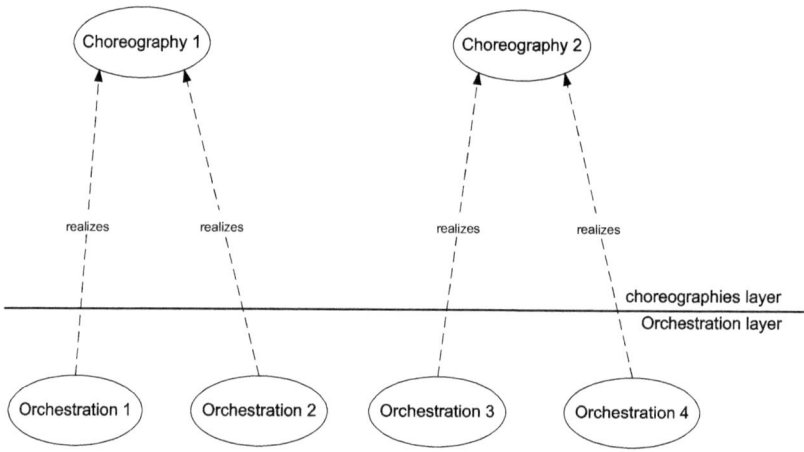

Figure 9.2.: A set of independent choreographies

However, not necessarily all clusters all independent of each other. In some cases two choreographies may have the same realizing orchestrations, as depicted in figure 9.3. In this case the clusters are not temporally independent and through the shared orchestration they impose reciprocal restrictions on each other.

9.2. Conformance Issues

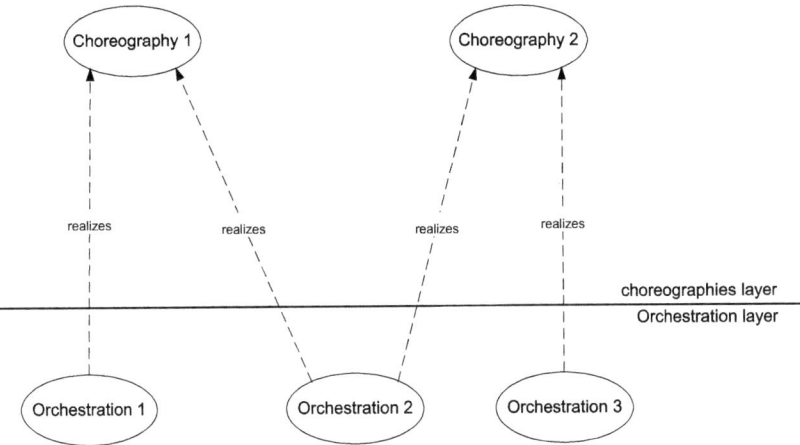

Figure 9.3.: A set of temporally dependent choreographies

The same conclusion about one choreography with multiple realizing orchestrations (as depicted in figure 8.27) can be derived about multiple choreographies with the same shared realizing orchestration as depicted in figure 9.4.

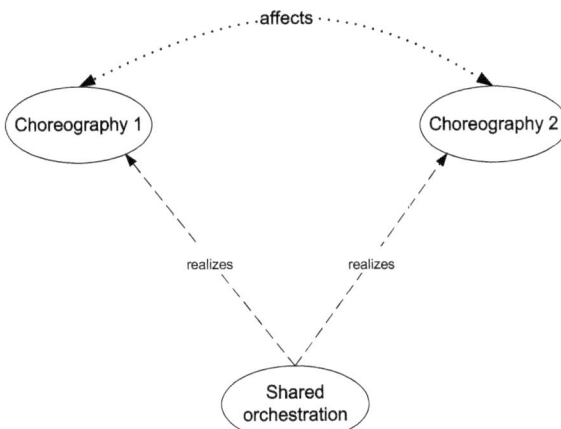

Figure 9.4.: Two choreographies with a shared orchestration

Here again two or more choreographies with the same shared orchestration affect each other even if they have no direct link to each other. Affecting each other means that one choreography imposes temporal restrictions on the other choreography. In this case the synchronization of choreographies are happened through the shared orchestration. In other words, even if the choreographies are independent of each other, they must be synchronized because of the shared orchestrations. In this case, after calculation of the valid temporal execution plans, it is clear which orchestration or choreography begins its execution first and when the other choreographies and orchestrations may start.

Let C be a choreography and O an orchestration such that the orchestration O (partially) realizes the choreography C. The modified version of the conformance checking algorithm is presented in algorithm *temporalConformance()*. Note that maximum duration (d.max) is considered for calculation of orchestration deadlines.

9.2.2.2. Probabilistic Calculations

In addition to the best case, worst case calculations in this subsection the probabilistic time management for the more general case of an interorganizational workflow is described in algorithm *temporalConformance(certainty)*.

9.2. Conformance Issues

The Algorithm temporalConformance()

```
   // -initialization and precalculation-
 1 conf := true;
 2 for all choreographies C in a topological order do
 3     initialize(C);
 4     calculate(C);
 5     conf := checkConformance (C);
 6     for all realizing orchestrations O of C in a topological order do
 7         initialize(O);
 8         change := propagate(C, O);
 9         if change = true then
10             O.deadline := O.first.eps + O.d.max;
11             calculate (O);
12         endif
13         change: = propagate(O, C);
14         if change = true then
15             calculate(C);
16             conf :=checkConformance(C);
17             mark all incoming edges of C;
18         endif
19     endfor
20 endfor
   // -recalculation and conformance checking-
21 repeat
22     select randomly a marked edge e such that C is the realized choreography and O
       the realizing orchestration;
23     change: = propagate(C, O);
24     if change = true then
25         calculate O;
26         conf := checkConformance (O);
27         mark all outgoing edges ∈ O;
28     endif
29     unmark e;
30     change: = propagate(O, C);
31     if change = true then
32         calculate C;
33         conf := checkConformance (C);
34         mark all incoming edges ∈ C;
35     endif
36 until all edges are unmarked ∨ conf = false ;
```

The Algorithm **temporalConformance(certainty)**

```
    // -initialization and precalculation-
 1  conf := true;
 2  for all choreographies C in a topological order do
 3      initialize(C);
 4      calculate(C);
 5      conf := checkConformance (C, certainty);
 6      for all realizing orchestrations O of C in a topological order do
 7          initialize(O);
 8          change := propagate(C,O,certainty);
 9          if change = true then
10              O.deadline := O.first.eps + O.d.max;
11              calculate (O);
12          endif
13          change: = propagate(O, C,certainty);
14          if change = true then
15              calculate(C);
16              conf :=checkConformance(C,certainty);
17              mark all incoming edges of C;
18          endif
19      endfor
20  endfor

    // -recalculation and conformance checking-
21  repeat
22      select randomly a marked edge e such that C is the choreography and O its realizing orchestration;
23      change: = propagate(C, O, certainty);
24      if change = true then
25          calculate(O);
26          conf := checkConformance(O, certainty);
27          mark all outgoing edges ∈ O;
28      endif
29      unmark e;
30      change: = propagate(O, C, certainty);
31      if change = true then
32          calculate C;
33          conf := checkConformance(C, certainty);
34          mark all incoming edges ∈ C;
35      endif
36  until all edges are unmarked ∨ conf = false ;
```

Chapter 10
Conclusions

Interorganizational workflows are workflows that interconnect partners that belong to autonomous organizations. Such workflows provide a framework for cooperation of independent entities. In order to ensure successful functionality of interorganizational workflows several requirements must be satisfied:

- The balance between autonomy and cooperation
- An architecture with adequate capabilities
- Verification of correctness

This book proposed the concept of workflow views to achieve the balance between the openness needed for cooperation and the isolation of internal workflows needed for protection of business logic. In this way only those parts of a process that are needed for communication are made accessible for external partners and business know-how which is coded in other parts of the internal workflow is made hidden. Techniques for correct construction of views and interorganizational workflows are proposed.

This work presented a nouvelle hierarchical architecture for web service based interorganizational workflows, called Federated choreographies, which consist of autonomous and interacting partners. Federated choreographies offer obvious advantages such as protection of business know-how, avoidance of unnecessary information, extendability and uniform modeling of both choraographies and orchestrations. In this approach both choreographies and orchestrations can be modeled uniformly and there is no need for different modeling languages. For the sake of better comprehensibility full-blocked workflows are chosen.

In order to ensure the correctness of interorganizational workflows, several techniques for checking the structural and temporal conformance of the federated choreographies and the correctness of interorganizational workflows are presented. By application of these techniques at design time, it can be checked if the model is conflict-free or there is any necessary modifications and redesign to guarantee the correct execution of the flow. In order to provide adequate means for different requirements, three different approaches for checking the temporal conformance have been proposed. The presented approaches provide means for checking and modeling choreographies and orchestrations with a deterministic fixed duration of activities, variable duration of activities and a probabilistic approach for modeling associated uncertainties with activity duration and branching probabilities. In addition to algorithms for checking the structural and temporal conformance, their mathematical background and related concepts have been presented and discussed. This book has presented a stand alone tool for temporal conformance checking. The conformance checking approach focuses on prevention of errors rather on detecting errors at run time and then repairing them. Application of the presented techniques on the one hand guarantees a conflict-free execution of the involved choreographies and orchestrations and on the other hand reduces the cost of process execution because of two reasons:

- Errors detected at design time cause less costs for process reengineering and redesign than those detected at run time

- Avoidance of exception handling mechanisms

Additionally a more general framework for interorganizational workflows has been presented and adapted versions of the conformance checking algorithms for the more general case have been as well proposed.

The approaches presented in this work (e.g. correct construction of workflow views, temporal conformance checking) are not limited to the federated choreographies but can be applied to many other scenarios independently. Besides, this approach is langauge and platform independent and algorithms work in a distributed manner.

Limitations of the Proposed Approach

The proposed approach focuses only on control-flow aspects and do not consider data flow issues. Data-Flow issues are essential and central aspects for a correct functionality of the model but they are out of scope of this work. In addition the conformance checking considers only structural and temporal issues of the model. In order to assure full conformance, data flow conformance and messaging conformance must be also taken into account. Further, the modeling technique does not consider loops.

Future Work

The future work shall focus on extending its capabilities and solving its limitations, which are:

- Consideration of loops

- Consideration of Data-flow

- Full consistency of the model

At this stage, each phase (process modeling, structural conformance and temporal conformance) can be performed with stand alone tools. An important improvement is a software suite with a common interface that unifies all required tools in one framework.

An interesting improvement and contribution is the extension of available standards such as WS-BPEL with capabilities that enables them to apply the concepts presented in this book, for example temporal annotation of WS-BPEL processes and extension of WS-BPEL engine to enable temporal conformance checking.

Appendix A

Calculation of Timed Graphs

In this appendix the detailed calculations of the timed graphs of the choreograhies G, S1 and S2 are presented. The dependency between these choreographies is depicted in figure 8.27. The bold number in the timed graphs shows that this value has been changed compared to the previous stage. Note that in figure A.11 the deadline is set to $S1.deadline := S1.first.eps + S1.d.max$ which is $50 + 2 = 52$.

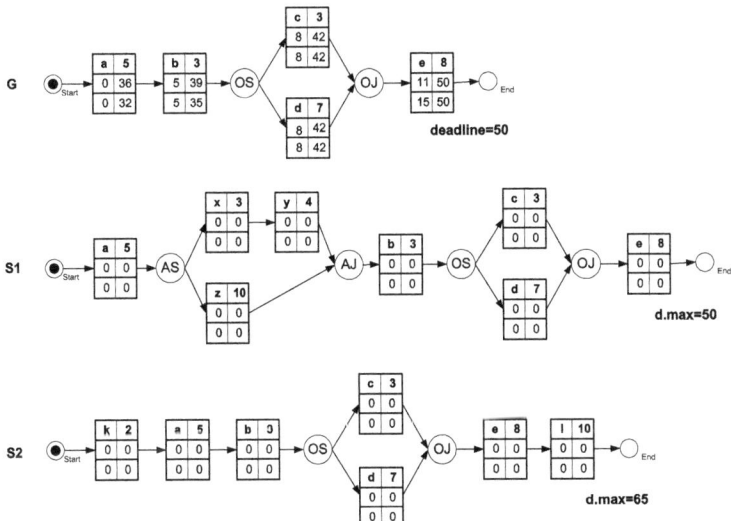

Figure A.1.: After initialization and calculation of G

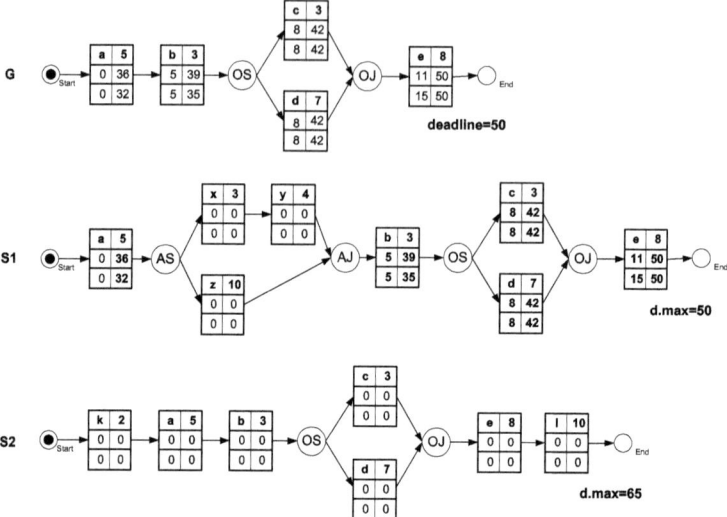

Figure A.2.: After propagation from G to S1

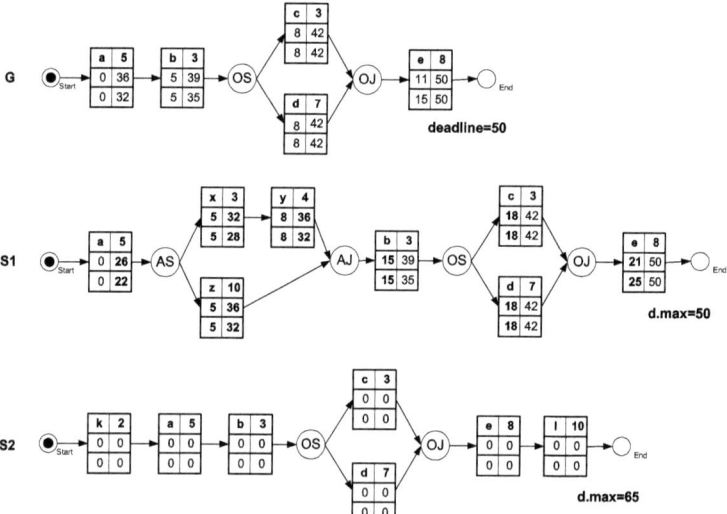

Figure A.3.: After calculation of S1

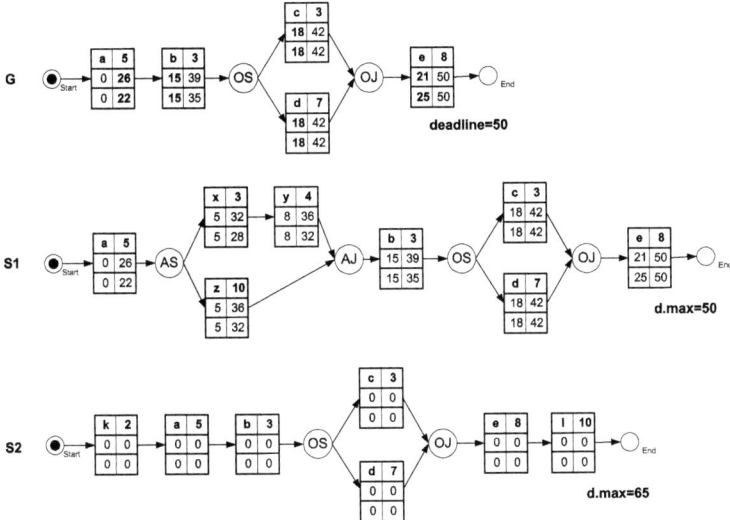

Figure A.4.: After propagation from S1 back to G

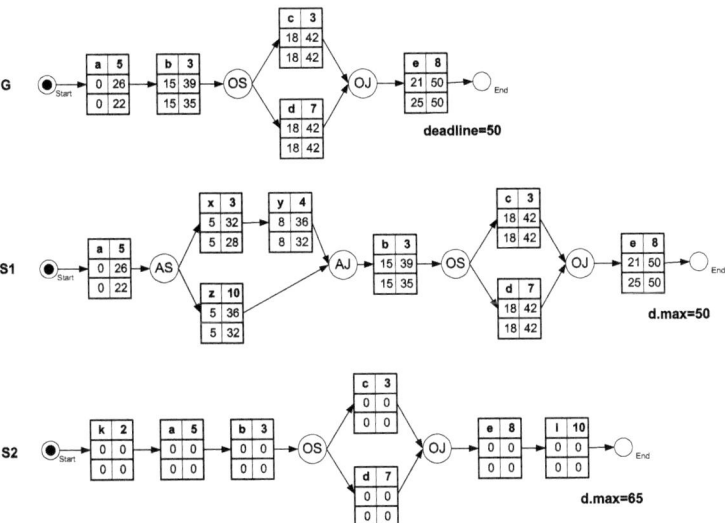

Figure A.5.: After recalculation of G

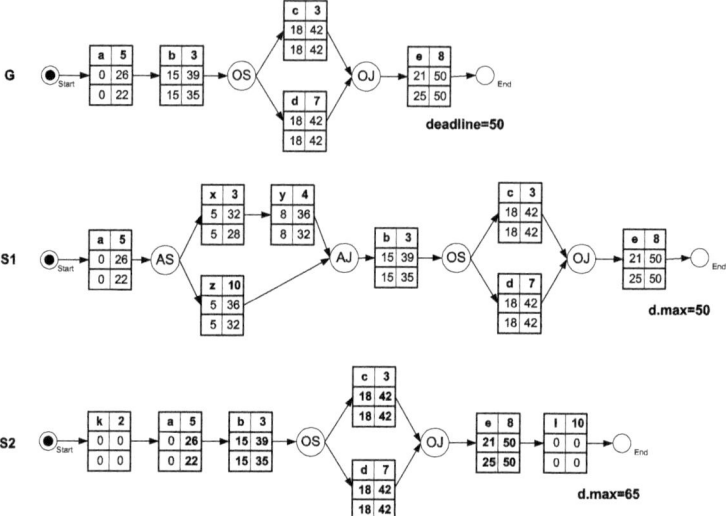

Figure A.6.: After propagation from G to S2

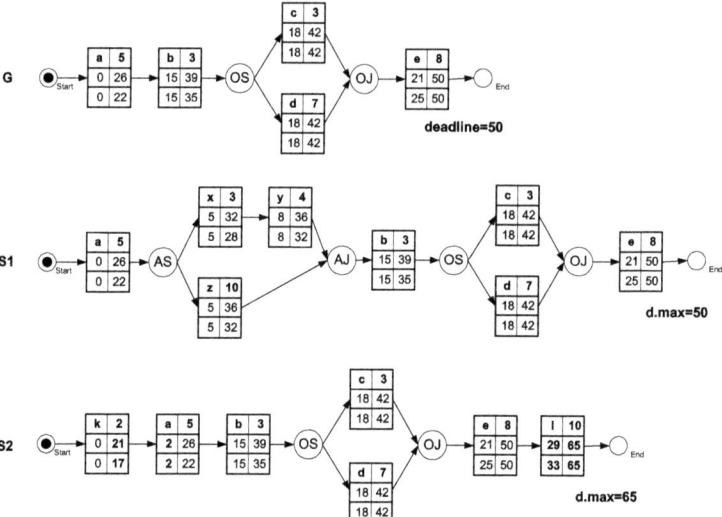

Figure A.7.: After calculation of S2

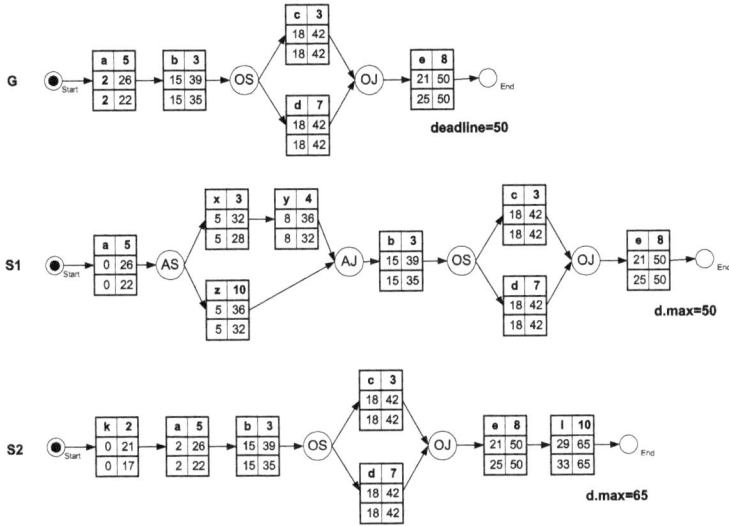

Figure A.8.: After propagation from S2 back to G

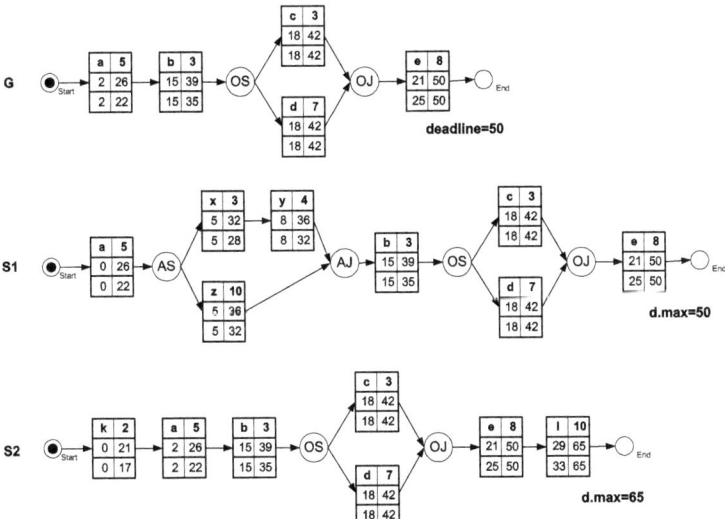

Figure A.9.: After recalculation of G

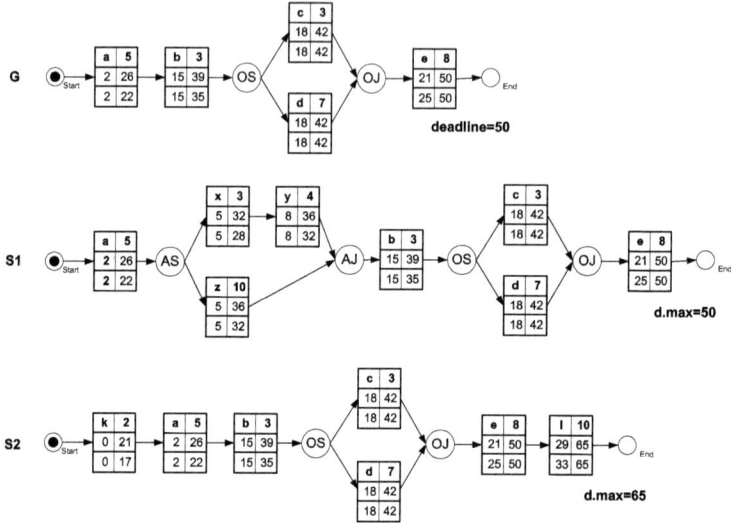

Figure A.10.: After propagation from G to S1

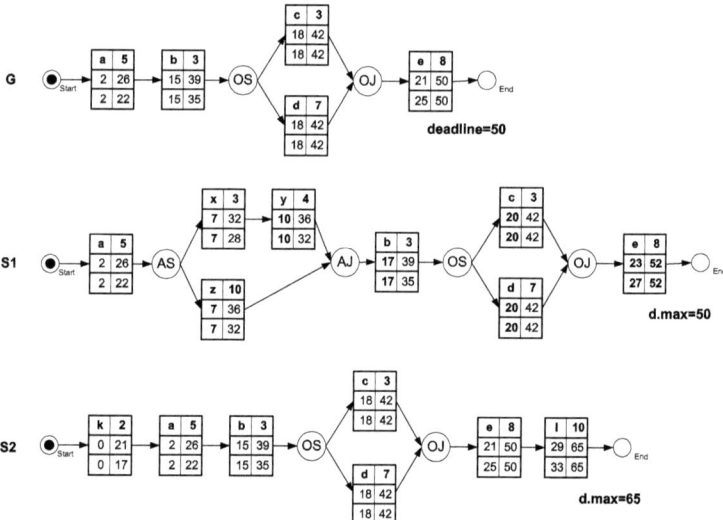

Figure A.11.: After calculation of S1

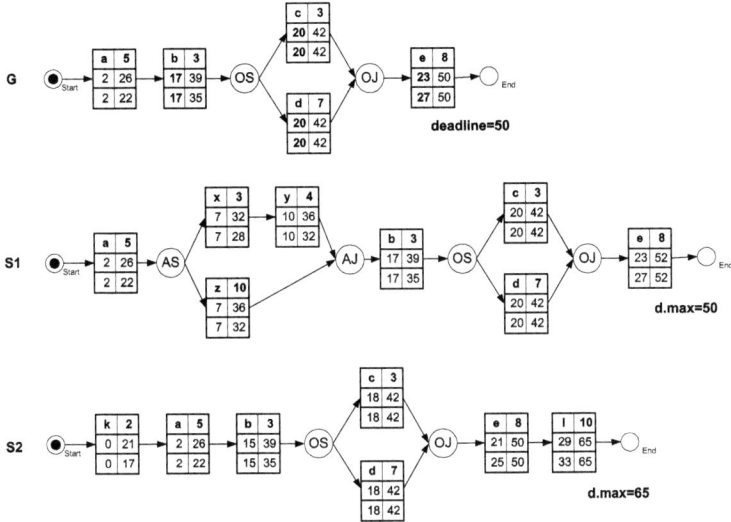

Figure A.12.: After propagation from S1 back to G

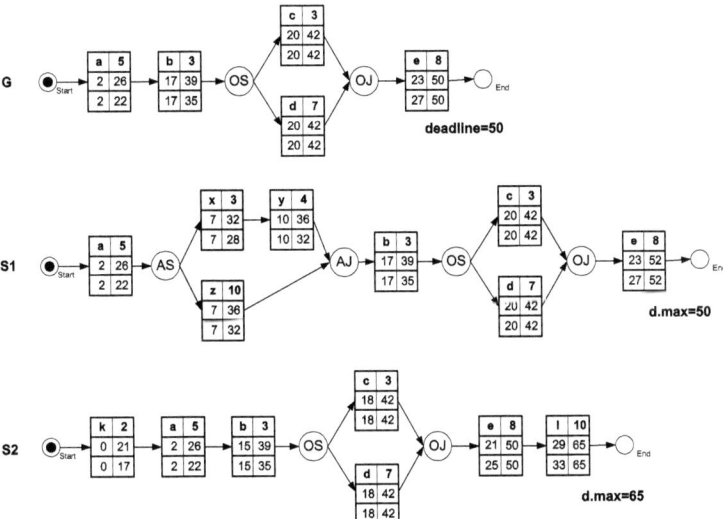

Figure A.13.: After recalculation of G

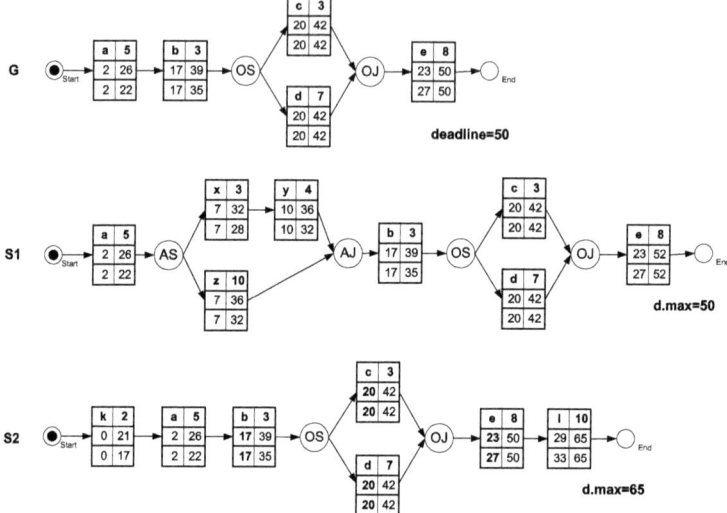

Figure A.14.: After propagation from G to S2

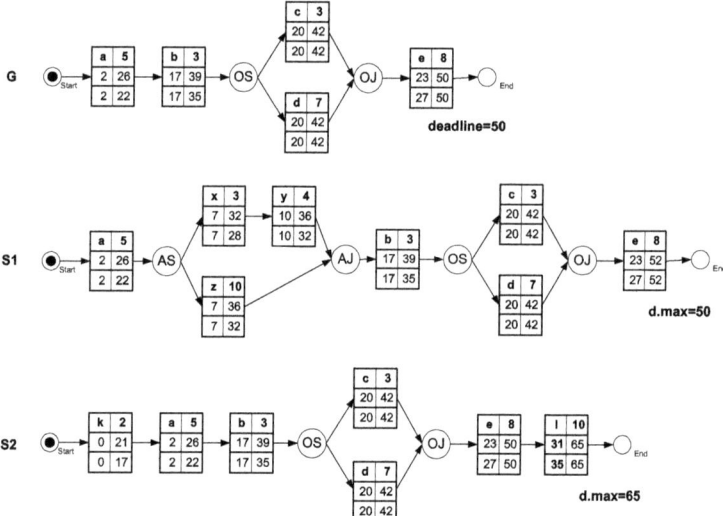

Figure A.15.: After recalculation of S2

Appendix B

Calculation of The Probabilistic Values

	Forward Calculation: starting with time point 0
start.eps =	$\{(1.0,0)\}$
start.epe =	start.eps + start.d = $\{(1.0,0)\} + \{(1.0,0)\} = \{(1.0,0)\}$
a.eps =	start.epe = $\{(1.0,0)\}$
a.epe =	a.eps + a.d = $\{(1.0,0)\} + \{(0.2,1),(0.5,5),(0.3,10)\}$ = $\{(0.2,1),(0.5,5),(0.3,10)\}$
b.eps =	a.epe = $\{(0.2,1),(0.5,5),(0.3,10)\}$
b.epe =	b.eps+ b.d= $\{(0.2,1),(0.5,5),(0.3,10)\} + \{(0.5,4),(0.5,8)\}= \{(0.1,5),(0.1,9),(0.25,9),(0.25,13),(0.15,14),(0.15,18)\}= \{(0.1,5),(0.35,9),(0.25,13),(0.15,14),(0.15,18)\}$
OS.eps =	b.epe=$\{(0.1,5),(0.35,9),(0.25,13),(0.15,14),(0.15,18)\}$
OS.epe =	OS.eps+ OS.d= $\{(0.1,5),(0.35,9),(0.25,13),(0.15,14),(0.15,18)\}+ \{(1.0,0)\}= \{(0.1,5),(0.35,9),(0.25,13),(0.15,14),(0.15,18)\}$
c.eps =	OS.epe = $\{(0.1,5),(0.35,9),(0.25,13),(0.15,14),(0.15,18)\}$
c.epe =	OS.epe= c.eps+ c.d = $\{(0.1,5),(0.35,9),(0.25,13),(0.15,14),(0.15,18)\}+ \{(0.1,8),(0.9,15)\}= \{(0.01,13),(0.035,17),(0.09,20),(0.025,21),(0.015,22),(0.315,24),(0.015,26),(0.225,28),(0.135,29),(0.135,33)\}$
d.eps =	OS.epe= $\{(0.1,5),(0.35,9),(0.25,13),(0.15,14),(0.15,18)\}$
d.epe =	d.eps+ d.d= $\{(0.1,5),(0.35,9),(0.25,13),(0.15,14),(0.15,18)\}+ \{(1.0,7)\}= \{(0.1,12),(0.35,16),(0.25,20),(0.15,21),(0.15,25)\}$
OJ.eps =	(c.epe* 0.40) $\vee$ (d.epe* 0.60) = $\{(0.01,13),(0.035,17),(0.09,20),(0.025,21),(0.015,22),(0.315,24),(0.015,26),(0.225,28),(0.135,29),(0.135,33)\}$ * (0.4) $\vee$ $\{(0.1,12),(0.35,16),(0.25,20),(0.15,21),(0.15,25)\}$ *(0.6)= $\{(0.004,13),(0.014,17),(0.036,20),(0.01,21),(0.006,22),(0.126,24),(0.006,26),(0.09,28),(0.054,29),(0.054,33)\}$ $\vee$ $\{(0.06,12),(0.21,16),(0.15,20),(0.09,21),(0.09,25)\}= \{(0.06,12),(0.004,13),(0.21,16),(0.014,17),(0.15,20),(0.036,20),(0.09,21),(0.01,21),(0.006,22),(0.126,24),(0.09,25),(0.006,26),(0.09,28),(0.054,29),(0.054,33)\}= \{(0.06,12),(0.004,13),(0.21,16),(0.014,17),(0.186,20),(0.1,21),(0.006,22),(0.126,24),(0.09,25),(0.006,26),(0.09,28),(0.054,29),(0.054,33)\}$

Table B.1.: Forward Calculation: starting with time point 0

	Forward Calculation: starting with time point 0 (cntd.)
OJ.epe =	OJ.eps + OJ.d= {(0.06,12), (0.004,13), (0.21,16), (0.014,17), (0.186,20), (0.1,21), (0.006,22), (0.126,24), (0.09,25), (0.006,26), (0.09,28), (0.054,29), (0.054,33)}+ {(1.0,0)}= {(0.06,12), (0.004,13), (0.21,16), (0.014,17), (0.186,20), (0.1,21), (0.006,22), (0.126,24), (0.09,25), (0.006,26), (0.09,28), (0.054,29), (0.054,33)}
AS.eps =	OJ.epe= {(0.06,12), (0.004,13), (0.21,16), (0.014,17), (0.186,20), (0.1,21), (0.006,22), (0.126,24), (0.09,25), (0.006,26), (0.09,28), (0.054,29), (0.054,33)}
AS.epe =	AS.eps + AS.d= {(0.06,12), (0.004,13), (0.21,16), (0.014,17), (0.186,20), (0.1,21), (0.006,22), (0.126,24), (0.09,25), (0.006,26), (0.09,28), (0.054,29),(0.054,33)}+ {(1.0,0)}= {(0.06,12), (0.004,13), (0.21,16), (0.014,17), (0.186,20), (0.1,21), (0.006,22), (0.126,24), (0.09,25), (0.006,26), (0.09,28), (0.054,29), (0.054,33)}
e.eps =	AS.epe= {(0.06,12), (0.004,13), (0.21,16), (0.014,17), (0.186,20), (0.1,21), (0.006,22), (0.126,24), (0.09,25), (0.006,26), (0.09,28), (0.054,29), (0.054,33)}
e.epe =	e.eps + e.d= {(0.06,12), (0.004,13), (0.21,16), (0.014,17), (0.186,20), (0.1,21), (0.006,22), (0.126,24), (0.09,25), (0.006,26), (0.09,28), (0.054,29), (0.054,33)}+ {(0.4,4), (0.6,6)} = {(0.024,16), (0.0016,17), (0.084,20), (0.0056,21),(0.0744,24), (0.04,25), (0.0024,26), (0.0504,28), (0.036,29), (0.0024,30), (0.036,32), (0.0216,33), (0.0216,37), (0.036,18), (0.0024,19), (0.126,22), (0.0084,23), (0.1116,26), (0.06,27), (0.0036,28), (0.0756,30), (0.054,31), (0.0036,32), (0.054,34), (0.0324,35), (0.0324,39)}= {(0.024,16), (0.0016,17), (0.036,18), (0.0024,19), (0.084,20), (0.0056,21), (0.126,22), (0.0084,23), (0.0744,24), (0.04,25), (0.114,26), (0.06,27), (0.054,28), (0.036,29), (0.078,30), (0.054,31), (0.0396,32), (0.0216,33), (0.054,34), (0.0324,35), (0.0216,37), (0.0324,39)}
f.eps =	AS.epe= {(0.06,12), (0.004,13), (0.21,16), (0.014,17), (0.186,20), (0.1,21), (0.006,22), (0.126,24), (0.09,25), (0.006,26), (0.09,28), (0.054,29), (0.054,33)}
f.epe =	f.eps + f.d= {(0.06,12), (0.004,13), (0.21,16), (0.014,17), (0.186,20), (0.1,21), (0.006,22), (0.126,24), (0.09,25), (0.006,26), (0.09,28), (0.054,29), (0.054,33)} + {(0.7,3), (0.3,7)}= {(0.042,15), (0.0028,16), (0.147,19), (0.0098.20), (0.1302,23), (0.07,24), (0.0042,25), (0.0882,27), (0.063,28), (0.0042,29), (0.063,31), (0.0378,32), (0.0378,36), (0.018,19), (0.0012,20), (0.063,23), (0.0042,24), (0.0558,27), (0.03,28), (0.0018.29), (0.0378,31), (0.027,32), (0.0018,33), (0.027,35), (0.0162,36), (0.0162,40)}= {(0.042,15), (0.0028,16), (0.165,19), (0.011,20), (0.1932,23), (0.0742,24), (0.0042,25), (0.144,27), (0.093,28), (0.006.29), (0.1008,31), (0.0648,32), (0.0018,33), (0.027,35), (0.054,36), (0.0162,40)}
AJ.eps =	e.epe $\wedge_{max}$ f.epe= {(0.024,16), (0.0016,17), (0.036,18), (0.0024,19), (0.084,20), (0.0056,21), (0.126,22), (0.0084,23), (0.0744,24), (0.04,25), (0.114,26), (0.06,27), (0.054,28), (0.036,29), (0.078,30), (0.054,31), (0.0396,32), (0.0216,33), (0.054,34), (0.0324,35), (0.0216,37), (0.0324,39)} $\wedge_{max}$ {(0.042,15), (0.0028,16),

Table B.2.: Forward Calculation: starting with time point 0 (cntd.)

Forward Calculation: starting with time point 0 (cntd.)
(0.165,19), (0.011,20), (0.1932,23), (0.0742,24), (0.0042,25), (0.144,27), (0.093,28), (0.006.29), (0.1008,31), (0.0648,32), (0.0018,33), (0.027,35), (0.054,36), (0.0162,40)}= {(0,001008,16), (0,0000672,17), (0,001512,18), (0,0001008,19), (0,003528,20), (0,0002352,21), (0,005292,22), (0,0003528,23), (0,0031248,24)(0,00168,25), (0,004788,26), (0,00252,27), (0,002268,28), (0,001512,29), (0,003276,30), (0,002268,31)(0,0016632,32), (0,0009072,33), (0,002268,34), (0,0013608,35), (0,0009072,37), (0,0013608,39), (0,0000672,16), (0,00000448,17), (0,0001008,18), (0,00000672,19), (0,0002352,20), (0,00001568,21), (0,0003528,22), (0,00002352,23), (0,00020832,24), (0,000112,25), (0,0003192,26), (0,000168,27), (0,0001512,28), (0,0001008,29), (0,0002184,30)(0,0001512,31), (0,00011088,32), (0,00006048,33), (0,0001512,34), (0,00009072,35), (0,00006048,37), (0,00009072,39), (0,00396,19), (0,000264,19), (0,00594,19), (0,000396,19), (0,01386,20), (0,000924,21), (0,02079,22), (0,001386,23), (0,012276,24), (0,0066,25), (0,01881,26), (0,0099,27), (0,00891,28), (0,00594,29), (0,01287,30), (0,00891,31), (0,006534,32), (0,003564,33), (0,00891,34), (0,005346,35), (0,003564,37), (0,005346,39), (0,000264,20), (0,0000176,20), (0,000396,20), (0,0000264,20), (0,000924,20), (0,0000616,21), (0,001386,22), (0,0000924,23), (0,0008184,24), (0,00044,25), (0,001254,26), (0,0066,27), (0,000594,28), (0,000396,29), (0,000858,30), (0,000594,31), (0,0004356,32), (0,0002376,33), (0,000594,34), (0,0003564,35), (0,0002376,37), (0,0003564,39), (0,0046368,23), (0,00030912,23), (0,0069552,23), (0,00046368,23), (0,0162288,23), (0,00108192,23), (0,0243432,23), (0,00162288,23), (0,01437408,24), (0,007728,25), (0,0220248,26), (0,011592,27), (0,0104328,28), (0,0069552,29), (0,0150696,30), (0,0104328,31), (0,00765072,32), (0,00417312,33), (0,0104328,34), (0,00625968,35), (0,00417312,37), (0,00625968,39), (0,0017808,24), (0,00011872,24), (0,0026712,24), (0,00017808,24), (0,0062328,24), (0,00041552,24), (0,0093492,24), (0,00062328,24), (0,00552048,24), (0,002968,25), (0,0084588,26), (0,004452,27), (0,0040068,28), (0,0026712,29), (0,0057876,30), (0,0040068,31), (0,00293832,32), (0,00160272,33), (0,0040068,34), (0,00240408,35), (0,00160272,37), (0,00240408,39), (0,0001008,25), (0,00000672,25), (0,0001512,25), (0,00001008,25), (0,0003528,25), (0,00002352,25), (0,0005292,25), (0,00003528,25), (0,00031248,25), (0,000168,25), (0,0004788,26), (0,000252,27), (0,0002268,28), (0,0001512,29), (0,0003276,30), (0,0002268,31), (0,00016632,32), (0,00009072,33), (0,0002268,34), (0,00013608,35), (0,00009072,37), (0,00013608,39), (0,003456,27), (0,0002304,27), (0,005184,27), (0,0003456,27), (0,012096,27), (0,0008064,27), (0,018144,27), (0,0012096,27), (0,0107136,27), (0,00576,27), (0,016416,27), (0,00864,27), (0,007776,28), (0,005184,29), (0,011232,30), (0,007776,31), (0,0057024,32), (0,0031104,33), (0,007776,34), (0,0046656,35), (0,0031104,37), (0,0046656,39), (0,002232,28), (0,0001488,28), (0,003348,28), (0,0002232,28), (0,007812,28), (0,0005208,28), (0,011718,28), (0,0007812,28), (0,0069192,28), (0,00372,28), (0,010602,28), (0,00558,28), (0,005022,28), (0,003348,29), (0,007254,30), (0,005022,31), (0,0036828,32), (0,0020088,33), (0,005022,34), (0,0030132,35), (0,0020088,37),

Table B.3.: Forward Calculation: starting with time point 0 (cntd.)

Forward Calculation: starting with time point 0 (cntd.)
(0,0030132,39), (0,000144,29), (0,0000096,29), (0,000216,29), (0,0000144,29),(0,000504,29), (0,0000336,29), (0,000756,29), (0,0000504,29), (0,0004464,29), (0,00024,29), (0,000684,29), (0,00036,29), (0,000324,29), (0,000216,29), (0,000468,30), (0,000324,31), (0,0002376,32), (0,0001296,33), (0,000324,34), (0,0001944,35), (0,0001296,37), (0,0001944,39), (0,0024192,31), (0,00016128,31), (0,0036288,31), (0,00024192,31), (0,0084672,31), (0,00056448,31), (0,0127008,31), (0,00084672,31), (0,00749952,31), (0,004032,31), (0,0114912,31), (0,006048,31), (0,0054432,31), (0,0036288,31), (0,0078624,31), (0,0054432,31), (0,00399168,32), (0,00217728,33), (0,0054432,34), (0,00326592,35), (0,00217728,37), (0,00326592,39), (0,0015552,32), (0,00010368,32), (0,0023328,32), (0,00015552,32), (0,0054432,32), (0,00036288,32), (0,0081648,32), (0,00054432,32), (0,00482112,32), (0,002592,32), (0,0073872,32), (0,003888,32), (0,0034992,32), (0,0023328,32), (0,0050544,32), (0,0034992,32), (0,00256608,32), (0,00139968,33), (0,0034992,34), (0,00209952,35), (0,00139968,37), (0,00209952,39), (0,0000432,33), (0,00000288,33), (0,0000648,33), (0,00000432,33), (0,0001512,33), (0,00001008,33), (0,0002268,33), (0,00001512,33), (0,00013392,33), (0,000072,33), (0,0002052,33), (0,000108,33), (0,0000972,33), (0,0000648,33), (0,0001404,33), (0,0000972,33), (0,00007128,33), (0,00003888,33), (0,0000972,34), (0,00005832,35), (0,00003888,37), (0,00005832,39), (0,000648,35), (0,0000432,35), (0,000972,35), (0,0000648,35), (0,002268,35), (0,0001512,35), (0,003402,35), (0,0002268,35), (0,0020088,35), (0,00108,35), (0,003078,35), (0,00162,35), (0,001458,35), (0,000972,35), (0,002106,35), (0,001458,35), (0,0010692,35), (0,0005832,35), (0,001458,35), (0,0008748,35), (0,0005832,37), (0,0008748,39), (0,001296,36), (0,0000864,36), (0,001944,36), (0,0001296,36), (0,004536,36), (0,004536,36), (0,006804,36), (0,0004536,36), (0,0040176,36), (0,00216,36), (0,006156,36), (0,00324,36), (0,002916,36), (0,001944,36), (0,004212,36), (0,002916,36), (0,0021384,36), (0,0011664,36), (0,002916,36), (0,0017496,36), (0,0011664,37), (0,0017496,39), (0,0003888,40), (0,00002592,40), (0,0005832,40), (0,00003888,40), (0,0013608,40), (0,00009072,40), (0,0020412,40), (0,00013608,40), (0,00120528,40), (0,000648,40), (0,0018468,40), (0,000972,40), (0,0008748,40), (0,0005832,40), (0,0012636,40), (0,0008748,40), (0,00064152,40), (0,00034992,40), (0,0008748,40), (0,00052488,40), (0,00034992,40), (0,00052488,40)}= {(0,001008,16), (0,0000672,16), (0,0000672,17), (0,00000448,17), (0,001512,18), (0,0001008,18), (0,0001008,19), (0,00000672,19), (0,00396,19), (0,000264,19), (0,00594,19), (0,000396,19), (0,003528,20), (0,0002352,20), (0,01386,20), (0,000264,20), (0,0000176,20), (0,000396,20), (0,0000264,20), (0,000924,20), (0,0002352,21), (0,00001568,21), (0,000924,21), (0,0000616,21), (0,005292,22), (0,0003528,22), (0,02079,22), (0,001386,22), (0,0003528,23), (0,00002352,23), (0,001386,23), (0,0000924,23), (0,0046368,23), (0,00030912,23), (0,0069552,23), (0,00046368,23), (0,0162288,23)(0,00108192,23), (0,0243432,23), (0,00162288,23), (0,0031248,24), (0,00020832,24), (0,012276,24), (0,0008184,24), (0,01437408,24), (0,0017808,24), (0,00011872,24),

Table B.4.: Forward Calculation: starting with time point 0 (cntd.)

Forward Calculation: starting with time point 0 (cntd.)
(0,0026712,24), (0,00017808,24)(0,0062328,24), (0,00041552,24), (0,0093492,24), (0,00062328,24), (0,00552048,24), (0,00168,25), (0,000112,25), (0,0066,25), (0,00044,25), (0,007728,25), (0,002968,25), (0,0001008,25), (0,00000672,25),(0,0001512,25), (0,00001008,25), (0,0003528,25), (0,00002352,25), (0,0005292,25), (0,00003528,25), (0,00031248,25), (0,000168,25) (0,004788,26), (0,0003192,26), (0,01881,26), (0,001254,26), (0,0220248,26), (0,0084588,26), (0,0004788,26), (0,00252,27), (0,000168,27), (0,0099,27), (0,00066,27), (0,004452,27), (0,000252,27), (0,003456,27), (0,0002304,27), (0,005184,27), (0,0003456,27), (0,012096,27), (0,0008064,27), (0,018144,27), (0,0012096,27), (0,0107136,27)(0,00576,27), (0,016416,27), (0,00864,27), (0,011592,27), (0,002268,28), (0,0001512,28), (0,00891,28), (0,000594,28), (0,0104328,28), (0,0040068,28), (0,0002268,28), (0,007776,28), (0,002232,28), (0,0001488,28), (0,003348,28), (0,0002232,28), (0,007812,28), (0,0005208,28), (0,011718,28), (0,0007812,28)(0,0069192,28), (0,00372,28), (0,010602,28), (0,00558,28), (0,005022,28), (0,001512,29), (0,0001008,29), (0,00594,29), (0,000396,29), (0,0069552,29), (0,0026712,29), (0,0001512,29), (0,005184,29), (0,003348,29), (0,000144,29), (0,0000096,29), (0,000216,29), (0,0000144,29), (0,000504,29), (0,000336,29), (0,000756,29)(0,0000504,29), (0,0004464,29), (0,00024,29), (0,000684,29), (0,00036,29), (0,000324,29), (0,000216,29), (0,003276,30), (0,0002184,30), (0,01287,30), (0,000858,30), (0,0150696,30), (0,0057876,30), (0,0003276,30), (0,011232,30), (0,007254,30), (0,000468,30), (0,002268,31), (0,0001512,31), (0,00891,31), (0,000594,31), (0,0104328,31), (0,0040068,31), (0,0002268,31), (0,007776,31), (0,005022,31), (0,000324,31), (0,0024192,31), (0,00016128,31), (0,0036288,31), (0,00024192,31), (0,0084672,31), (0,00056448,31), (0,0127008,31), (0,00084672,31), (0,00749952,31), (0,004032,31), (0,0114912,31), (0,006048,31), (0,0054432,31)(0,0036288,31), (0,0078624,31), (0,0054432,31), (0,0016632,32), (0,00011088,32), (0,006534,32), (0,0004356,32), (0,00765072,32), (0,00293832,32), (0,00016632,32), (0,0057024,32), (0,0036828,32), (0,00399168,32), (0,0015552,32), (0,00010368,32), (0,0023328,32), (0,00015552,32), (0,00054432,32)(0,00036288,32), (0,0081648,32), (0,00054432,32), (0,00482112,32), (0,002592,32), (0,0073872,32), (0,003888,32)(0,0034992,32), (0,0023328,32), (0,0050544,32), (0,0034992,32), (0,00256608,32), (0,0002376,32), (0,0009072,33), (0,00006048,33), (0,003564,33), (0,0002376,33), (0,00417312,33), (0,00160272,33), (0,00009072,33), (0,0031104,33), (0,0020088,33), (0,00217728,33), (0,00139968,33), (0,0000432,33), (0,00000288,33), (0,0000648,33), (0,00000432,33), (0,0001512,33), (0,00001008,33), (0,0002268,33), (0,00001512,33), (0,00013392,33), (0,000072,33), (0,0002052,33), (0,000108,33), (0,0000972,33), (0,0000648,33), (0,0001404,33), (0,0000972,33), (0,00007128,33), (0,00003888,33), (0,0001296,33), (0,002268,34), (0,0001512,34), (0,00891,34), (0,000594,34), (0,0104328,34), (0,0040068,34), (0,0002268,34), (0,007776,34), (0,005022,34), (0,000324,34), (0,0054432,34), (0,0034992,34), (0,0000972,34), (0,0013608,35), (0,00009072,35), (0,005346,35), (0,0003564,35), (0,00625968,35), (0,00240408,35), (0,00013608,35),

Table B.5.: Forward Calculation: starting with time point 0 (cntd.)

	Forward Calculation: starting with time point 0 (cntd.)
	(0,0046656,35), (0,0030132,35), (0,0001944,35), (0,00326592,35), (0,00209952,35), (0,000648,35), (0,0000432,35), (0,000972,35), (0,0000648,35), (0,002268,35), (0,0001512,35), (0,003402,35), (0,0002268,35), (0,00005832,35), (0,0020088,35), (0,00108,35), (0,003078,35), (0,00162,35), (0,001458,35), (0,000972,35), (0,002106,35), (0,001458,35), (0,0010692,35), (0,0005832,35), (0,001458,35), (0,0008748,35), (0,001296,36), (0,0000864,36), (0,001944,36), (0,0001296,36), (0,004536,36), (0,004536,36), (0,006804,36), (0,004212,36), (0,002916,36), (0,0021384,36), (0,0011664,36), (0,002916,36), (0,0017496,36), (0,0004536,36), (0,0040176,36), (0,00216,36), (0,006156,36), (0,00324,36), (0,002916,36), (0,001944,36), (0,0009072,37), (0,00006048,37), (0,003564,37), (0,0002376,37), (0,00417312,37), (0,00160272,37), (0,00009072,37), (0,0020088,37), (0,0001296,37), (0,00217728,37), (0,00139968,37), (0,00003888,37), (0,0005832,37), (0,0011664,37), (0,0031104,37), (0,0013608,39), (0,00009072,39), (0,005346,39), (0,0003564,39), (0,00625968,39), (0,00240408,39), (0,00013608,39), (0,0046656,39), (0,0030132,39), (0,0001944,39), (0,00326592,39), (0,00209952,39), (0,0008748,39), (0,0017496,39), (0,00005832,39), (0,0003888,40), (0,00002592,40), (0,0005832,40), (0,00003888,40), (0,0013608,40), (0,00009072,40), (0,0020412,40), (0,00013608,40)(0,00120528,40), (0,000648,40), (0,0018468,40), (0,000972,40), (0,0008748,40), (0,0005832,40), (0,0012636,40), (0,0008748,40), (0,00064152,40), (0,00034992,40), (0,0008748,40), (0,00052488,40), (0,00034992,40), (0,00052488,40)}= {(0,0010752,16), (0,00007168,17), (0,0016128,18), (0,01066752,19), (0,0192512,20), (0,00123648,21), (0,0278208,22), (0,05749632,23), (0,05769168,24), (0,02121808,25), (0,0561336,26), (0,1125456,27), (0,0929928,28), (0,0302568,29), (0,0573612,30), (0,12019032,31), (0,08088192,32), (0,02100888,33), (0,0487512,34), (0,05479272,35), (0,0553176,36), (0,02125008,37), (0,03187512,39), (0,0162,40)}
AJ.epe =	AJ.eps + AJ.d= {(0,0010752,16), (0,00007168,17), (0,0016128,18), (0,01066752,19), (0,0192512,20), (0,00123648,21), (0,0278208,22), (0,05749632,23), (0,05769168,24), (0,02121808,25), (0,0561336,26), (0,1125456,27), (0,0929928,28), (0,0302568,29), (0,0573612,30), (0,12019032,31), (0,08088192,32), (0,02100888,33), (0,0487512,34), (0,05479272,35), (0,0553176,36), (0,02125008,37), (0,03187512,39), (0,0162,40)}+ {(1,0)}= {(0,0010752,16), (0,00007168,17), (0,0016128,18), (0,01066752,19), (0,0192512,20), (0,00123648,21), (0,0278208,22), (0,05749632,23), (0,05769168,24), (0,02121808,25), (0,0561336,26), (0,1125456,27), (0,0929928,28), (0,0302568,29), (0,0573612,30), (0,12019032,31), (0,08088192,32), (0,02100888,33), (0,0487512,34), (0,05479272,35), (0,0553176,36), (0,02125008,37), (0,03187512,39), (0,0162,40)}
j.eps =	AJ.eps = {(0,0010752,16), (0,00007168,17), (0,0016128,18), (0,01066752,19), (0,0192512,20), (0,00123648,21), (0,0278208,22), (0,05749632,23), (0,05769168,24), (0,02121808,25), (0,0561336,26), (0,1125456,27),

Table B.6.: Forward Calculation: starting with time point 0 (cntd.)

	Forward Calculation: starting with time point 0 (cntd.)
	(0,0929928,28), (0,0302568,29), (0,0573612,30), (0,12019032,31), (0,08088192,32), (0,02100888,33), (0,0487512,34), (0,05479272,35), (0,0553176,36), (0,02125008,37), (0,03187512,39), (0,0162,40)}
j.epe =	j.eps + j.d = {(0,0010752,16), (0,00007168,17), (0,0016128,18), (0,01066752,19),(0,0192512,20), (0,00123648,21), (0,0278208,22), (0,05749632,23), (0,05769168,24), (0,02121808,25), (0,0561336,26), (0,1125456,27), (0,0929928,28), (0,0302568,29), (0,0573612,30), (0,12019032,31), (0,08088192,32), (0,02100888,33), (0,0487512,34), (0,05479272,35), (0,0553176,36), (0,02125008,37), (0,03187512,39), (0,0162,40)} + {(1.0,5)}= {(0,0010752,21), (0,00007168,22), (0,0016128,23), (0,01066752,24), (0,0192512,25), (0,00123648,26), (0,0278208,27), (0,05749632,28), (0,05769168,29), (0,02121808,30), (0,0561336,31), (0,1125456,32), (0,0929928,33), (0,0302568,34), (0,0573612,35), (0,12019032,36), (0,08088192,37), (0,02100888,38), (0,0487512,39), (0,05479272,40), (0,0553176,41), (0,02125008,42), (0,03187512,44), (0,0162,45)}
End.eps =	j.epe= {(0,0010752,21), (0,00007168,22), (0,0016128,23), (0,01066752,24), (0,0192512,25), (0,00123648,26), (0,0278208,27), (0,05749632,28), (0,05769168,29), (0,02121808,30), (0,0561336,31), (0,1125456,32), (0,0929928,33), (0,0302568,34), (0,0573612,35), (0,12019032,36), (0,08088192,37), (0,02100888,38), (0,0487512,39), (0,05479272,40), (0,0553176,41), (0,02125008,42), (0,03187512,44), (0,0162,45)}
End.epe =	End.eps + End.d = {(0,0010752,21), (0,00007168,22), (0,0016128,23), (0,01066752,24), (0,0192512,25), (0,00123648,26), (0,0278208,27), (0,05749632,28), (0,05769168,29), (0,02121808,30), (0,0561336,31), (0,1125456,32), (0,0929928,33), (0,0302568,34), (0,0573612,35), (0,12019032,36), (0,08088192,37), (0,02100888,38), (0,0487512,39), (0,05479272,40), (0,0553176,41), (0,02125008,42), (0,03187512,44), (0,0162,45)} + {(1.0,0)}= {(0,0010752,21), (0,00007168,22), (0,0016128,23), (0,01066752,24), (0,0192512,25), (0,00123648,26), (0,0278208,27), (0,05749632,28), (0,05769168,29), (0,02121808,30), (0,0561336,31), (0,1125456,32), (0,0929928,33), (0,0302568,34), (0,0573612,35), (0,12019032,36), (0,08088192,37), (0,02100888,38), (0,0487512,39), (0,05479272,40), (0,0553176,41), (0,02125008,42), (0,03187512,44), (0,0162,45)}

Table B.7.: Forward Calculation: starting with time point 0 (cntd.)

Backward Calculation: starting with deadline= 50	
End.lae =	{ 1.0, 50)}
End.las =	End.lae - End.d = { 1.0, 50)}-{ 1.0, 0)} = { 1.0, 50)}
j.lae =	End.las ={ 1.0, 50)}
j.las =	j.lae - j.d ={ 1.0, 50)} - {(1.0, 5)} = {(1.0,45)}
AJ.lae =	j.las ={(1.0,45)}
AJ.las =	AJ.lae - AJ.d= {(1.0,45)} - {(1.0,0)}= {(1.0,45)}
e.ale =	AJ.las= {(1.0,45)}
e.las =	e.lae - e.d= {(1.0,45)} -{((0.4,4), (0.6,6))}= {(0.4,41), (0.6,39)}
f.ale =	AJ.las ={(1.0,45)}
f.las =	f.lae - f.d= {(1.0,45)} -{(0.7,3), (0.3,7)}= {(0.7,42), (0.3,38)}
AS.lae =	e.las $\wedge_{min}$ f.las= {(0.4,41), (0.6,39)}$\wedge_{min}$ {(0.7,42), (0.3,38)}= {(0.28,41), (0.12,38), (0.42,39), (0.18,38)}= {(0.3,38), (0.42,39), (0.28,41)}
AS.las =	AS.lae - AS.d= {(0.3,38), (0.42,39), (0.28,41)}-{(1.0,0)}= {(0.3,38), (0.42,39), (0.28,41)}
OJ.lae =	AS.las ={(0.3,38), (0.42,39), (0.28,41)}
OJ.las =	AOJ.lae - OJ.d ={(0.3,38), (0.42,39), (0.28,41)} - {(1.0,0)}= {(0.3,38), (0.42,39), (0.28,41)}
c.lae =	OJ.las ={(0.3,38), (0.42,39), (0.28,41)}
c.las =	c.lae - c.d= {(0.3,38), (0.42,39), (0.28,41)} - {(0.1,8), (0.9,15)}= {(0.27,23), (0.378,24), (0.252,26), (0.03,30), (0.042,31), (0.028,33)}
d.lae =	OJ.las ={(0.3,38), (0.42,39), (0.28,41)}
d.las =	d.lae - d.d= {(0.3,38), (0.42,39), (0.28,41)} - {(1.0,7)}= {(0.3,31), (0.42,32), (0.28,34)}

Table B.8.: Backward Calculation: starting with deadline= 50

	Backward Calculation: starting with deadline= 50 (cntd.)
OS.lae =	(c.las*0.4)$\vee$ (d.las*0.6)= {(0.27,23), (0.378,24), (0.252,26), (0.03,30), (0.042,31), (0.028,33)}*0.4 $\vee$ {(0.3,31), (0.42,32), (0.28,34)}*0.6={(0.108,23), (0.1512,24), (0.1008,26), (0.012,30), (0.0168,31), (0.0112,33)} $\vee$ {(0.18,31), (0.252,32), (0.168,34)} ={(0.108,23), (0.1512,24), (0.1008,26), (0.012,30), (0.18,31), (0.0168,31), (0.252,32), (0.0112,33), (0.168,34)}={(0.108,23), (0.1512,24), (0.1008,26), (0.012,30), (0.1968,31), (0.252,32), (0.0112,33), (0.168,34)}
OS.las =	OS.lae - OS.d={(0.108,23), (0.1512,24), (0.1008,26), (0.012,30), (0.1968,31), (0.252,32), (0.0112,33), (0.168,34)}- {(1.0,0)}={(0.108,23), (0.1512,24), (0.1008,26), (0.012,30), (0.1968,31), (0.252,32), (0.0112,33), (0.168,34)}
b.lae =	OS.las={(0.108,23), (0.1512,24), (0.1008,26), (0.012,30), (0.1968,31), (0.252,32), (0.0112,33), (0.168,34)}
b.las =	b.lae - b.d={(0.108,23), (0.1512,24), (0.1008,26), (0.012,30), (0.1968,31), (0.252,32), (0.0112,33), (0.168,34)} - {(0.5,4), (0.5,8)}= {(0,054,15), (0,0756,16), (0,0504,18), (0,054,19), (0,0756,20), (0,006,22), (0,0504,22), (0,0984,23), (0,126,24), (0,0056,25), (0,084,26), (0,006,26), (0,0984,27), (0,126,28), (0,0056,29), (0,084,30)} ={(0,054,15), (0,0756,16), (0,0504,18), (0,054,19), (0,0756,20), (0,0564,22), (0,0984,23), (0,126,24), (0,0056,25), (0,09,26), (0,0984,27), (0,126,28), (0,0056,29), (0,084,30)}
a.lae =	b.las= {(0,054,15), (0,0756,16), (0,0504,18), (0,054,19), (0,0756,20), (0,0564,22), (0,0984,23), 0,126,24), (0,0056,25), (0,09,26), (0,0984,27), (0,126,28), (0,0056,29), (0,084,30)}
a.las =	a.lae - a.d= {(0,054,15), (0,0756,16), (0,0504,18), (0,054,19), (0,0756,20), (0,0564,22), (0,0984,23), (0,126,24), (0,0056,25), (0,09,26), (0,0984,27), (0,126,28), (0,0056,29), (0,084,30)} - {(0.2,1), (0.5,5), (0.3,10)}= {(0,0108,14), (0,01512,15), (0,01008,17), (0,0108,18), (0,01512,19), (0,01128,21), (0,01968,22), (0,0252,23), (0,00112,24), (0,018,25), (0,01968,26), (0,0252,27), (0,00112,28), (0,0168,29), (0,027,10), (0,0378,11), (0,0252,13), (0,027,14), (0,0378,15), (0,0282,17), (0,0492,18), (0,063,19), (0,0028,20), (0,045,21), (0,0492,22), (0,063,23), (0,0028,24), (0,042,25), (0,0162,5), (0,02268,6), (0,01512,8), (0,0162,9), (0,02268,10), (0,01692,12), (0,02952,13), (0,0378,14), (0,00168,15), (0,027,16), (0,02952,17), (0,0378,18), (0,00168,19), (0,0252,20)}={(0,0162,5), (0,02268,6), (0,01512,8), (0,0162,9), (0,027,10), (0,02268,10), (0,0378,11), (0,01692,12), (0,0252,13), (0,02952,13), (0,027,14), (0,0108,14), (0,0378,14), (0,0378,15), (0,01512,15), (0,00168,15), (0,027,16), (0,0282,17), (0,01008,17), (0,02952,17), (0,0108,18), (0,0492,18), (0,0378,18), (0,01512,19), (0,063,19), (0,00168,19), (0,0028,20), (0,0252,20), (0,01128,21), (0,045,21), (0,01968,22), (0,0492,22), (0,0252,23), (0,063,23), (0,00112,24), (0,0028,24), (0,018,25), (0,042,25), (0,01968,26), (0,0252,27), (0,00112,28), (0,0168,29)} ={(0,0162,5), (0,02268,6), (0,01512,8), (0,0162,9), (0,04968,10), (0,0378,11), (0,01692,12), (0,05472,13), (0,0756,14), (0,0546,15), (0,027,16), (0,0678,17), (0,0978,18), (0,0798,19), (0,028,20), (0,05628,21), (0,06888,22), (0,0882,23), (0,00392,24), (0,06,25), (0,01968,26), (0,0252,27), (0,00112,28), (0,0168,29)}

Table B.9.: Backward Calculation: starting with deadline= 50 (cntd.)

Backward Calculation: starting with deadline= 50 (cntd.)	
Start.lae =	a.las= {(0,0162,5), (0,02268,6), (0,01512,8), (0,0162,9), (0,04968,10), (0,0378,11), (0,01692,12), (0,05472,13), (0,0756,14), (0,0546,15), (0,027,16), (0,0678,17), (0,0978,18), (0,0798,19), (0,028,20), (0,05628,21), (0,06888,22), (0,0882,23), (0,00392,24), (0,06,25), (0,01968,26), (0,0252,27), (0,00112,28), (0,0168,29)}
Start.las =	Start.lae-Start.d= {(0,0162,5), (0,02268,6), (0,01512,8), (0,0162,9), (0,04968,10), (0,0378,11), (0,01692,12), (0,05472,13), (0,0756,14), (0,0546,15), (0,027,16), (0,0678,17), (0,0978,18), (0,0798,19), (0,028,20), (0,05628,21), (0,06888,22), (0,0882,23), (0,00392,24), (0,06,25), (0,01968,26), (0,0252,27), (0,00112,28), (0,0168,29)}

Table B.10.: Backward Calculation: starting with deadline— 50 (cntd.)

Bibliography

[1] http://www.w3.org/TR/soap/.

[2] http://uddi.xml.org/.

[3] *http : //publib.boulder.ibm.com/infocenter/wasinfo/v6r0/index.jsp?topic = /com.ibm.websphere.express.doc/info/exp/ae/twsu_ep.html.*

[4] http://udditest.sap.com/webdynpro/dispatcher/sap.com/tc uddi webui wdp/UDDIWebUI.

[5] http://www.ebxml.org/.

[6] http://www.microsoft.com/germany/biztalk/default.mspx.

[7] http://unece.org/cefact/.

[8] http://www.oasis-open.org/committees/uddi-spec/doc/spec/v3/uddi-v3.0.2-20041019.htm.

[9] http://dev2dev.bea.com/webservices/BPEL4WS.html.

[10] Active endpoints. http://www.activevos.com/.

[11] The european project ws-diamond. http://wsdiamond.di.unito.it/.

[12] The north american industry classification system. http://www.census.gov/epcd/www/naics.html.

[13] Oracle bpel designer. http://www.oracle.com/technology/products/ias/bpel/index.html.

[14] United nations standard product and services classification (unspsc) code organization. http://www.unspsc.org/.

[15] The woekflow management coalition. http://www.wfmc.org/.

[16] Xml schema ver. 1.1. http://www.w3.org/XML/Schema.

[17] Ccitt recomendation z.120: Message sequence chart (msc92). Technical report, CCITT, Geneva, 1992.

[18] Itu-ts recomendation z.120: Message sequence chart 1996 (msc96). Technical report, ITU-TS, Geneva, 1996.

[19] Interoperability abstract specification, wfmc-tc-1012. Technical report, Workflow Management Coalition, 1999.

[20] Terminology and glossary, wfmc-tc-1011. Technical report, The Workflow Management Coalition, 1999.

[21] Workflow process definition interface- xml process definition language. Technical Report WFMC-TC-1025, Workflow Management Coalition, 2002.

[22] Workflow process definition interface Ű xml process definition language version 1.15. Technical Report WFMC-TC-1025, Workflow Management Coalition, $http://www.wfmc.org/standards/documents/TC - 1025/_xpdl/_2/_2005 - 10 - 03.pdf$, October 2005.

[23] Bpmn specification, version 1.1. Technical Report formal/2008-01-17, Object Management Group, Business Process Management Initiative, http://www.omg.org/spec/BPMN/1.1/PDF, February 2008.

[24] A. Abecker, A. Bernardi, H. Maus, M. Sintek, and C. Wenzel. Information supply for business processes: coupling workflow with document analysis and information retrieval. *Knowledge-Based Systems*, 13(5):271–284, 2000.

[25] S. Abramsky. Observation equivalence as a testing equivalence. *Theoretical Computer Science*, 53:225–241, 1987.

[26] N.R. Adam, V. Atluri, and W.K. Huang. Modeling and analysis of workflows using petri nets. *Journal of Intelligent Information Systems*, 10:131–158, 1998.

[27] C. Adams and S. Boeyen. Uddi and wsdl extensions for web service: a security framework. In *Proc. of the ACM workshop on XML security*, 2002.

[28] C.C. Albrecht. How clean is the future of soap? *Communications of the ACM*, 47(2):66–68, 2004.

[29] J.F. Allen. Maintaining knowledge about temporal intervals. *Communications of the ACM*, 26(11):832–843, 1983.

[30] R. Alur, C. Courcoubetis, and T.A. Henzinger. The observational power of clocks. In *Proc. of the Concurrency Theory*, 1994.

[31] A. DŠ Ambrogio. A model-driven wsdl extension for describing the qos ofweb services. In *Proc. of the IEEE International Conference on Web Services*, 2006.

[32] T. Andrews and et al. Business process execution language for web services (bpel4ws), ver. 1.1. BEA, IBM, Microsoft, SAP, Siebel Systems, 2003.

[33] N. Aoumeur and G. Saake. Dynamically evolving concurrent information systems specification and validation: a component-based petri nets proposal. *Data & Knowledge Engineering*, 50(2):117–173, 2004.

[34] A. Arkin. Business process modeling language (bpml), ver. 1.0. Technical report, eBPML, 2002.

[35] V. Atluri and W.K. Huang. A petri net based safety analysis of workflow authorization models. *Journal of Computer Security*, 8(2-3):209–240, 2000.

[36] J.C.M. Baeten and J.A. Bergstra. Ready-trace semantics for concrete process algebra with the priority operator. *The Computer Journa*, 30(6):498 – 506, 1987.

[37] J.C.M. Baeten and R.J. van Glabbeek. Another look at abstraction in process algebra (extended abstract). In *Proc. of the 14th International Colloquium, on Automata, Languages and Programming, Lecture Notes In Computer Science, Volume 267, pages 84-94*, 1987.

[38] J.C.M. Baeten and W.P. Weijland. *Process algebra, Volume 18 of Cambridge tracts in theoretical computer science*. Cambridge University Press, 1990.

[39] S. Bajaj, D. Box, D. Chappell, F. Curbera, G. Daniels, P. Hallam-Baker, M. Hondo, C. Kaler, D. Langworthy, A. Nadalin, N. Nagaratnam, H. Prafullchandra, C. von Riegen, D. Roth, J. Schlimmer, C. Sharp, J. Shewchuk, A. Vedamuthu, U. Yalçinalp, and D. Orchard. Web services policy framework (ws-policy). Technical report, BEA Systems, IBM, Microsoft, SAP, Sonic Software, VeriSign, 2006.

[40] G. BALBO, S. DONATELLI, and G. FRANCESCHINIS. Understanding parallel program behavior through petri net models. *Journal of parallel and distributed computing*, 15(3):171–187, 1992.

[41] N.S. Barghouti and G.E. Kaiser. Concurrency control in advanced database applications. *ACM Computing Surveys (CSUR)*, 23(3):269–317, 1991.

[42] A. Barros, M. Dumas, and P. Oaks. A critical overview of the web services choreography description language(ws-cdl). Technical report, Business Process Trends, 2005.

[43] P.A. Barros, M. Dumas, and P. Oaks. Standards for web service choreography and orchestration: Status and perspectives. In *BPM 2005 Work- shops, LNCS 3812*, 2005.

[44] T. Basten. Branching bisimilarity is an equivalence indeed! *Information Processing Letters*, 58(3):141–147, 1996.

[45] T. Basten. *In Terms of Nets: System Design with Petri Nets and Process Algebra*. PhD thesis, TU Eindhoven, 1998.

[46] T. Basten and W.M.P. Van der Aalst. Inheritance of behavior. *Journal of Logic and Algebraic Programming*, 47(2):47–145, 2001.

[47] T. Basten and W.M.P. van der Aalst. Inheritance of behavior. *Journal of Logic and Algebraic Programming*, 47(2):47–145, 2001.

[48] B. Benatallah, F. Casati, J. Ponge, and F. Toumani. On temporal abstractions of web service protocols. In *Proc. of CAiSE Forum*, 2005.

[49] B. Benatallah, Q.Z. Sheng, and M. Dumas M. The self-serv environment for web services composition. *Internet Computing*, 7(1):40–48, 2003.

[50] N. Berge, M. Samaan, G. Juanole, and Y. Atamna. Methodology for lan modeling and analysis using petri nets basedmodels. In *Proc. of the Second International Workshop on Modeling, Analysis, and Simulation of Computer and Telecommunication Systems (MASCOTS 94)*, 1994.

[51] J.A. Bergstra and J.W. Klop. Algebra of communicating processes with abstraction. *Comput. Sci.*, 37:77–121, 1985.

[52] J.A. Bergstra, J.W. Klop, and E.R. Olderrog. Readies and failures in the algebra of communicating processes. *SIAM Journal on Computing*, 17(6):1134 – 1177, 1988.

[53] M. Bernauer, G. Kappel, and G. Kramler. Comparing wsdl-based and ebxml-based approaches for b2b protocol specification. In *Proc. of the international conference on service-oriented computing*, 2003.

[54] P.A. Bernstein, D.W. Shipman, and W.S. Wong. Formal aspects of serializability in database concurrency control. *IEEE Transactions on Software Engineering*, SE-5(3):203–216, 1979.

[55] B. Bloom. Structural operational semantics for weak bisimulations. *Theoretical Computer Science*, 146:25–68, 1995.

[56] B. Bloom, S. Istrail, and A.R. Meyer. Bisimulation cant be traced. *Journal of the ACM*, 42(1):232–268, 1995.

[57] S.L. Bloom and D.R. Troeger. Logical characterization of observation equivalence. *Theoretical Computer Science*, 35(1):43–53, 1985.

[58] T. Bolognesi and S.A. Smolka. Fundamental results for the verification of observational equivalence: A survey. In *Proc. of the IFIP WG6.1 Seventh International Conference on Protocol Specification, Testing and Verification VII*, 1987.

[59] M. Boreale and R. De Nicola. Testing equivalence for mobile processes. *Information and Computation*, 120(2):279 Ű303, 1995.

[60] M. Boreale, R. De Nicola, and R. Pugliese. Trace and testing equivalence on asynchronous processes. *Information and Computation*, 172(2):139–164, 2002.

[61] S. Bowers and B. Ludaescher. A calculus for propagating semantic annotations through scientific workflow queries. In *Proc. of the 11th International Conference on Current Trends in Database Technology (EDBT 06)*, 2006.

[62] D. Box and F. Curbera (Eds). Web services addressing (ws-addressing). Technical report, BEA, IBM and Microsoft, 2003.

[63] M.A. Bragen. Go with the flow. *PC Magazine*, pages 253–302, 19994.

[64] S.D. Brookes. On the relationship of ccs and csp. In *Proc. of the 10th Colloquium on Automata, Languages and Programming*, 1983.

[65] S.D. Brookes, C.A.R. Hoare, and A.W. Roscoe. A theory of communicating sequential processes. *Journal of the ACM*, 31(3):560–599, 1984.

[66] S.D. Brookes and A.W. Roscoe. *An Improved Failures Model for Communicating Processe*, volume Volume 197 of *LNCS*, pages 281–305. Springer-Verlag, London, UK, 1985.

[67] S.D. Brookes and W.C. Rounds. Behavioural equivalence relations induced by programming logics. In *Proc. of the 10th Colloquium on Automata, Languages and Programming*, 1983.

[68] G. Bruzzone, M. Caccia, P. Coletta, and G. Veruggio. Execution control of robotic tasks: estimators representation. In *Proc. of the IEEE International Conference on Robotics and Automation*, 2002.

[69] I. Budinska, V. Oravec, E. Gatial, M. Laclavik, M. Seleng, Z. Balogh, B. Frankovic, R. Forgac, I. Mokris, and L. Hluchy. Raport - a knowledge support system for administrative workflow processes. In *Proc. of the Seventh International Conference on Application of Concurrency to System Design*, 2007.

[70] D. Burdett and N. Kavantzas. Ws choreography model overview. Technical report, W3C, 2004.

[71] F. Casati and A. Discenza. Supporting workflow cooperation within and across organizations. In *Proc. of the 2000 ACM symposium on Applied computing - Volume 1*, 2000.

[72] S. Ceri, E. Di Nitro, A. Discenza, A. Fuggetta, and G. Valetto. Derpa: a generic distributed eventbased reactive processing architecture. Technical report, CEFRIEL, Milano, Italy, 1998.

[73] A.T. Chamillard and L.A. Clarke. Improving the accuracy of petri net-based analysis of concurrent programs. In *Proc. of the international symposium on Software testing and analysis (ACM SIGSOFT)*, 1996.

[74] I. Chebbi, S. Dustdar, and S. Tata. The view-based approach to dynamic interorganizational workflow cooperation. *Data and Knowledge Engineering*, 56(2):139–173, 2006.

[75] S.W. Chen, C.Y. Fang, and K.E. Chang. Neural simulation of petri nets. *Parallel Computing*, 25(2):183–207, 1999.

[76] F. Cherief and P.H. Schnoebelen. τ-bisimulations and full abstraction for refinement of actions. *Information Processing Letters*, 40(4):219–222, 1991.

[77] R. Chinnici, J.J. Moreau, A. Ryman, and S. Weerawarana. Web services description language (wsdl) version 2.0 part 1: Core language. Technical report, The World Wide Web Consortium, 2007.

[78] D.K.W. Chiu, S.C. Cheung, K. Karlapalem, Q. Li, and S. Till. Workflow view driven cross-organizational interoperability in a web-service environment. In *Proc. of the Web Services, E-Business, and the Semantic Web, CAiSE 2002 International Workshop*, 2002.

[79] E. Christensen, F. Curbera, G. Meredith, and S. Weerawarana. The web services description language wsdl. http://www-4.ibm.com/software/solutions/webservices/resources.html, 2001.

[80] N.K. Cicekli and I. Cicekli. Formalizing the specification and execution of workflows using the event calculus. *Information Sciences*, 176(15):2227–2267, 2006.

[81] N.K. Cicekli and Y. Yildirim. Formalizing workflows using the event calculus. In *Proc. of the 11th International Conference on Database and Expert Systems Applications (DEXA 00)*, 2000.

[82] J. Clark and S. DeRose. Xml path language (xpath. Technical report, The World Wide Web Consortium, 1999.

[83] R. Cleaveland and M.C.B. Hennessy. Testing equivalence as a bisimulation equivalence. In *Proc. of the Workshop on Automatic Verification Methods for Finite-State Systems*, 1989.

[84] J. Colgrave and K. Januszewski. Using wsdl in a uddi registry, version 2.0. 2. Technical report, OASIS, 2004.

[85] R.S. Cost, Y. Chen, T.W. Finin, Y. Labrou, and Y. Peng. Using colored petri nets for conversation modeling. In *Issues in Agent Communication*, 2000.

[86] W.D. Cottrell. Simplified program evaluation and review technique (pert). *Journal Of Construction Engineering and Management*, 125(1):16–22, 1999.

[87] N.P. Dalal, M. Kamath, W.J. Kolarik, and E. Sivaraman. Toward an integrated framework for modeling enterprise processes. *Communications of the ACM*, 47(3):83 – 87, 2004.

[88] P. Darondeau. An enlarged definition and complete axiomatization of observational congruence of finite processes. In *Proc. of the 5th Colloquium on International Symposium on Programming*, 1982.

[89] P.H. Darondeau and P. Degano. About semantic action refinement. *Fundamenta Informaticae*, 14(2):221–234, 1991.

[90] G. Decker, H. Overdick, and J.M. Zaha. On the suitability of ws-cdl for choreography modeling. In *Proc. of the Methoden, Konzepte und Technologien fuer die Entwicklung von dienstebasierten Informationssystemen (EMISA 06)*, 2006.

[91] J. Dehnert and P. Rittgen. Relaxed soundness of business processes. In *Proc. of the 13th International Conference on Advanced Information Systems Engineering (CAiSE)*, 2001.

[92] I. Demongodin and N.T. Koussoulas. Differential petri nets: representing continuous systems in adiscrete-event world. *IEEE Transactions on Automatic Control*, 43(4):573–579, 1998.

[93] Y. Deng, S.K. Chang, J.C. A. de Figueired, and A. Perkusich. Integrating software engineering methods and petri nets for the specification and prototyping of complex information systems. In *Proc. of the 14th International Conference on Application and Theory of Petri Nets*, 1993.

[94] W.M.P. Van der Aalst. Verification of workflow nets. In *Proc. of the 18th International Conference on Application and Theory of Petri Nets*, 1997.

[95] W.M.P. Van der Aalst. The application of petri nets to workflow management. *The Journal of Circuits, Systems and Computers*, 8:21–66, 1998.

[96] W.M.P. Van der Aalst. The application of petri nets toworkflow management. *The Journal of Circuits, Systems and Computers*, 8(1):21Ű66, 1998.

[97] W.M.P. Van der Aalst. Modeling and analyzing interorganizationalworkflows. In *Proc. of the International Conference on Application of Concurrency to System Design (CSDŠ98)*, 1998.

[98] W.M.P. Van der Aalst. Interorganizational workflows: An approach based on message sequence charts and petri nets. *Systems Analysis - Modelling - Simulation*, 34(3):335–367, 1999.

[99] W.M.P. Van der Aalst. Woflan: a petri-net-based workflow analyzer. *Systems Analysis Modelling Simulation*, 35(3):345–357, 1999.

[100] W.M.P. Van der Aalst. Inheritance of interorganizational workflows: How to agree to disagree without loosing control? *Information Technology and Management*, 4(4):345 – 389, 2003.

[101] W.M.P. Van der Aalst and T. Basten. Inheritance of workflows: an approach to tackling problems related to change. *Theoretical Computer Science*, 270(1-2):125 – 203, 2002.

[102] R.M. Dijkman and M. Dumas. Service-oriented design: A multi-viewpoint approach. *Int. J. Cooperative Inf. Syst.*, 13(4):337Ű368, 2004.

[103] A. Discenza. Filtering events in a distributed architecture. Technical report, Dipartimento di Elettronica e Informazione, Politecnico di Milano, 1998.

[104] J. Eder and W. Gruber. A meta model for structured workflows supporting workflow transformations. In *In Proc. of the 6th East European Conference on the Advances in Databases and Information Systems (ADBIS 2002)*, 2002.

[105] J. Eder, W. Gruber, and E. Panagos. Temporal modeling of workflows with conditional execution paths. In *Proc. of the 11th International Conference on Database and Expert Systems Applications*, 2000.

[106] J. Eder and H.Pichler. Duration histograms for workflow systems. In *Proc. of the IFIP TC8 / WG8.1 Working Conference on Engineering Information Systems in the Internet Context*, 2002.

[107] J. Eder, M. Lehmann, and A. Tahamtan. Choreographies as federations of choreographies and orchestrations. In *Proc. of International Workshop on Conceptual Modeling of Service-Oriented Software Systems*, 2006.

[108] J. Eder, M. Lehmann, and A. Tahamtan. Conformance test of federated choreographies. In *Proc. of the 3rd International Conference on Interoperability for Enterprise Software and Applications*, 2007.

[109] J. Eder and E. Panagos. *WfMC WorkFlow Handbook 2001*, chapter Managing Time in Workflow Systems. J. Wiley & Sons, 2001.

[110] J. Eder, E. Panagos, and M. Rabinovich. Time constraints in workflow systems. In *Proc. of the 11th International Conference on Advanced Information Systems Engineering (CAiSE)*, 1999.

[111] J. Eder, H. Pichler, and A. Tahamtan. Probabilistic time management of choreographies. In *Proc. of the 1st International Workshop on QoS in Self-healing Web Services in*

conjunction with BPM 2008 6th International Conference on Business Process Management, 2008.

[112] J. Eder, H. Pichler, and S. Vielgut. Avoidance of deadline-violations for inter-organizational business processes. In *Proc. of the 7th International Baltic Conference on Databases and Information Systems*, 2006.

[113] J. Eder, H. Pozewaunig, and W. Liebhart. epert: Extending pert for workflow management systems. In *Proc. of the First East-European Symposium on Advances in Database and Information Systems*, 1997.

[114] J. Eder and A. Tahamtan. Temporal conformance of federated choreographies. In *Proc. of the 19th International Conference on Database and Expert Systems Applications*, 2008.

[115] J. Eder and A. Tahamtan. Temporal consistency of view based interorganizational workflows. In *Proc. of the 2nd International United Information Systems Conference*, 2008.

[116] R. Elfwing, U. Paulsson, and L. Lundberg. Performance of soap in web service environment compared to corba. In *Proc. of the Ninth Asia-Pacific Software Engineering Conference*, 2002.

[117] J. Eloranta. Minimizing the number of transitions with respect to observation equivalence. *BIT*, 31(4):576–590, 1991.

[118] J. Engelfriet. Determinacy arrow right (observation equivalence = trace equivalence). *Theoretical Computer Science*, 36(1):21–25, 1985.

[119] R. ESSER. *An Object Oriented Petri Net Approach to Embedded System Design*. PhD thesis, ETH Zuerich, 1996.

[120] G.L. Ferrari, U. Montanari, and P. Quaglia. The weak late pi-calculus semantics as observation equivalence. In *Proc. of the 6th International Conference on Concurrency Theory*, 1995.

[121] M.J. Fischer and R.E. Ladner. Propositional dynamic logic of regular programs. *Journal of Computer and System Sciences*, 18:194–211, 1979.

[122] H. Foster, S. Uchitel, J. Magee, and J. Kramer. Model-based verification of web service compositions. In *Proc. of 18th IEEE International Conference on Automated Software Engineering*, 2003.

[123] H. Foster, S. Uchitel, J. Magee, and J. Kramer. Model-based verification of web service compositions. In *Proc. of the 18th IEEE International conference on Automated Software Engineering*, 2003.

[124] H. Foster, S. Uchitel, J. Magee, and J. Kramer. Compatibility verification for web service choreography. In *Proc. of IEEE International Conference on Web Services*, 2004.

[125] G. Franceschinis S. Haddad G. Chiola, C. Dutheillet. Stochastic well-formed colored nets and symmetric modelingapplications. *IEEE Transactions on Computers*, 42(11):1343–1360, 1993.

[126] H. Garcia-Molina and K. Salem. Sagas. In *Proc. of the ACM special interest group on management of data annual conference*, 1987.

[127] S. Gatziu and K.R. Dittrich. Detecting composite events in active database systems using petrinets. In *Proc. of the Fourth International Workshop on Research Issues in Data Engineering*, 1994.

[128] S. Genc and S. Lafortune. Distributed diagnosis of discrete-event systems using petri nets. In *Proc. of the international conference on applications and theory of Petri nets*, 2003.

[129] R.J. Van Glabbeek and W.P. Weijland. Branching time and abstraction in bisimulation semantics. *Journal of ACM*, 43(3):555–600, 1996.

[130] R.J. Van Glabbeek and W.P. Weijland. Branching time and abstraction in bisimulation semantics (extended abstract). In *Proc. of IFIP 11th World Comput. Congr*, 1998.

[131] J.F. Groote and F. W. Vaandrager. An efficient algorithm for branching bisimulation and stuttering equivalence. In *Proc. 17th International Colloquium of the Automata, Languages and Programming (ICALP 90)*, 1990.

[132] M. Hack. Decision problems for petrl nets and vector addition systems. Technical report, Massachusetts Institute of Technology, 1975.

[133] D. Harel, A. Pnueli, and J. Stavi. Propositional dynamic logic of nonregular programs. *Journal of Computer and System Sciences*, 26:222–243, 1983.

[134] P. Heinl, S. Horn, S. Jablonski, J. Neeb, K. Stein, and M. Teschke. A comprehensive approach to flexibility in workflow management systems. *ACM Sigsoft Software Engineering Notes*, 24(2):79–88, 1999.

[135] M. Hennessy and R. Milner. On observing nondeterminism and concurrency. In *Proc. of the 7th Colloquium on Automata, Languages and Programming*, 1980.

[136] M. Hennessy and R. Milner. Algebraic laws for nondeterminism and concurrency. *Journal of the ACM*, 32(1):137–161, 1985.

[137] C.A. Heuser and G. Richter. Constructs for modeling information systems with petri nets. In *Proc. of the 13th International Conference on Application and Theory of Petri Nets*, 1992.

[138] Y. Hishfeld. Petri nets and the equivalence problem. In *Proc. of the 7th Workshop on Computer Science Logic*, 1993.

[139] G.T.S. Ho, H.C.W. Lau, C.K.M. Lee, A.W.H. Ip, and K.F. Pun. An intelligent production workflow mining system for continual quality enhancement. *The International Journal of Advanced Manufacturing Technology*, 28(7-8):792–809, 2006.

[140] CAR Hoare. In *On the construction ofprograms*, chapter Communicationg sequential processes, pages 229–254. Cambridge University Press, Cambridge, England, 1980.

[141] C.A.R. Hoare. A model for communicating sequential processes. Technical Report PRG-22, Programming Research Group, University of Oxford, 1981.

[142] C.A.R. Hoare. *Communicating Sequential Processes. Series in Computer Science*. Prentice-Hall International, London, 1985.

[143] C.A.R. Hoare, S.D. Brookes, and A.W. Roscoe. A theory of communicating sequential processes. Technical Report PRG-16, Programming Research Group, University of Oxford, 1981.

[144] S. Holmstroem. A refinement calculus for specifications in hennessy-milner logic with recursion. *Formal Aspects of Computing*, 1(3):242–272, 1989.

[145] J.E. Hopcroft and J.D. Ullman. *Introduction To Automata Theory, Languages, And Computation*. Addison-Wesley Longman Publishing Co., Inc., Boston, MA, USA, 1990.

[146] H. Huettel. Undecidable equivalences for basic parallel processes. In *Proc. of the International Conference on Theoretical Aspects of Computer Software*, 1994.

[147] C. Huth, I. Erdmann, and L. Nastansky. Groupprocess: using process knowledge from the participative design and practical operation of ad hoc processes for the design of structured workflows. In *Proc. of the 34th Annual Hawaii International Conference on System Sciences*, 2001.

[148] L. Jategaonkar and A. Meyer. Testing equivalence for petri nets with action refinement: Preliminary report. In *Proc. of the Third International Conference on Concurrency Theory (CONCUR 92)*, 1992.

[149] L. Jategaonkar and A.R. Meyer. Deciding true concurrency equivalences on finite sate nets. In *Proc. of the 20th International Colloquium on Automata, Languages and Programming*, 1993.

[150] K. Jensen, L.M. Kristensen, and L. Wells. Coloured petri nets and cpn tools for modelling and validation of concurrent systems. *International Journal on Software Tools for Technology Transfer*, 9(3-4):213–254, 2007.

[151] T. Jepsen. Soap cleans up interoperability problems on the web. *IT Professional*, 3(1):52–55, 2001.

[152] P. Jiang, Q. Mair, and J. Newman. Using uml to design distributed collaborative workflows: from uml to xpdl. In *Proc. of the Twelfth IEEE International Workshops on Enabling Technologies: Infrastructure for Collaborative Enterprises*, 2003.

[153] W.T. Jong, Y.S. Shiau, Y.J. Horng, H.H. Chen, and S.-M. Chen. Temporal knowledge representation and reasoning techniques usingtime petri nets. *IEEE Transactions on Systems, Man, and Cybernetics*, 29(4):541–545, 19999.

[154] C.C. Jou and S.A. Smolka. Equivalences, congruences, and complete axiomatizations for probabilistic processes. In *Proc. of the Theories of concurrency : unification and extension: unification and extension*, 1990.

[155] J.Y. Jung, W. Hur, S.H. Kang, and H. Kim. Business process choreography for b2b collaboration. *Internet Computing*, 8(1):37–45, 2004.

[156] P.C. Kanellakis and S.A. Smolka. Ccs expressions, finite state processes, and three problems of equivalence. In *Proc. of the second annual ACM symposium on Principles of distributed computing*, 1983.

[157] P.C. Kanellakis and S.A. Smolka. Ccs expressions finite state processes, and three problems of equivalence. *Information and Computation*, 86(1):43–68, 1990.

[158] N. Kavantzas and et al. Web services choreography description language (ws-cdl) 1.0. Technical report, W3C, 2004.

[159] T. Kawamura, J.A. De Blasio, T. Hasegawa, M. Paolucci, and K. Sycara. Preliminary report of public experiment of semantic service matchmaker with uddi business registry. In *Proc. of the First International Conference on Service-Oriented Computing*, 2003.

[160] R. Kazhamiakin, P. Pandya, and M. Pistore. Representation, verification, and computation of timed properties in web service compositions. In *Proc. of ICWS 06*, 2006.

[161] R. Kazhamiakin, P. Pandya, and M. Pistore. Timed modelling and analysis in web service compositions. In *Proc. of ARESŠ06*, 2006.

[162] R.M. Keller. Generaltzed petrz nets as models for system verification. Technical report, Princeton University, 1975.

[163] P.M. Kelly, P.D. Coddington, and A.L. Wendelborn. Lambda calculus as a workflow model. In *Proc. of the The 3rd International Conference on Grid and Pervasive Computing.*, 2008.

[164] J.K. Kennaway. *Formal semantics of nondeterminism and parallelism*. PhD thesis, University of Oxford, 1981.

[165] R. Kennaway and C.A.R. Hoare. A theory of nondeterminism. In *Proc. of the 7th Colloquium on Automata, Languages and Programming*, 1980.

[166] R. Khalaf and F. Leymann. E role-based decomposition of business processes using bpel. In *Proc. of IEEE International Conference on Web Services (ICWS 06)*, 2006.

[167] A. Khetawat, H. Lavana, and F. Brglez. Collaborative workflows: A paradigm for distributed benchmarking and design on the internet. Technical report, North Carolina State University, 1997.

[168] S.O. Kimbrough and S.A. Moore. On automated message processing in electronic commerce and work support systems: speech act theory and expressive felicity. *ACM Transactions on Information Systems*, 15(4):321–367, 1997.

[169] J. Klingemann and J. Waesch J K. Aberer. Adaptive outsourcing in cross-organizational workflows. Technical report, GMD Ű German National Research Center for Information Technology, 1998.

[170] J. Klingemann and J. Waesch J K. Aberer. Deriving service models in cross-organizational workflows. In *Proc. of Ninth International Workshop on Research Issues in Data Engineering:Virtual Enterprise, RIDE-VE 99*, 1999.

[171] S.Y. Kung, S.C. Lo, and P.S. Lewis. Timing analysis and design optimization of vlsi data flow arrays. In *Proc. of the International Conference on Parallel Processing*, 1986.

[172] M. Z. Kwiatkowska and G. Norman. A testing equivalence for reactive probabilistic processes. *Electronic Notes in Theoretical Computer Science*, 16(2):114Ű132, 1998.

[173] C. Lambrinoudakis, S. Kokolakis, M. Karyda, V. Tsoumas, D. Gritzalis, and S. Katsikas. Electronic voting systems: security implications of the administrative workflow. In *Proc. of the 14th International Workshop on Database and Expert Systems Applications*, 2003.

[174] K.G. Larsen. Proof systems for satisfiability in hennessy-milner logic with recursion. *Theoretical Computer Science*, 72(2-3):265 – 288, 1990.

[175] F. Leymann. *Production workflow: concepts and techniques*. Prentice Hall PTR Upper Saddle River, NJ, USA, 19999.

[176] F. Leymann. Web services flow language (wsfl 1.0). Technical report, IBM, 2001.

[177] Q. Li, Z. Shan, P.C.K. Hung, D.K.W. Chiu, and S.C. Cheung. Flows and views for scalable scientific integration. In *Proc. of InfoScale 06, ACM International Conference Proceeding Series, Vol. 152*, 2006.

[178] S.H. Liao. Expert system methodologies and applicationsŮa decade review from 1995 to 2004. *Expert Systems with Applications*, 28(1):93–103, 2005.

[179] C. Lin, Y. Qu, F. Ren, and D.C. Marinescu. Performance equivalent analysis of workflow systems based on stochastic petri net models. In *Proc. of the First International Conference on Engineering and Deployment of Cooperative Information Systems*, 2002.

[180] D.R. Liu and M. Shen. Workflow modeling for virtual processes: An order-preserving process-view approach. *Information Systems*, 28(6):505–532, 2003.

[181] D.R. Liu and M. Shen. Business-to-business workflow interoperation based on process-views. *Decision Support Systems*, 38(3):399–419, 2004.

[182] D.R. Liu and M. Shen. Discovering role-relevant process-views for disseminating process knowledge. *Expert Systems with Applications*, 26(3):301–310, 2004.

[183] I.A. Lomazova. Nested petri nets - a formalism for specification and verification of multi-agent distributed systems. *Fundamenta Informaticae*, 43(1-4):195–214, 2000.

[184] D. Lowe, X. Chen, T. Mondor, T. Rus, N. Rynearson, S. Wright, and T. Xu. *BizTalk Server: The Complete Reference*. McGraw-Hill Professional, 2001.

[185] G. Luo, G. von Bochmann, and A. Petrenko. Test selection based on communicating nondeterministic finite-statemachines using a generalized wp-metho. *IEEE Transactions on Software Engineering*, 20(2):149–162, 1994.

[186] M. Makela. Applying compiler techniques to reachability analysis of high-level models. In *Proc. of the Workshop on Concurrency, Specification & Programming*, 2000.

[187] O. Marjanovic. Dynamic verification of temporal constraints in production workflows. In *Proc. of the Australasian Database Conference*, 2000.

[188] A. Martens. *Verteilte Geschaeftsprozesse-Modellierung und Verifikation mit Hilfe von Web Services*. PhD thesis, Humbolst-Universitaet Zu Berlin, 2004.

[189] A. Martens. Consistency between executable and abstract processes. In *Proc. of IEEE International Conference on e-Technology, e-Commerce and e-Service*, 2005.

[190] J. Martinez, P.R. Muro, M. Silva, S. Smith, and J.L. Villarroel. Merging artificial intelligence techniques and petri nets for real-time scheduling and control of production systems. In *Proc. of the 12th IMACS world congress on scientific computation*, 1988.

[191] J. Metso and L. Kutvonen. Managing virtual organizations with contracts. In *Proc. of Workshop on Contract Architectures and Languages, Enschede, The Netherlands*, 2005.

[192] R. Milner. *A Calculus of Communicating Systems (Lecture Notes in Computer Science, Volume 92)*. Springer Verlag, 1980.

[193] R. Milner. A modal characterisation of observable machine-behaviour. In *Proc. of the 6th Colloquium on Trees in Algebra and Programming, Lecture Notes In Computer Science, Volume 112, Pages 25-34*, 1981.

[194] R. Milner. Calculi for synchrony and asynchrony. *Theoretical Computer Science*, 25:267–310, 1983.

[195] R. Milner. Lectures on a calculus for communicating systems. In *Proc. of the Seminar on Concurrency, Lecture Notes in Computer Science, volume 97, pages 197-220*, 1985.

[196] R Milner. *Communication and concurrency.* Prentice-Hall International Computer Science Series, London, England, 1989.

[197] R. Muehlberger, M.E. Orlowska, and B. Kiepuszewski. Backward step: The right direction for production workflow systems. In *Proc. of the Australian Database Conference*, 1999.

[198] T. Murata. Petri nets: Properties, analysis and applications. *Proceedings of the IEEE*, 77:541–580, 1989.

[199] W. Naqvi and M.T. Ibrahim. Reflex active database model: Application of petri-nets. In *Proc. of the 4th International Conference on Database and Expert Systems Applications*, 1993.

[200] R. De Nicola and M.C.B. Hennessy. Testing equivalences for processes. Technical Report CSR-123-82, University of Edinburgh, 1982.

[201] R. De Nicola and M.C.B. Hennessy. Testing equivalence for processes. In *Proc. of the 10th Colloquium on Automata, Languages and Programming, Lecture Notes In Computer Science, Volume 154*, 1983.

[202] R. De Nicola and M.C.B. Hennessy. Testing equivalences for processes. *Theoretical computer science*, 34:83–133, 1984.

[203] R. De Nicola, U. Montanari, and F.W. Vaandrager. Back and forth bislmulations. In *Proc. of CONCUR '90, Lecture Notes in Computer Science, vol. 458. Springer-Verlag, New York, pp. 152-165.*, 1990.

[204] R. De Nicola and F.W. Vaandrager. Three logics for branching bisimulation. *Journal of ACM*, 42(2):458–487, 1995.

[205] M. Nielsen and P.S. Thiagarajan. Degrees of non-determinism and concurrency: A petri net view. In *Proc. of the Fourth Conference on Foundations of Software Technology and Theoretical Computer Science*, 1984.

[206] A. Oberweis and P. Sander. Information system behavior specification by high level petri nets. *ACM Transactions on Information Systems*, 14(4):380 – 420, 1996.

[207] E.R. Olderog. Specification oriented programming in tcsp. In *Proc. of the NATO Advanced Study Institute in Logics and Models of Concurrent Systems*, 1985.

[208] E.R. Olderog. *Nets, Terms and Formulas*. Cambridge University Press, 1991.

[209] E.R. Olderog and C.A.R. Hoare. Specification-oriented semantics for communicating processes. *Acta Informatica*, 23(1):9–66, 1986.

[210] C. Ouyang and J. Billington. Formal analysis of the internet open trading protocol. In *Proc. of the Applying Formal Methods: Testing, Performance, and M/E-Commerce*, 2004.

[211] A. Overkamp. Supervisory control using failure semantics and partialspecifications. *IEEE transactions on Automatic Control*, 42(4):498–510, 1997.

[212] E. Panagos and M. Rabinovich. Predictive workflow management. In *Proc. of the 3rd Int. Workshop on Next Generation Information Technologies and Systems*, 1997.

[213] M. Paolucci, T. Kawamura, T.R. Payne, and K.P. Sycara. Importing the semantic web in uddi. In *Proc. of the International Workshop on Web Services, E-Business, and the Semantic Web*, 2002.

[214] C. Papadimitriou. *The theory of database concurrency control*. Computer Science Press, Inc., 1986.

[215] D.M.R. Park. Concurrency and automata on infinite sequences. In *Proc. of he 5th GI Conference. Lecture Notes in Computer Science, vol. 104*. Springer-Verlag, New York, 1981.

[216] K.M. Passino and P.J. Antsaklis. Artificial intelligence planning problems in a petri net framework. In *Proc. of the American Control Conference*, 1988.

[217] C. Peltz. Web services orchestration and choreography. *IEEE Computer*, 36(10):46Ű53, 2003.

[218] J.L. Peterson. Petri nets. *ACM Computing Surveys (CSUR)*, 9:223–252, 1977.

[219] S. Philipose. *Operations Research A Practical Approach*. Tata McGrawHill, New Delhi, New York, 1986.

[220] I. Phillips. Refusal testing. *Theoretical Computer Science*, 50(3):241–284, 1987.

[221] H. Pichler. *Time Management for Workflow Systems. A probabilistic Approach for Basic and Advanced Control Flow Structures*. PhD thesis, Alpen-Adria-Universitaet Klagenfurt. Fakultaet fuer Wirtschaftswissenschaften und Informatik, 2006.

[222] A. Pnueli. Linear and branching structures in the semantics and logics of reactive systems. In *Proc. of the 12th Colloquium on Automata, Languages and Programming, Lecture Notes In Computer Science, Volume 194*, 1985.

[223] L. Pomello. Some equivalence notions for concurrent systems. an overview. In *Proc. of the 6th European Workshop on Applications and Theory in Petri Nets*, 1985.

[224] L. Pomello, G. Rozenberg, and C. Simone. A survey of equivalence notions for net based systems. In *Proc. of the Advances in Petri Nets*, 1992.

[225] L. Pudhota, A. Tierney, and E. Chang. Services integration monitor for collaborative workflow management. In *Proc. of the 14th IEEE International Workshops on Enabling Technologies: Infrastructure for Collaborative Enterprise*, 2005.

[226] F. Puhlmann and M. Weske. Using the pi-calculus for formalizing workflow patterns. In *Proc. of the 3rd International Conference on Business Process Management (BPM 05)*, 2005.

[227] H. Qin and P. Lewis. Factorization of finite state machines under observational equivalence. In *Proc. of the Theories of concurrency : unification and extension: unification and extension*, 1990.

[228] G.M. Reed and A.W. Roscoe. The timed failures-stability model for csp. *Theoretical Computer Science*, 211(1-2):85 – 127, 1999.

[229] W. Reisig. *Petri nets: an introduction.* Springer-Verlag New York, Inc., 1985.

[230] W. Reisig. Embedded system description using petri nets. In *Lecture Notes in Computer Science, Volume 284*, 1987.

[231] S. Rinderle, A. Wombacher, and M. Reichert. On the controlled evolution of process choreographies. In *Proc. of 22nd International Conference on Data Engineering*, 2006.

[232] A.W. Roscoe. An alternative order for the failures model. *Journal of Logic and Computation*, 2(5):557–577, 1992.

[233] W.C. Rounds and S.D. Brookes. Possible futures, acceptances, refusals and communicating processes. In *Proc. of the 22 thAnnual Symposium on Foundations of Computer Science*, 1981.

[234] A. Ryman. Simple object access protocol (soap) and web services. In *Proc. of the 23rd International Conference on Software Engineering*, 2001.

[235] W. Sadiq, S. Shazia, and K. Schulz. Model driven distribution of collaborative business processes. In *Proc. of IEEE International Conference on Services Computing*, 2006.

[236] S. Sakthivel and M.R. Tanniru. Information system verification and validation during requirement analysis using petri nets. *Journal of Management Information Systems*, 5(3):33–50, 1989.

[237] K. Salimifard and M. Wright. Petri net-based modelling of workflow systems: An overview. *European Journal of Operational Research*, 134(3):664–676, 2001.

[238] D. Sannella and A. Tarlecki. On observational equivalence and algebraic specification. *Journal of Computer and System Sciences*, 34(2-3):150–178, 1987.

[239] K. Sarshar, T. Theling, P. Loos, and M. Jerrentrup. Integrating process and organization models of collaborations through object petri nets. In *Proc. of the Third GI-Workshop XML4BPM - XML Integration and Transformation for Business Process Management*, 2006.

[240] H.J. Schek and M.H. Scholl. The relational model with relation-valued attributes. *Journal of Information Systems*, 11(2):137–147, 1986.

[241] H. Schlinglof, A. Martens, and K. Schmidt. Modeling and model checking web services. *Electronic Notes in Theoretical Computer Science*, 126:3–26, 2005.

[242] K. Schulz and ME. Orlowska. Architectural issues for cross-organisational b2b interactions. In *Proc. International Conference on Distributed Computing Systems*, 2001.

[243] K.A. Schulz and M.E. Orlowska. Facilitating cross-organisational workflows with a workflow view approach. *Data and Knowledge Engineering*, 51(1):109–147, 2004.

[244] K. Scribner, K. Scribner, and M.C. Stiver. *Understanding Soap: Simple Object Access Protocol*. Sams Indianapolis, 2000.

[245] S. Seely. *SOAP: Cross Platform Web Service Development Using XML*. Prentice Hall, 2001.

[246] L.R. Shaffer, J.B. Ritter, and W.L. Meyer. *The Critical-path Method*. McGraw-Hill Education, 1965.

[247] Z. Shan, Z. Long, Y. Luo, and Z. Peng. Object-oriented realization of workflow views for web services Ű an object deputy model based approach. In *Proc. of the 5th International Conference on Advances in Web-Age Information Management*, 2004.

[248] T. Smigelski, T. Murata, and M. Sowa. A timed petri net model and simulation of a dataflow computer. In *Proc. of the nternational Workshop on Timed Petri Nets*, 1985.

[249] J. Snell, D. Tidwell, and P. Kulchenko. *Programming Web services with SOAP*. O Reilly & Associates, Inc., 2002.

[250] UK Springer-Verlag London. *Workflow Verification: Finding Control-Flow Errors Using Petri-Net-Based Techniques*, chapter Business Process Management, Models, Techniques, and Empirical Studies, Lecture Notes In Computer Science; Vol. 1806., pages 161–183. Springer-Verlag, London, UK, 2000.

[251] M.O. Stehr, J. Meseguer, and P. Csaba Oelveczky. Rewriting logic as a unifying framework for petri nets. In *Lecture Notes In Computer Science, Vol. 2128*, 2001.

[252] R.S. Streett. Propositional dynamic logic of looping and converse. In *Proc. of the thirteenth annual ACM symposium on Theory of computing*, 1981.

[253] Z. Tan, C. Lin, H. Yin, Y. Hong, and G. Zhu. Approximate performance analysis of web services flow using stochastic petri net. In *Proc. of the Grid and Cooperative Computing*, 2004.

[254] Y. Tang, L. Chen, K.T. He, and N. Jing. Srn: an extended petri-net-based workflow model for web service composition. In *Proc. of the IEEE International Conference on Web Services*, 2004.

[255] S. Thatte. Xlang: Web services for business process design. Technical report, Microsoft, 2001.

[256] I.L. Traiger. Trends in systems aspects of database management. In *Proc. of the 2nd International Conference on Databases*, 1983.

[257] W.T. Tsai, R. Paul, Z. Cao, L. Yu, and A. Saimi. Verification of web services using an enhanced uddi server. In *Proc. of the Eighth International Workshop on Object-Oriented Real-Time Dependable Systems*, 2003.

[258] G. Tuncel and G.M. Bayhan. A high-level petri net based decision support system for real-time scheduling and control of flexible manufacturing systems: An object-oriented approach. In *Proc. of the International Conference on Computational Science*, 2005.

[259] A. Valmari. Failure-based equivalences are faster than many believe. In *Proc. of the Structures in Concurrency Theory*, 1995.

[260] W.M.P. van der Aalst and A.H.M. ter Hofstede. Yawl: Yet another workflow language. *Information Systems*, 30(4):245–275, 2005.

[261] W.M.P. van der Aalst and K.M. van Hee. Business process redesign: A petri-net-based approach. *Computers in Industry*, 29(1-2):15–26, 1996.

[262] R.J. van Glabbee. *Mathematical Foundations of Computer Science 1993*, chapter A Complete Axiomatization for Branching Bisimulation Congruence of Finite-State Behaviours., pages 473–484. Springer-Verlag, New York-Berlin, 1993.

[263] R.J. van Glabbeek. The linear time branching time spectrum ii: The semantics of sequential systems with silent moves (extended abstract). In *Proc. of CONCUR 93, 4th. International Conference on Concurrency Theory, Lecture Notes in Computer Science, volume 715, pp. 66-81*, 1993.

[264] H.M.W. Verbeek. *Verification of WF-nets*. PhD thesis, TU Eindhoven, 2004.

[265] H.M.W. Verbeek and W.M.P. van der Aalst. Woflan 2.0 a petri-net-based workflow diagnosis tool. In *Proc. of Application and Theory of Petri Nets 2000*, 2000.

[266] W. Vogler. Failures semantics and deadlocking of modular petri nets. In *Proc. of the Mathematical Foundations of Computer Science*, 1988.

[267] L.C. Wang. Object-oriented petri nets for modelling and analysis of automated manufacturing systems. *Computer Integrated Manufacturing Systems*, 9(2):111–125, 1996.

[268] Y. Wang and D.L. Parnas. Simulating the behavior of software modules by trace rewriting. *IEEE Transactions on Software Engineering*, 20(10):750–759, 1994.

[269] Y. Wang, C. Wu, and K. Xu. Study on pi-calculus based equipment grid service chain model. In *Proc. of the IFIP International Conference on Network and Parallel Computing (NPC 05)*, 2005.

[270] D. Webber and A. Dutton. Understanding ebxml, uddi and xml/edi. *XML Global*, online at: http://www.touchbriefings.com/pdf/977/webber.pdf, 2000.

[271] H. Weigand and WJ. van den Heuvel. Cross-organizational workflow integration using contracts. *Decision Support Systems*, 33 (3):247–265, 2002.

[272] W.P. Weijland. *Synchrony and Asynchrony in Process Algebra*. PhD thesis, University of Amsterdam, Department of Mathematics and Computer Science, 1989.

[273] G. Weikum. Principles and realization strategies of multilevel transaction management. *ACM Transactions on Database Systems (TODS)*, 16(1):132–180, 1991.

[274] A. Wombacher, P. Fankhauser, B. Mahleko, and E. Neuhold. Matchmaking for business processes based on choreographies. In *Proc. of IEEE International Conference on e-Technology, e-Commerce and e-Service*, 2004.

[275] WOMBAT4WS. Workflow modeling and business analysis toolkit for web services. http://www.informatik.hu-berlin.de/top/wombat/.

[276] P.Y.H. Wong and J. Gibbons. A process-algebraic approach to workflow specification and refinement. In *Proc. of the 6th International Symposium on Software Composition (SC 07)*, 2007.

[277] Jr. W.W. McLendon and R.F. Vidale. Analysis of an ada system using coloured petri nets and occurrence graphs. In *Proc. of the 13th International Conference on Application and Theory of Petri Nets*, 1992.

[278] Q. Xiaoqiang and J. Wei. A decentralized services choreography approach for business collaboration. In *Proc. of IEEE International Conference on Services Computing (SCC 06)*, 2006.

[279] F. Xu and Z. Yu. A workflow verification method based on calculus. In *Proc. of the First Joint IEEE/IFIP Symposium on Theoretical Aspects of Software Engineering*, 2007.

[280] B.S. Yang, S.K. Jeong, Y.M. Oh, and A.C.C. Tan. Case-based reasoning system with petri nets for induction motor fault diagnosis. *Expert Systems with Applications*, 27(2):301–311, 2004.

[281] A.K. Zaidi. On temporal logic programming using petri nets. *IEEE Transactions on Systems, Man and Cybernetics*, 29(3):245–254, 1999.

[282] X. Zhao, C. Liu, and Y. Yang. An organisational perspective on collaborative business processes. In *Proc. of the 3rd International Conference on Business Process Management*, 2005.

[283] D. Zimmer, A. Meckenstock, and R. Unland. Using petri nets for rule termination analysis. In *Proc. of the workshop on on Databases: active and real-time*, 1996.

[284] J. Zwiers. Compositionality, concurrency and partial correctness:proof theories for networks of processes and their relationship. In *Lecture Notes In Computer Science, Volume: 231*, 1989.

VDM Verlagsservicegesellschaft mbH

Die VDM Verlagsservicegesellschaft sucht für wissenschaftliche Verlage abgeschlossene und herausragende

Dissertationen, Habilitationen, Diplomarbeiten, Master Theses, Magisterarbeiten usw.

für die kostenlose Publikation als Fachbuch.

Sie verfügen über eine Arbeit, die hohen inhaltlichen und formalen Ansprüchen genügt, und haben Interesse an einer honorarvergüteten Publikation?

Dann senden Sie bitte erste Informationen über sich und Ihre Arbeit per Email an *info@vdm-vsg.de*.

Sie erhalten kurzfristig unser Feedback!

VDM Verlagsservicegesellschaft mbH
Dudweiler Landstr. 99
D - 66123 Saarbrücken
www.vdm-vsg.de

Telefon +49 681 3720 174
Fax +49 681 3720 1749

Die VDM Verlagsservicegesellschaft mbH vertritt

Printed by Books on Demand GmbH, Norderstedt / Germany